THE AMERICAN FRONTIER

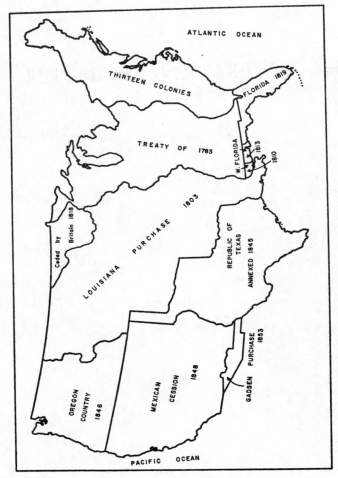

ATLANTIC OCEAN

THIRTEEN COLONIES

FLORIDA 1819

TREATY OF 1783

W. FLORIDA

1813

1810

Ceded by Britain 1818

LOUISIANA PURCHASE 1803

REPUBLIC OF TEXAS

ANNEXED 1845

GADSEN PURCHASE 1853

OREGON COUNTRY 1846

MEXICAN CESSION 1848

PACIFIC OCEAN

TERRITORIAL ACQUISITIONS OF THE UNITED STATES

A CONCISE STUDY GUIDE
to the
American Frontier

by

NELSON KLOSE

UNIVERSITY OF NEBRASKA PRESS · LINCOLN

First printing: May, 1964
Second printing: October, 1966
Third printing: January, 1969

MANUFACTURED IN THE UNITED STATES OF AMERICA

Preface

It is better to see the main outlines of a subject before plunging into the mass of its details; it is helpful to have a convenient guide for reference as one proceeds; and one can learn better if the more significant details are pointed out after he has read them in a detailed textbook. In these ways this book, a synopsis, should aid the student and teacher of the American frontier and of westward expansion.

This compact book provides a topical treatment of the various main subjects of frontier history. First, the various regional frontiers are sketched to provide the student both a perspective of these geographical frontiers and, at the same time, the necessary chronology of leading events. Thus, the chronology and .the framework of frontier history are provided, since they are both difficult to follow in detailed textbooks where insufficient, if any, headings are supplied. Under the regional frontiers, political and military events and population movements are treated. Next, the various problems are discussed in separate sections to isolate them from the confusion of other contemporaneous developments. The leading types of frontiers, as seen by reference to the Table of Contents, are treated apart from chronology also. Types of frontiers are determined mainly on the basis of the predominant economic development.

A topical treatment and organization such as this is helpful, since we are studying different aspects of a phenomenon rather than a political or geographical unit where a more traditional chronological organization would be required. The traditional subject matter of American history not directly related to the frontier has been omitted. Also material about the West as a geographical region *per se* has been omitted. Provided for each section is a list of references selected on a basis of readability, availability, and authoritativeness. Also in the back of the book a list of the most recently published paperbacks has been provided. A full index and adequate maps have been added to help make this a more useful handbook for both teacher and student.

NELSON KLOSE

January, 1964

Contents

Contents

Textbooks on the History of the West

BILLINGTON, RAY ALLEN. *Westward Expansion: A History of the American Frontier* (2d ed.; New York: Macmillan, 1960).

CLARK, DAN ELBERT. *The West in American History* (New York: T. Y. Crowell, 1937).

CLARK, THOMAS D. *The Story of the Westward Movement* (New York: Scribner, 1959).

HAFEN, LEROY R., and CARL COKE RISTER. *Western America: The Exploration, Settlement, and Development of the Region beyond the Mississippi* (2d ed.; Englewood Cliffs, N. J.: Prentice-Hall, 1950).

HINE, ROBERT V., and EDWIN R. BINGHAM. *The Frontier Experience: Readings in the Trans-Mississippi West* (Belmont, Calif.: Wadsworth Publishing Co., 1963).

PAXSON, F. L. *History of the American Frontier* (Boston: Houghton Mifflin, 1924).

RIEGEL, ROBERT E. *America Moves West* (3d ed.; New York: Holt, 1956).

Paperbacks with documents or maps:

BILLINGTON, RAY ALLEN. *The Westward Movement in the United States* (Princeton, N. J.: Van Nostrand, 1959). A brief survey with documents.

SALE, RANDALL D., and EDWIN D. KERN. *American Expansion: A Book of Maps* (Homewood, Ill.: Dorsey Press, 1962).

STILL, BAYRD. *The West: Contemporary Records of America's Expansion Across the Continent, 1607–1890* (New York: Capricorn Books, 1961).

OLD AND NEW SURVEY HISTORIES AND READINGS ON THE AMERICAN FRONTIER
(Correlation and Analysis of Available Textbooks)

Sections of this Book	Billington, Westward Expansion (2d ed.)	Billington, Westward Movement (Readings)	D. E. Clark, The West...	T. D. Clark, Frontier America	Hafen and Rister, Western America (2d ed.)	Hine and Bingham, Frontier Experience (Readings)	Paxson, Hist. of the Amer. Frontier	Riegel, America Moves West (3d ed.)	Still, The West (Readings)
Frontier Hypothesis 1	1	8		1		1		41	(265-72)
Frontier in Wide Perspecitve 2	37	1							
Seaboard Frontier 3	2-4	(12-18)(95-98)	1		6				(1-15,17-25)
Old West 4	5, 6	(18-24)(99-103)		2, 3			1-3	1	(27-43)
Eastern Mississippi Region 5	7-14,24	(24-46)(103-13)	3-12,15,23	4-8,11	(28-41),8,9,10,12		4,8-14,16,18,19,22,33	2,3,9,12,13	(44-61)
To the 98th Meridian 6	16,23,29	(53-55)(134-37)	13,24	10,13,16,25,26	(41-47),4,(166-73),16,17,21	6	15,20,24,32,34,43	18,23	(88-124)
Pacific and Mexican War 7	21,25,27,28	(55-64)(137-47)	2,29	20,21,23	5,14,18,19	4,5,7	37,39,40,41	24,25,38	(161-79)
Intermountain and Last States 8	20,26	(64-66,73-75)(177-84)	31	22,28	1,2,20,22,24,31,33	8	38,46,58,59	26 (580-83)	(157-61)
Great Plains (Environment) 9	34	(81-86)			23	14		(564-77)	
Indians 10	32	(75-78)(114-17)(167-71)	16,35	19,30	28,29	11	31,51,53	5,21,31,32	(210-17)
Public Domain 11	18	(121-23)	17,18(604-7)		7		5-7,25,42,50	4,27	
Financial Problems 12	17	.	22	(331-36)			26-28,35,54	19	

OLD AND NEW SURVEY HISTORIES AND READINGS ON THE AMERICAN FRONTIER
(Correlation and Analysis of Available Textbooks)

Sections of this Book		Billington, Westward Expansion (2d ed.)	Billington, Westward Movement (Readings)	D. E. Clark, The West ...	T. D. Clark, Frontier America	Hafen and Rister, Western America (2d ed.)	Hine and Bingham, Frontier Experience (Readings)	Paxson, Hist. of the Amer. Frontier	Riegel, America Moves West (3d ed.)	Still, The West (Readings)
Transportation	13	16, 19, 31	(70–72) (162–67)	14, 19, 32, 34	14, 29	27, 30	12	17, 29, 30, 44, 45, 49, 52, 57	15, 16, 17, 29, 30, 36	(184–210)
Government and Politics	14			23, 24, 31	8, 13, 25	26		11, 12, 14, 22, 28, 33, 58	4 (93–98) (405–8) 39	
People and Religion	15		(117–20)	21, 25	9, 12, 22				6, 7, 14	Part IV. (also 258–65)
Culture	16			26	15	37	15		8, 30, 35, (596–600), 40	
Early Agricultural Frontiers	17	15				35		21, 23		
Fur Business	18	22	(49–53)	28	18	13	3		11	
Explorations and Trails	19		(47–49) (124–34) (147–52)	27, 30	17	(173–91), 15	2	36	10, 22	(125–57)
Mining	20	30	(66–70) (152–61)	33	34	24, 26, 36	9	47, 48	28, 33	(217–19)
Cattlemen's Frontier	21	33	(78–81) (171–74)	(587–604)	27	32	10	56	34	(220–34)
Farmers in Far West	22	35, 36	(175–77)	37	31, 32	(646–52)	14	55	(577–80), 39	(234–57)
Urban Frontier	23				311–14	34	13			
Bibliography		759–854	185–88	629–54	765–97	Chapter Bibliographies	Chapter Bibliographies	No Bibliographies	Chapter Bibliographies	(273–79)

THE HISTORIANS' THEORY
OF THE FRONTIER

The Historians' Theory of the Frontier

1

THE FRONTIER HYPOTHESIS,
OR TURNER THESIS

In recent decades historians in America have given much attention to the study of the frontier as a momentous factor in the development of the United States. This attention began with the influence of Frederick Jackson Turner; it will be helpful first to consider his teachings.

Interpretations of American History Before the Turner Thesis.—In seeking to discover the determinants that explain the unique features and qualities of American development, American historians, since 1893, began concentrating upon the formative influence of westward expansion. The concentration on this new interpretation of American development originated with Frederick Jackson Turner, professor of American History at Wisconsin and Harvard. This interpretation came to be known as the frontier hypothesis or the Turner thesis.

To understand the place of the frontier hypothesis, it is necessary to know what interpretations it superseded. At Johns Hopkins University, the first important graduate school in the United States, where Turner received his historical training, historical interpretation was concerned with the Germanic origins of Anglo-Saxon institutions as transmitted through England. American individualism and institutions were traced to the forests of Germanic ancestors and to European "germ cells."

Before Turner much attention was also given to American colonial history and to the Atlantic seaboard states. This attention persisted long after the newer states of the West had been settled, until it obviously amounted to an undue emphasis. The

Eastern point of view predominated, since the nation's historians were largely Easterners. Still another focus was upon constitutional issues; here the questions arising from the slavery controversy received central attention.

There were two historians before Turner who paid especially noteworthy attention to the West. Hubert Howe Bancroft, who in 1852 in San Francisco established himself as publisher and historian, was responsible for extensive writing on the Far West. Theodore Roosevelt interested himself in the frontier and produced *The Winning of the West* and other books on the West.

The Study of the Role of the Frontier in American History.— Major attention to the influence of the Western frontier in accounting for the unique development of American civilization began when Frederick Jackson Turner read his now famous paper. This young history teacher at the University of Wisconsin read an essay entitled "The Significance of the Frontier in American History" at a meeting of the American Historical Association held in conjunction with the World's Columbian Exposition in Chicago in 1893. The essay in time came to be recognized as a landmark in American historiography.

The Spread of Turner's Influence.—Turner's essays affected American historiography profoundly, and the influence of his ideas spread vigorously through the work of his disciples. Within a generation his stimulating ideas were thoroughly disseminated through historical writing in America. As an inspiring teacher at Wisconsin and later at Harvard, Turner caused many devoted students to investigate aspects of the history of the frontier, and they had much to do with the spread of his thesis. He was greatly admired as a person and as a teacher.

Turner was not a remarkably prolific writer, but he did write enough to assist the further spread of his ideas. Practically all of his ideas are in the original essay, "The Significance of the Frontier in American History," published in 1920 as one of a collection under the title *The Frontier in American History*. The essay altered the whole course of American historical scholarship. It proved to be the most influential single piece of historical writing ever done in the United States and gave rise to a large school of frontier historians.

Statement of the Turner Thesis.—Turner's own words best state the thesis: "The existence of an area of free land, its continuous recession, the advance of the American settlement westward, explain American development." Essentially, the thesis expounded the overwhelming importance of the frontier in the United States as a force fostering democracy and freeing the individual from Old World and Eastern influences and restrictions. Turner's purpose, instead of detailing the similarities to Europe, was to describe how America came to be different.

Turner explained that as men advanced into a new area they necessarily sloughed off or reshaped their original institutions and cultural baggage as they adapted themselves to new environments on the frontier. They left social, political, and economic controls behind them, because, as they left older communities, they abandoned a static social organization and entered an unorganized society where new conditions prevailed. The frontier environment demanded such qualities as industry, initiative, individual enterprise, ingenuity, optimism, and resourcefulness; it therefore attracted or produced men with these qualities. Later as the communities became populated and more complex institutions were needed, society began to crystallize with new characteristics. Thus, there occurred an Americanization of men and institutions. This process was repeated on new frontiers for three hundred years as the growing population pushed the frontier out in successive new waves of advance. Each advance represented a rebirth of society. The results of this process created certain common characteristics, but differences occurred on various frontiers due to differences in time, the geographic environment, and in the immigrants themselves. To some extent the political weight of the newer regions and other influences continued to affect the older sections in the East long after they had passed through the frontier stages.

Turner paid much attention to the effects of geographical environment and the consequent rise of sectionalism in America.

The West, he alleged, acted as a "safety valve" for democracy in the East, since those who were oppressed or exploited could always escape to the frontier. Thus, the dominant classes in the East had to make concessions to people to match the attraction of freedom and economic opportunity offered in the vacant lands of the West.

The Meaning of "Frontier."—The "frontier" is "the meeting point between savagery and civilization" and a region of sparse settlement. The frontier is all of these too: a region, a line, a process. More concretely, it often has been defined as a region having from two to six inhabitants to the square mile, and accordingly has been traced on population maps. Basic to the concept is the existence of cheap or free, vacant land. Usually it was the attraction of land and its resources that kept the line of the frontier moving westward; freedom was a second objective of the migrant, but it was the existence of vacant land that offered him the opportunity to escape his restrictions and realize the yearning for freedom. The frontier is that advancing line of civilization where it comes in contact with the Indians and the wilderness.

Turner and other historians of his time use the terms "West" and "frontier" synonymously, as if they mean the same thing. This is the case, of course, because the frontier has advanced necessarily to the west more than in any other direction. Actually, however, our subject is the *frontier* wherever it may have occurred, and we are interested here in the West only as a frontier. For this reason "Western" history, unless it treats the West as a *region,* ends with the disappearance of its frontier features.

The Frontier in Time.—American historians assume that the frontier in the United States began at Jamestown in 1607 and came to an end in 1890. The termination date of 1890 is taken because the census report for that year announced that all suitable land for homesteading had been taken up. And this is actually the best approximate date of the closing of the frontier as a well-defined line of advancing population. The American frontier differed from that of other countries because of its longer existence.

Influence of the Frontier.—Turner pointed out certain characteristic traits of frontier people: equalitarianism, individualism, love of freedom, coarseness, restlessness, inquisitiveness, and self-reliance; they were optimistic, materialistic, and nationalistic in outlook.

The frontier created and established firmly American democracy; it did not come over by importation on the *Mayflower*. At first Westerners were fairly equal in wealth and in social status; the West favored political equality and showed faith in the ability of the average man. As typified by Jacksonian democracy, the West favored freedom of opportunity and abhorred privilege.

Influence of the West in National Politics.—Historians, beginning with Turner, spotlighted the crucial role of Western influence in determining the outcome of various political issues. Strongly affected by the West were the national land laws, federal aid to internal improvements, protective tariffs, growth of the authority of the central government, the nation's territorial expansion, and various expressions of nationalism. The role of the West comes up for much attention in the history of the American Revolution, in the purchase of Louisiana, in the War of 1812, in the development of the slavery controversy, in the money question, and in the Civil War.

The Regional Appeal of the Turner Thesis.—Turner repeatedly asserted that after men crossed the Appalachians into the Mississippi Basin they became separated from European influences of the East coast and in the frontier backwoods they developed into Americans. He thought of the Mississippi Valley as more remote from European influences and therefore as being more American. In various essays he emphasized the centrality and preeminence of the Mississippi Valley as a shaping force in America. He was therefore accused of a Middle-West sectional interpretation of American history, an emphasis upon his own section of the country. Some historians deprecated his concentration upon American factors in explaining our history and his diverting attention from our European connections at a time when we needed to look outward; his work promoted a narrow nationalism and self-conceit.

The popularity of Turner's thesis is partly explained by its appeal to the whole country west of the Appalachians; it deemphasized the role of the East and the significance of the colonial period. But it was a salutary change since it called attention to developments and regions hitherto neglected. And when many historians were interpreting American history in terms of North-South divergences as a fundamental theme, Turner called for an interpretation in terms of East-West interaction.

Criticism of the Frontier Hypothesis.—Naturally emphasis upon any single explanation of American development and particularly upon one that called for a novel interpretation was challenged by other historians. The Turner thesis evoked endless discussion, especially in the 1930's.

The leading criticisms of Turner may be summarized as follows:

1. The "safety valve" effect of the West was not operative, because the main source of migrants was not oppressed wage earners in the shops of the Eastern cities but farmers moving from an adjoining frontier settled just previously.

2. Turner was too much concerned with a single frontier, that of the farmer in the Middle West; this offers only a narrow, sectional explanation. In offering a single explanation of American development, he omitted the effects of industrialization, urbanization, and European intellectual influences. The theory tends to distract attention from these and other important influences.

3. The theory was introspective, isolationist, and parochial. It ignored and belittled the enormous influences of America's heritage from Europe and the reforms originating there. Democracy was a product of this heritage, not of the American forests. The West was not outstanding for innovation, it is alleged by the critics.

4. Turner used the concepts "frontier" and "West," as well as other terms, loosely, inexactly, and interchangeably.

5. The Marxian influence in American historiography deplored his neglect of class conflict as a factor in our history.

6. Turner is criticized as being poetic rather than scientific in his observations—he generalizes, he is vague where he should be specific and exact.

7. Finally, it should be noted that the opening of the frontier in America and its consequences are the results of a larger and prior movement in European civilization rather than a cause. The discovery was the result of the technological advance of man in Europe that made possible an expansion that had already begun on a world scale. The American frontier itself was a part and continuation of this worldwide movement.

2

THE FRONTIER IN WIDE PERSPECTIVE

For the sake of orientation and perspective certain broad aspects and outlines of the study of the American frontier and the implications of its termination may be observed. The frontier hypothesis has been applied to other parts of the world and also may be considered to apply to a frontier of Western civilization, as centered in Europe.

A LARGER VIEW OF THE AMERICAN FRONTIER

Before we consider the separate regional frontiers in America, as taken up in the next part of this book, certain facts about the frontier must be viewed in a larger perspective and viewed for purposes of introduction to the subject.

The Momentum of the Frontier Advance.—The movement of Europeans was slow at first as the English colonies took root in North America along the Atlantic seaboard. For some time they remained dependent upon Europe and in danger of Indian attack and therefore were unwilling to relinquish ocean-going transportation. As time passed the rate of advance gained momentum. The United States reached the Pacific much sooner than Jefferson and others had calculated. They did not take into account the future improvements in technology that would accelerate the advance.

Effect of the Wealth of Natural Resources.—Fertile, virgin soil, waiting for the mining it would receive in the harvest of abundant crops, opened opportunity for freedom from political, economic, social, and religious domination; the vacant land offered opportunity for the persecuted and exploited to shape their own destinies. Non-conformists could escape organized society and find economic independence. The wealth of animal, plant, and mineral resources waiting to be harvested gave economic opportunity and attracted ambitious and aggressive types. The abundance of material wealth was to shape profoundly life and institutions in America, for example, the effects of gold and oil discoveries upon our society.

Geographical Stages in the Frontier.—Several different separate advances of waves of people across the continent present clearly discernible geographical stages in the frontier. The chronological treatment of the frontier in this book surveys these seven successive geographic or regional frontiers in as many chapters. These stages may be distinguished as follows: (1) the advance from the Atlantic seacoast to the fall line—the upper limits of navigation up the rivers flowing into the Atlantic; (2) the advance from the fall line to the crest of the Appalachian Mountains; (3) the advance from the Appalachians to the Mississippi River; (4) the advance from the Mississippi to the approximate line of the 98th meridian, or edge of the Great Plains. (5) In the next stage the advance jumped the plains and intermountain region of the Rockies to the Pacific Coast. (6) Then the intermountain region and the Rockies were settled by population moving in from both the west and the east. (7) Last of all to be settled, in spite of its proximity to the frontier advancing from the east, was the then formidable Great Plains, with an unfriendly environment for Anglo-American institutions. These stages may be labeled (1) the Atlantic tidewater, (2) the Piedmont or Old West, (3) the eastern Mississippi region, (4) the valley of the Mississippi up to the 98th meridian, (5) the Pacific slope, (6) the intermountain region, and (7) the Great Plains.

Economic Zones and Phases in the Evolution of the Frontier.— The fur traders and trappers were the first to open any new frontier. Their way of life was often not much above the beasts they preyed upon and about on a par with the aborigines they sometimes lived with. They learned the geography of the land and brought information to or served as guides to those who followed them—cattlemen, miners, or pioneer farmers. Usually next behind the fur men were the cattle grazers, not only in the Far West but in the early colonies on the Atlantic Coast. They occupied the outward edge of frontier farming zones and usually preceded the farmer. The mining frontier, when mineral deposits were present, represented an early zone of advance. The fourth zone in this idealized, evolving frontier was that of the pioneer, self-sufficient, or subsistence, farmer. These were the frontiersmen who changed the landscape; often they had to withstand Indian attacks, to begin clearing the trees, and later they sold out to a more progressive type of farmer. The progressive, money-minded, "equipped" farmers or planters with capital came next and bought out the pioneers and engaged in the production of staples for the market. The arrival of this progressive cultivator actually represented the passing of the frontier. The urban frontier of commerce and industry, of skilled labor and the professions, represents the final transformation of any given zone but often accompanied and aided the other kinds of frontiers.

Whether the term *phase* or *zone* is applied depends upon whether one is viewing the successive frontier economic transformations that any given region passed through or the frontier characteristics being experienced by different geographical zones at any given time.

Implications of the Closing of the American Frontier.—If we accept the Turner thesis, then a corollary must be drawn from it. If the existence of the frontier gave rise to certain changes in institutions, then its disappearance might halt such changes. The implication is that such products of the frontier as democracy and freedom are in danger of being replaced by a trend to concentration of authority and to regimentation in government. For illustration, American society now looks with respect to specialists and experts instead of relying with simple faith upon the ability and wisdom of the unschooled common man. It is further suggested that the splintering and fragmenting effects of the frontier experience will give way to centralizing and unifying forces, e.g., religious denominations that once split off from each other are merging and local government everywhere is looking more to larger units of government to solve its problems. Democracy is in danger if it thrived because of the frontier environment.

Observable Effects of the Disappearance of the Frontier.—The passing of the frontier required Americans to pay more attention to the rest of the world. The frontier had kept America busy settling the continent and exploiting it; she belittled the rest of the world, presumed superiority to it, and grew provincial. American leaders have taken an increased interest in foreign affairs since 1890, when the frontier came to an end. At first Americans reacted by waging the imperialistic Spanish-American War but since then have moved more and more in the direction of world cooperation.

The rugged individualism of the pioneer has been rapidly giving way since 1900 to governmental economic controls. Theodore Roosevelt and the Progressives realized the need to bring under public control the plutocrats who were undermining popular government and the corporations that were exploiting the people; that the lavish and wasteful use of natural resources that Americans had practiced for three centuries could not go on forever was recognized by Theodore Roosevelt and the conservationists in 1900. Franklin D. Roosevelt was influenced by the closing of the frontier; he said in 1935: "We can no longer escape into virgin territory; we must master our environment." He promoted agencies for social security and economic protection to remedy the weaknesses of outdated frontier individualism. Realization that we no longer had vacant land to occupy nor sufficient jobs helped bring severe restrictions on immigration beginning in 1921.

The Corporation and the Frontier.—Walter Prescott Webb in *The Great Frontier* (1952) pointed to the corporation as the modern institution under which society is crystallizing. Feudal institutions were destroyed by the world frontier but are being replaced by the device of the corporation. The corporation, public and private, in various forms and spheres of activity, is performing the functions formerly managed by feudal institutions; in the modern world the individual is becoming subordinated to the corporation. The corporation, a device usually associated with private business enterprise, is used by government and private organizations other than business firms.

Corporations in many areas have replaced private enterprise; they direct individuals and perform functions formerly left to individuals. Social security and social welfare are organized along corporate lines. Labor organizations and government agencies are often organized as corporations and exercise controls over individuals similar to those of corporations. These corporations have brought greater economic well-being, but they limit the freedom of individuals and regiment them. In fact, the old freedoms sometimes ring hollow as compared with the economic and social benefits of more organized society.

THE WORLDWIDE FRONTIER OF MODERN HISTORY

Historians more recently are turning their attention to the study of other frontiers and the application of the Turner thesis to other parts of the world than the frontiers in the United States. Wider effects of the frontier than those observed by Turner are being studied, including the effects of the opening of the new continents upon the Old World. Some other views should be stated here before proceeding with the specific details of the frontier history of the United States.

The World Frontier, the Result of European Dynamism.— The opening of the European frontier in America was first a result of a renewed dynamism among the nations of Europe; after the discovery of America the opening of the new lands accelerated the causative forces in Europe. The expansion of European civilization into America was the fruition of a preceding movement of expansion in the Old World. This expansion first expressed itself in the Crusades or Holy Wars against the Moslems to the east and south of the Mediterranean Sea. This renewed energy of Europe brought conquests of foreign lands and pushed European rule outward along many new frontiers in Europe, Asia, and Africa.

In the eastern Mediterranean contact of the now aggressive Europeans with the more advanced but effete culture of Asia stimulated an appetite for the fine goods and commodities of the East. The consequent expansion of commerce, with the search for new sources of goods, carried Europeans outward farther and farther. It reached the point where European merchants came to yearn for an all-water trade route by which they could obtain the spices, among other goods, of eastern Asia. The development of the technology of navigation and the accumulation of geographical knowledge, combined with the merchants' profit motive, led to the discovery of America after the expansion had already borne fruit in the opening of an all-water route to India by Vasco da Gama. Thus, the discovery of America was one result of expansive forces already underway in Europe.

Webb's The Great Frontier.—In 1952 Walter Prescott Webb published *The Great Frontier,* a study of the frontier thesis in world dimensions. This work discusses the effects of the world frontier upon Europe, the great "Metropolis." It emphasizes the economic and cultural enrichment of Europe consequent to the easy harvest of material wealth in the new lands. Webb calls attention to the parallel growth of democracy in Europe with colonial expansion and the growth of world trade of European nations. He suggests that the close of Europe's frontier may bring an end to an epoch in Western civilization; many institutions designed to function in a society dominated by frontier conditions find themselves in strain and crisis today.

As to the effects of the frontier upon European civilization, Webb attributes the rise of individualism to the frontier. In America hard work in exploiting the resources of the land brought rich rewards and respect for those who worked and accumulated wealth; America made a religion of work. As for the economic institutions of Europe, the world frontier transformed economies highly regulated under mercantilistic theory and opened the way for the rugged individualism of laissez faire economics. Adam Smith declared economic independence for the individual at the same time that the British-American colonies declared political independence in order to create a system favoring individual liberty.

Some Cultural Influences of the World Frontier.—Webb points out that since Columbus the findings of observers in various fields of science have helped to overthrow medieval misconceptions. Scientists concluded that all natural phenomena could be explained by natural causes. It was the worldwide accessibility of natural phenomena that made it possible, after the whole world was opened by exploration, to see the whole picture in many fields of science. Information not previously available helped to construct the complete picture. These data included astronomical observations, geological studies, and observations of plant and animal life. Darwin was able to travel and make biological observations in various parts of the world. This great accretion of scientific information made classification and systematization necessary and this in turn disclosed meaningful relationships. England sent out many scientific expeditions over the world during her rise to world power. International law was forced to expand with the opening of overseas areas to rival European nations.

Webb observed further that the great wealth from the new world and the new subject matter influenced literature. Men's imaginations were stimulated. Europeans wrote about new subjects such as primitive man, nature, Eldorado, Utopia, and of civilized man in conflict with nature. Among writers affected by the new world were Sir Thomas More, Shakespeare, and Coleridge. Art became more functional. In America a more functional type of architecture produced the skyscraper. Artists took more interest in people at work. The appropriation of abundant vacant lands for the support of education brought relatively lavish expenditures as compared with what had been made before. Public schools received early support from appropriations of land by the federal government under the Ordinance of 1785; later the Morrill Act appropriated parts of the federal domain to institute a more democratic type of college in each of the states.

THE SUCCESSIVE REGIONAL FRONTIERS

3

THE SEABOARD-COLONIAL FRONTIER, 1492–1700

America was not Europe's first frontier after the decline of the Roman Empire. Europe had already started pushing outward centuries before under the Vikings, the Teutonic Knights, and the Mediterranean Crusaders. Just before Columbus the Iberian states were making great progress in pushing back the Moslems and in exploring the African coast. Vasco da Gama (1487) had just discovered the long-desired sea route giving direct access to the trade of the Orient. In the search for a westward sea route, Columbus stumbled upon America.

Europe's first frontier in America was carried by the Spanish into the West Indies and the lands bordering the Gulf of Mexico. Exploration, fishing, and the fur trade preceded colonization in the exploitation of North America by the French, Dutch, and English. Of most importance to the United States, however, was the colonization by the English of the Atlantic seaboard, the first English frontier in the United States. We are concerned with the movement of this frontier and some of its major effects in these colonies.

The seaboard frontier of colonial times in British America ended about 1700. It extended from the coast westward to the fall line, an imaginary line running from north to south drawn through the waterfalls or rapids that prevented the further upstream movement on the rivers flowing into the Atlantic Ocean. A temporary halt occurred after most of these tidelands or coastal plains had been occupied. Contact with the mother country was maintained by the accessibility of ocean shipping. The frontier influences were therefore not as effective at first as they were later when the population had less contact with the Old World.

EARLY FRONTIERS IN AMERICA

The Spanish.—The Spanish opened the first frontier in America, with Columbus leading the way. Unlike many of the Spanish, Columbus was enthusiastically in favor of colonizing the new world. He was responsible for the first attempted European settlement in America when, on his first voyage to America, he left a garrison on the island of Hispaniola upon his return to Spain; the Indians destroyed this force of Spaniards. On the second voyage (1493) he brought 1,500 colonists to Hispaniola and founded the first permanent settlement in America. The gold mining frontier opened there was accompanied by features similar to later Anglo-American mining booms. Gross exploitation of the Indians was a prominent feature in Hispaniola.

Hispaniola became a base, along with other West Indian islands, for the expansion of Spanish frontiers by exploration and conquest. From these islands the Spanish launched expeditions into Florida under Ponce de Leon (1513) and then into Mexico under Cortez (1519) and into Peru by Pizarro (1528). The Spanish were motivated in this expansion by the desire for gold and silver, the exploitation of the land with Indian labor, and a zeal to spread Christianity among the natives.

The Spanish next explored parts of the southern United States under such leaders as Panfilo de Narvaez (1528) and Hernando de Soto (1539–1543). In the Southwest, Cabeza de Vaca (1528–1534) and Francisco de Coronado (1540–1542) explored the regions of present Texas, New Mexico, Arizona, and the southern Great Plains. Missionaries were sent northward from Mexico into New Mexico, Arizona, and Texas. St. Augustine, Florida, was founded in 1565 as the first permanent white settlement in what would become a part of the United States. Other Spanish settlements were founded subsequently in the present states of the southeastern United States. The Spanish remained here until American ownership was completed by the acquisition of Florida in 1819. Thus, for over a century and a half the Spanish were a factor in the frontier of the Southeast. Later they extended the northwestern frontiers of Mexico in New Mexico and Arizona, and into California.

The French in North America.—When the French tried to found settlements in Florida and in the region of Carolina they were annihilated by the Spanish. But Cartier's exploration of the St. Lawrence (1534) gave the French a claim to more northerly territory. Fish and furs lured the French to Newfoundland year after year.

In 1603 Champlain began his explorations up the St. Lawrence. In the next year the French built their first homes in America in the present region of New Brunswick, which they called Acadia. In 1608 Champlain founded Quebec. After this the French gave their main attention in the St. Lawrence Valley to the fur trade with the natives. Their missionaries, fur traders, and explorers carried forward French civilization, founded numerous settlements, and extended territorial claims to the whole of the Great Lakes region and to much of the Mississippi Valley.

The English in America.—Early English interest in America centered in fishing and in searching for a northwest passage through America to the Orient. In these pursuits they conducted several explorations. The English established a claim to the New England region when it was discovered by John Cabot (1497). In the reign of Elizabeth, the Protestant daughter of Henry VIII, the English vigorously challenged Catholic Spain's monopoly in America. They plundered Spanish ships and coastal towns and under the protection of their ships' guns conducted illegal trade with Spanish settlements.

During this time of rivalry with Spain the English tried to establish colonies under Raleigh in the region of Virginia but failed because of inexperience, lack of financial support, and interference and distraction caused by the war with Spain (1588). The famous defeat of the Spanish navy in the battle of the Armada gave the English superiority on the seas and helped open the way for successful English colonization on the Atlantic Coast.

[21]

THE ENGLISH IN THE SOUTH

The establishment of peace with Spain in 1603 enabled James I of England to proceed with plans for the establishment of colonies in America.

The Settlement of Virginia.—In 1607 the first permanent English settlement in America was founded by the London Company at Jamestown. This joint-stock company was composed of a group of merchant adventurers who hoped to find gold and who sought to profit from the exploitation of the natural resources of the country, including the soil.

The settlers learned from experience in their environment and from the Indians how to survive and make a living in Virginia. The early failure in Virginia, the starving time, was caused partly by the members of the Company who tried to live as gentlemen did in the old country and partly by their unfamiliarity with the new continent. Success came when an early prototype of the frontiersman, the seasoned adventurer John Smith, rolled up his sleeves, went to work, and made others do the same. Smith, a commoner with qualities of initiative, bravery, and resourcefulness, was elevated, by the environment of danger and forest wilderness, above the gentlemen and became their "president." Such men as Smith would continue to rise to leadership in the frontier regions of America.

Expansion in Virginia.—The permanence of the Virginia colony was assured when John Rolfe introduced a variety of tobacco that suited the English market. Thus began the tobacco prosperity of the colony. Farmers rapidly took up land to the west to grow this crop, for which there was a ready market. The methods of farming, especially in the production of tobacco, rapidly exhausted the fertility of the soil. Instead of restoring the lost fertility, virgin soil was cleared to secure heavier yields. In this way tobacco cultivation pushed the line of settlement outward. The same process occurred in Maryland. By the 1670's the whole tidewater region of both Virginia and Maryland was settled by farmers.

The Westward movement advanced with the migration from England, especially during the English Civil War in the 1640's. The evolution of a system of land distribution that enabled planters to secure their farms cheaply contributed to the expansion. At first headrights of 50 acres were given as rewards for various services, such as bringing an indentured servant to Virginia. For a time almost all passengers on incoming ships were awarded headrights upon application. Indentured servants and redemptioners upon completion of their term of service usually migrated to the outward fringe of settlement and bought the cheaper land.

Maryland.—The settlement of Maryland began in 1634 with the founding of St. Mary's. The colony prospered from the beginning, since it benefited from the experience of Virginia. As in Virginia, corn, tobacco, and livestock were produced.

The colonists soon picked up the spirit of frontier independence. When Lord Baltimore tried to set up the feudal institutions of Europe and restricted the legislature to advisory functions, the settlers strongly resisted, and in fifteen years the Maryland assembly practically ruled the colony. The existence of unoccupied land on the edge of the settlements made men more independent. Urgent need rendered labor valuable and placed men in a stronger position to make heavy demands upon ruling groups. Religious toleration was granted because Protestants outnumbered Catholics, who, as a minority, were in danger of losing their freedom of worship.

Early Pioneer Life in the South.—Out of the adjustment of the Englishman to the raw wilderness the pattern of establishing a home on the frontier soon developed. The settler usually moved out in the autumn. He built a log house and dug a well by hand near the door. A plank roof covered the house and sliding panels took the place of windows. Holes were bored in the logs to make openings for muskets. Nails were used very sparingly and the cabin might be burned when the pioneer moved so as to recover the precious metal.

In the spring the settler would plant his first crop of corn in a clearing where the trees had been killed by girdling and burning brush under them. His foodstuffs were made up of bread from his corn crop, of turnips or other vegetables, and acorn-fattened hogs. From this originated the traditional Southern frontier diet of hog, hominy, bacon, greens, and cornbread.

In the second year a field of tobacco would be grown, harvested, and packed for shipment to England. The tobacco paid for the commodities he could not produce himself—sugar, tea, gunpowder, and iron implements. Almost everything else he used he made at home. Clothing was sewn from skins or made of wool produced in the neighborhood. The life of the pioneer differed from that of the pretentious planters on the lower tidewater. These class differences helped provide the setting for Bacon's Rebellion. (For further discussion of colonial agriculture see Section 17.)

Bacon's Rebellion.—During the conservative reaction of the period following the Stuart Restoration in 1660, the governors in Virginia and Maryland, Berkeley and Calvert, attempted to deprive the frontier settlers of the few political rights they enjoyed. Berkeley, an irritable old man, raised taxes and used his power as governor to keep his loyal followers in office. Economic depression due to the low tobacco prices, caused by overproduction during the 1670's gave rise to serious discontent, particularly among the backwoods debtor farmers.

Under such provocations Bacon's Rebellion was set off when Indian outrages that took a great toll of lives beginning in 1675 reached a peak in January, 1676. By March, several hundred whites had lost their lives, but Governor Berkeley did nothing to prevent the Indian ravages. The settlers believed the profits from trade with the Indians kept officials from acting against the savages. The frontiersmen decided to take matters into their own hands and punish the natives. Nathaniel Bacon was persuaded to lead them; three hundred settlers won a decisive victory over the Indians. But Bacon and his men attacked any Indians, even those that were friendly. Berkeley tried to arrest the rebel leader, but popular resentment against the eastern governing class prevented it. In the course of the quarrel Bacon raised an army of six hundred men, took Jamestown from the conservatives, and burned it completely. At the peak of victory Bacon suddenly died of fever. Without adequate leadership among the farmers, Berkeley was able to regain the upper hand and began a bloody purge in which over twenty of his opponents were hanged. These troubles in Virginia caused an exodus of settlers who helped populate the first settlements of North Carolina around Albemarle Sound. Bacon's Rebellion is significant as an early expression of backwoods farmer discontent with aristocratic domination during the colonial period.

Backwoods Discontent in Maryland.—In Maryland discontented backwoods farmers who followed a Bacon-inspired rebellion were crushed for lack of support from most of the settlers. But the dislike of the domineering aristocrats smouldered through the 1680's. When the Glorious Revolution came in England in 1689, the dissatisfied backwoodsmen took advantage of it to revolt against the governing class in Maryland. They marched to St. Mary's, took over the government, and called a popular assembly which abolished the proprietary control of the Calverts. Maryland was made a royal colony in 1691. This frontier revolt had succeeded.

The Carolina Frontier.—Carolina, at first including both North and South Carolina of the present time, began officially when the region was granted in 1663 to the eight Lords Proprietors. The first settlers in Carolina were sent by Virginia into the region around the Albemarle Sound in 1653 to guard the southern approach. Typical frontier settlers moved into the region in succeeding years for refuge from zealous tax collectors and ministers. In 1670 the Proprietors colonized Charleston, and it became the nucleus of South Carolina.

The important early economic foundation of Charleston, until rice became a profitable staple after 1700, was the fur trade with Indian tribes to the west and south. Through this profitable trade the friendship of the Indians was gained. The Spanish were driven back, unfriendly Indians defeated, and a long prospering trade with the western Indians established and expanded. During the fall and winter, traders moved from one tribe to another gathering pelts. In the spring the deer skins and pelts were taken to Charleston, where the traders indulged in a few weeks of riotous living. Later, plantation agriculture superseded the economic importance of the fur traders' frontier.

THE FRONTIER IN NEW ENGLAND

The English first encountered the problems of frontier settlement in New England in the founding of Plymouth Colony in 1620 and Massachusetts Bay Colony in 1630.

The Settlement of Plymouth.—The Pilgrim founders of Plymouth, upon finding themselves landing on a section of the Atlantic Coast not granted in their charter, on their own initiative drew up the Mayflower Compact. By it they established for their "civil body politic" the principle of the rule of the majority. This agreement foreshadowed many similar compacts made by Americans as they advanced to different frontiers and found themselves beyond the jurisdiction of established governments.

The provision that the members of the colony work for seven years for the joint-stock company they all belonged to broke down in 1623; the members were made private owners of the land they held. This was another development repeated in the frontier colonies, where it was found that private ownership would best bring out man's energy to develop the land. The Plymouth settlers, lacking any agricultural staple, very early began to engage in the fur trade with the Indians. Cattle-raising soon became the leading industry as settlers occupied the adjoining coastal areas and then the river valleys.

Massachusetts Bay Colony.—As with the Plymouth settlers, the Massachusetts Bay colonists at Boston migrated to the new world, not only for economic reasons, but because the vacant spaces offered an opportunity to worship freely according to their own ideas and to escape the papistic High Church leaders in England. Thus, America offered opportunities for religious and other dissenters to live according to their own precepts. The large colony founded at Boston quickly threw off population that

[26]

founded new satellite towns beyond the settled areas. Immigrants poured in by the thousands from England during the 1630's when the High Church authorities persisted in their attempt to establish religious uniformity in England. Some came to escape poverty.

The Widening of the New England Frontier.—Although the Puritans had left England to worship as they liked, they were only seeking religious freedom for themselves and did not wish to extend toleration to those who held different religious beliefs. The great concern among them over matters of religion and the gravity of minor differences seemed to breed dissenters. Soon after the founding of Massachusetts Bay Colony, these disagreements with the ruling theocratic oligarchy caused settlers to move out and found new towns in every direction. Those who dissented did not have to submit but could go into exile, as did Roger Williams, and join others of a like mind and found a new settlement. Of the large stream of immigrants from England, few stayed in Boston, because the system of government there was nearly as autocratic as the one they had left.

At first the Puritan ministers tried to rule without the General Court, or legislature, but in 1634 popular demand forced them to permit delegates to be elected from the various towns. The right to vote, however, was limited to church members, and only men approved by the clergy could become members.

Population scattered rapidly over the lower New England regions of Rhode Island and Connecticut. The fur trade with the Indians began in 1631 and cattle-raising, too, became a general occupation.

Settlers in the new lands took matters of government into their own hands as much as they could. The Fundamental Orders of Connecticut and other developments in self-government show this.

Roger Williams, Anne Hutchinson, and other dissenters started settlements in what came to be chartered as the colony of Rhode Island. Towns in New Hampshire were also settled by dissenters.

Indian Wars and Expansion.—The Pequot War broke out in the summer of 1636. It was caused by the encirclement of blocks of Indian lands by the colonists. In retaliation the whole of the Pequot tribe was wiped out by the Massachusetts soldiers. Forty years of peace and expansion followed this victory. As usual, fur traders took the lead in moving into new areas and were quickly followed by cattle grazers and farmers.

Conflict of New Englanders with the Dutch in New Netherland over the fur trade and other events not related to the frontier resulted in 1664 in the English capture of New Netherland, which was renamed New York.

The Establishment of Towns in New England.—Individuals moving out helter-skelter settled the outlying lands in Virginia, but in New England the migration was planned by the colonial governments. Title to a township was secured from the General Court; settlers moved as a group and created towns by cooperative effort. Religious views explain why the New England colonies expanded differently from colonies to the south. The Puritans granted townsites to believers, after considering the fitness of the locality for a settlement. Townships, usually six miles square in size, were located next to settled areas. The grantees were expected to divide the land among themselves and bring in other settlers. The founders first laid out the townsite with its lots for residences. Arable land and meadow land were allotted by the laws of chance in drawings which gave divided strips to settlers. Thus, a settler would hold several strips according to the medieval custom on English feudal manors. This orderly system of founding towns assured that provisions would be made for churches, schools, and community life. Community spirit and discipline prevailed. Later, farmers exchanged or bought strips of land to form compact holdings. Agriculture was only self-sufficient, since the land was poor and no highly profitable staple was found for export.

King Philip's War.—In 1675 crowding of whites upon Indian lands caused an Indian war that raged throughout the New England settlements for two years. Losses were heavy on both sides.

Even Boston put up fortifications to defend itself. After their defeat the Indians were deprived of their lands, slaughtered, sold into slavery, or confined to reservations; and New England expansion was resumed.

4

THE OLD WEST, 1700–1776

The term "Old West" designates the Piedmont, or foothill, area west of the fall line and extending to the crest of the Appalachian Mountain ranges, thirteen hundred miles long, from New England to Georgia; the settlement of this frontier region lasted approximately from 1700 to 1776. The Old West includes the region of the Great Valley of the Appalachians in western Virginia and other interior valleys.

Early Movement into the Old West.—By 1700 the plains and valleys of the tideland region had been largely settled; new immigrants had to move farther into the West. First exploration of the Old West was conducted to extend the fur trade there. The actual fur trade itself brought further familiarity with the region and the choice lands were determined. By 1710 Virginia farmers were rapidly pushing into the region. At the head of these pioneers were the cattlemen. These ranchers grazed their herds in meadows, in canebreaks, or enclosed them in "cow-pens." The expansion of the plantations in the tidewater region caused small farmers to sell out and move west.

The Germans on the Frontier.—Differing considerably from the English were two new groups that came into the colonies, the Germans and the Scotch-Irish. Both created buffer settlements against the Indians. Their presence introduced an important non-English influence in the colonies. These settlers moved into the mountain valleys and hardly knew which colony they belonged to and thought of themselves as Americans rather than as Virginians or Carolinians. Thus, they became a nationalizing influence.

The Germans came to America after 1708; upon arriving in the colonies, they were encouraged to move out west to settle vacant land and fend for themselves against the Indians. These Germans migrated from the Palatinate along the Rhine to escape poverty, taxes, and war. As Protestants they were welcomed to America by the British, who encouraged the immigration in order to populate their colonies. The Germans settled first in New York along the Mohawk and soon afterward in the southeast of Pennsylvania in what became known as the Pennsylvania-Dutch section. The Scotch-Irish also moved in large numbers to the south, and the two groups founded alternating settlements in the back country.

The Scotch-Irish on the Frontier.—From Northern Ireland came the Scotch-Irish who were mostly lowland Scots but included a considerable addition of Highland Scots as well as Irish and English blood. The Scotch-Irish left their homeland to escape poverty partly caused by discriminatory tariff duties against their exports of cattle and woolen goods to England. Religious discrimination against Presbyterians was another cause.

Most of the Scotch-Irish went to Pennsylvania. This colony, founded by the Quaker William Penn in 1681, welcomed people of any religion or nationality. Heavy migration of the Scotch-Irish began in 1717; in the 1730's they were moving into the valleys of Pennsylvania and into the hillier country. The Scotch-Irish, like the Germans, also turned southward but into the western edges of the Great Valley; many moved west of the Appalachian divide into the upper tributaries of the Tennessee River. These people became typical Indian-hating, devout, aggressive pioneers.

New England Expansion.—In New England the fever of land speculation, with its opportunities to increase individual fortunes, replaced the religious motivation in originating land grants for new towns. Profit-minded speculative groups exerted pressure on the legislatures to grant townsites. The land was settled by the sons of New Englanders who were now undergoing a transformation into speculative-minded frontier farmers.

Distinctive Life in the Old West.—The typical frontier mode of living prevailed over the back country from New England to South Carolina. The axe, the long rifle, the log cabin, the Conestoga wagon were the leading symbols of their way of life. A common mode of living with common problems united the backwoods people; they became conscious of the differences between themselves and the aristocracy of plantation owners and wealthy merchants.

The conflict of interests between the East and the West began as these two groups sought fair representation in the colonial legislatures. They supported protest movements and several times waged war against the authorities to assert their rights. A frequent grievance was the disproportionate tax burden they had to pay to support colonial governments. They also complained of the inadequate military protection afforded by the governments against the marauding Indians.

Uprisings in the Old West.—In 1763 the "Paxton Boys" in Paxton County, Pennsylvania, in defiance of the Philadelphia legislature attacked peaceful Indians. Frontiersmen usually made little distinction between good and bad Indians. A military force was sent against the Paxton Boys, but fortunately a peace was arranged before bloodshed occurred.

In North Carolina "The Regulation" movement arose to protest multiple injustices. The grievances there were against corrupt officials, under-representation in government, and high taxes—all traceable to domination of backwoods county government by the Eastern aristocracy. Governor Tryon in 1771 marched against them at the Battle of Alamance. Nine men were killed on each side.

In South Carolina a similar Regulation movement occurred. About the same grievances angered the Westerners. Because of the inadequacy of government the Westerners organized vigilantes to punish criminals and protect property. Scattered fighting that broke out was climaxed by a pitched battle in March, 1769. The legislature appeased the rebels by passing a circuit court bill in answer to one of their grievances. Defeat of the Westerners

[31]

propelled them farther into the West and made cooperation with the East difficult and sometimes impossible during the American Revolution.

The French and Indian War, 1754–1763.—The most significant of the imperial wars between the British and the French was the French and Indian War, or Great War for Empire. The three colonial wars that had been fought earlier over trade and territory had been indecisive. English expansion in the Ohio Valley and rivalry with the French for its highly profitable fur trade brought on the last and greatest of these contests for empire; the war began in 1754. The French claimed the Ohio Valley as a part of their vast inland empire in the Mississippi Basin and resented the fur-trading activities of Pennsylvanians that extended far into the Ohio Valley. The intrusion of the Ohio Company, a British-chartered land company, intended to promote settlement into the West in the Allegheny River region, aroused the French to construct a string of forts across western Pennsylvania. George Washington was sent by the governor of Virginia to protest to the commanders of the French forts between Lake Erie and the Allegheny River. A fight between the French and the English at Washington's hastily built defenses at Fort Necessity touched off a world war, known in Europe as the Seven Years' War.

The early years of the war brought successive defeats to the British forces. General Edward Braddock suffered a shocking defeat in his march to take Fort Duquesne in 1755. The tide of war in America turned against the French after the energetic and brilliant William Pitt became Prime Minister in 1757. General John Forbes captured Fort Duquesne in 1758, but the contest in America was decided on the Plains of Abraham at Quebec, where Wolfe defeated Montcalm in 1759.

The consequences of the victory, written into the Treaty of Paris of 1763, removed the French barrier to the incipient westward movement of Americans over the mountains into the eastern Mississippi basin. The treaty transferred to other powers all French possessions on the continent of North America except the city of New Orleans and two small islands in the St. Lawrence

Bay. The English won Canada and the territory of eastern Louisiana. France gave to Spain the Louisiana territory west of the Mississippi in compensation for Spanish loss of Florida. The Spanish transferred Florida to Britain in exchange for Cuba, which the British had taken during the war.

5

THE FRONTIER OF THE EASTERN MISSISSIPPI REGION, 1763–1840

The British victory in the French and Indian War removed the French as an obstacle to the frontier advance into the attractive lands beyond the Appalachians. Land speculators, fur traders, and settlers were poised and waiting for this opportunity—in fact, had already begun the invasion. This vast area, from the Appalachians to the Mississippi River, was to be occupied quickly by American pioneer farmers. This eventful frontier, coinciding with the American Revolution and the War of 1812, was particularly formative in American development.

BRITISH WESTERN POLICY

The cession of French territory east of the Mississippi to Great Britain created difficult problems in policy-making for Britain. The two leading problems were, first, whether the territories should be opened for settlement or be reserved for traders and, second, whether the territories should be governed by the colonial legislatures or by the mother country.

The fur traders and land jobbers both exerted great influence in government circles. The traders wanted to close the West to settlement and reserve the territory for the Indians. Land jobbers and small frontier farmers wanted it opened to settlement. Also several of the colonies had claims under their charters to this territory and, of course, provincial land jobbers wanted the colonies rather than England to govern these territories and decide policy. Pennsylvania and Virginia land speculators had the largest interests in the West.

[33]

Pontiac's Rebellion, 1763–1764.—Soon after the British occupied the western territory taken from the French, the Indians became increasingly restless. In 1763 war began when the Indian leader Pontiac attacked the British posts at Detroit.

Causes of Pontiac's Rebellion may be enumerated: (1) French travellers encouraged the uprising by promising aid. (2) Unscrupulous fur traders cheated the Indians and aroused their resentment. (3) Threats of coming waves of English settlers into the fertile lands alarmed the Indians, and (4) the unfriendly attitude of the British and their decision to stop giving presents antagonized the Indians.

Peace was substantially restored in 1764. In 1765 Pontiac himself made terms. The Rebellion moved the British to issue the Proclamation of 1763 to prevent further trouble between Indians and Americans.

Colonial Land Speculation.—Early in colonial times land speculation became a leading business activity by which individuals might hope to accumulate large fortunes. As long as large areas of potential farm lands lay vacant, land jobbing remained relatively prominent among money-making opportunities in America. Land development and resale to settlers was carried on by large companies, since it required much capital to buy, survey, and improve the land. Some companies built towns and established sawmills and other industries needed by the new communities. Land companies brought the availability of land to the attention of settlers and sold the land under more attractive terms than governments did at this time. On the frontier east of the Mississippi land jobbers spied out the land about as early as did traders and hunters. Many prominent persons had financial interests in land companies and often it was basic to their political interests. George Washington, Benjamin Franklin, and many others among the Founding Fathers were interested in land jobbing and speculation. It should be observed that such business interests acting behind the scenes exerted much influence in many of the events prominent in American history in colonial times and for long afterward.

[34]

The Frontier of the Eastern Mississippi Region

The Proclamation of 1763.—At the end of the French and Indian War the British proceeded to settle permanently various problems in North America. As a solution of the Indian problem they set aside the land west of the Appalachians as an Indian Reserve and undertook to regulate entrance into this region by the Proclamation of 1763.

Provisions of the Proclamation (1) limited white settlement to the region east of the Appalachians by drawing the Proclamation Line and (2) reserved the land west of the mountains for the royal government of England. Colonial officials could not make further grants of land west of the line and settlers there were required to vacate. (3) In the future all lands were to be ceded by the Indians voluntarily so as not to give cause for retaliation. (4) To eliminate the unscrupulous and prevent friction with Indians, traders were required to obtain licenses.

The enmity aroused among the colonials by the Proclamation was prominent among the causes of the American Revolution. The powerful land speculators in the colonies were offended by the apparent intention of the British to monopolize the distribution of the western lands. But the Proclamation did not prevent innumerable speculators from staking out claims west of the mountains; three large companies worked to win large tracts by exercising their influence with government officials. Frontier traders and farmers hated the restrictions.

A revised Plan of 1764 established a detailed plan of regulation of the Indian trade and further angered Americans who saw it as a scheme to benefit the Indians. In 1768, yielding to pressure from land companies, the government negotiated Indian treaties to push the Proclamation Line farther west and open land for occupation by whites. This revision showed that when the land jobbers exerted sufficient pressure the western lands would be opened to settlement; at the same time the revision encouraged pioneers to disregard British restrictions, since they could look forward to their eventual removal. Thus, the Proclamation was not effective and imposed little restraint; the approaching

American Revolution reflected already the colonial attitude of disobedience toward British laws in general.

The Quebec Act, 1774.—By this measure the British Parliament extended religious freedom to Roman Catholic French-Canadians and provided civil government. The act placed the whole territory enclosed by the Ohio, the Mississippi, and the Great Lakes under the province of Quebec. The religious and political provisions were not particularly related to frontier problems but aroused intense resentment among the colonists. Virginia denied the right of the crown to give away territory that she claimed. Colonial land jobbers and traders resented being brought under regulations originating in Montreal.

THE OPENING OF SETTLEMENTS WEST OF THE APPALACHIANS

The Proclamation of 1763 did not stop pioneer movement into the eastern Mississippi Basin. The Indian attacks accompanying the American Revolution slowed settlement there, but the westward movement was quickly resumed after peace had been restored.

Leading Routes to the West.—Beginning in the north (1) the St. Lawrence River and the Great Lakes provided water routes for traders. (2) The next route westward followed the Hudson-Mohawk rivers to Lake Erie. (3) In north central Pennsylvania the Kittanning Path ran along the Susquehanna and Juniata rivers to Fort Pitt on the Ohio River. (4) Forbes Road, in southern Pennsylvania, was opened between Philadelphia and Fort Pitt in 1758 (the general route of the present Lincoln Highway). (5) Braddock's Road was opened in 1755 along the Potomac River to Cumberland. From there it cut across the country to Fort Pitt. Later the National or Cumberland Road followed this route but went through Wheeling instead of to Pittsburgh. (6) At the Cumberland Gap (no connection with the Cumberland Road), near the upper branches of the Tennessee and Cumberland rivers, the Wilderness Road began; it connected Virginia with central Kentucky at Boonesborough. (7) A final entrance to the Trans-Appalachian region skirted around the southern end of the Appalachians in Georgia.

Most of these routes had originally been buffalo trails used by the Indians. These forest paths were widened later into wagon roads.

PATHS ACROSS THE ALLEGHENIES, 1750–1790, AND THE PROCLAMATION LINE OF 1763

The Settlement of Pittsburgh.—The first large settlement west of the Appalachians was made in the forks of the Ohio at Pittsburgh. The vicinity of Pittsburgh, where the Monongahela and the Allegheny join and become the Ohio, was recognized early as of much strategic importance. Consequently the English and French clash here opened the French and Indian War. Fort Pitt was built here by the English in 1759. The road up from Virginia had been built by Braddock in the campaign that ended in his disaster. Two other routes from the east converged at the forks, the Forbes Road and the Kittanning Path.

The first settlers at Fort Pitt came up from Virginia in defiance of the Proclamation of 1763. In the United States Fort Pitt was the first permanent settlement of the English west of the mountains. For a long time, until the railroads came, this gateway to the West served as the staging or the jumping off place for western travellers. It was the eastern point at which men gained access to the Ohio and the great natural transportation system of the Mississippi River.

The Watauga Settlement in North Carolina.—A second point where large numbers of settlers crossed the mountains to enter the Mississippi Basin was along the Watauga River. The Watauga settlement, in Tennessee, began in 1769 but grew slowly. Their two ablest leaders, James Robertson and John Sevier, educated and cultured men, later came to be well known in Tennessee and Kentucky. But the most famous of the Watauga settlers was Daniel Boone.

Daniel Boone was well prepared for his exploits in the West. He was born in Pennsylvania and took part in Braddock's expedition. He returned after the Braddock expedition to his home on the Yadkin River, just east of the Watauga River. Most of his life was spent hunting in the wilderness farther out in the West.

After 1770 and the failure of the Regulator movement in North Carolina, many new migrants came to the Watauga settlement. As the population increased, they tried to induce North Carolina to organize local (county) government but were left to establish their own Watauga Association in 1772 with a written

[38]

constitution and representative assembly. It performed the functions of local administration that otherwise would have been provided by county government. In 1777 this region was organized as a county of North Carolina.

Kentucky.—A third region of settlement in the land to the west was in the Blue Grass region of Kentucky. Boone's hunting trips led him into this rich country; he became enthusiastic about the region. In 1775 the Transylvania Company, organized by Judge Richard Henderson to purchase land from the Indians, sent Boone out to mark the Wilderness Trail through the Cumberland Gap to the Blue Grass country along the Kentucky River; the same year he established the fort at Boonesborough on the Kentucky River near present Lexington. Other settlements grew up as frontier families poured into the region. Later Sevier and Robertson bought a large part of the state of Kentucky from the Cherokee tribe.

The Kentucky settlers, like the Watauga Association, established their own government. The constitution was written by Judge Henderson and accepted by popular vote.

Migration to Kentucky was slowed during the American Revolution because of Indian hostility encouraged by the British. The settlements suffered severely from Shawnee and Delaware attacks. Boone himself underwent great dangers and was held captive for four months by the Shawnee. After 1778 the Indian menace subsided and settlers began to return. In time these settlements were organized by Virginia as the County of Kentucky.

The American Revolution and the West.—The settlements in both Kentucky and Tennessee suffered great harassment and loss of life due to British incitement of the Indians to warfare during the American Revolution. George Rogers Clark, who was commissioned by the Virginia legislature to lead a force into the Ohio Valley, captured the British posts there. Other American leaders were forced to campaign in western New York and in Tennessee to quell bloody Indian uprisings. The victories over the Indians brought a large new migration westward in the closing years of the Revolution.

The Treaty of Paris of 1783 recognized the independence of the thirteen American states and ceded to them the British western territory from the Appalachians to the Mississippi River on the West. Florida was returned to Spain and marked the southern boundary; in the north the Great Lakes separated Canada and the United States.

Tennessee.—The next large center of settlement was opened when Judge Richard Henderson in 1779 turned to the development of the land in central Tennessee granted to him in lieu of his claim to Kentucky. He founded what was to become Nashville, on the Cumberland River. Within a year five hundred settlers had arrived. The old process of pioneers exercising their capacity of self-government was re-enacted once again as the settlers drew up a compact in 1780 providing for government, headed by a committee of twelve.

Beginning in 1782 a movement for independence from North Carolina resulted, two years later, in the organization of the State of Franklin. John Sevier was elected governor and members of a legislature were chosen.

In 1788 North Carolina took advantage of an internal quarrel in the State of Franklin to assert her control over the region but ceded her western lands to the federal government. Tennessee was admitted to the Union as a separate state in 1796.

AMERICAN GOVERNMENT WEST OF THE APPALACHIANS

Three difficult problems in the West were inherited by the United States government with the signing of the Treaty of Independence in 1783: land policy, the establishment of government, and Indian relations.

Determination of American Land Policy.—The first problem requiring attention was whether state possession of the western lands should be recognized or federal control substituted. Maryland led the five other states without claims to western lands in the movement to refuse to ratify the Articles of Confederation unless the lands were ceded by the claimant states to the national government. States with claims, originating with the sea-to-sea charters, included Massachusetts, Connecticut, New York, Virginia, North Carolina, South Carolina, and Georgia.

When New York and then Virginia ceded their land claims in 1781, most other states with claims followed their example. It was the influence of land jobbers in the Maryland legislature that caused that state to take the stand it did; a particularly influential group of jobbers expected to find the federal government more amenable to their influence. Other land jobbers also believed the federal government would be more liberal in selling land to speculative companies. The Federal Congress in 1785 passed the Land Ordinance providing for the survey and distribution of the western public domain. (Policies governing the distribution of public lands are discussed in Section 11.) Georgia did not give up her claims until 1802; she did so then because it relieved her of the dispute over the Yazoo land sales.

The Northwest Ordinance of 1787.—By this legislation Congress provided for the Northwest Territory the necessary framework for successive phases of government leading to statehood. Provisions of government were intended to promote settlement and the sale of lands to provide much-needed revenue for the national treasury. (1) In the first phase of territorial government an unorganized territory was placed under the administration of a governor appointed by Congress. (2) When the population of a territory reached 5,000 adult males, it could organize and enjoy a limited degree of self-government through an elected legislature and could send one delegate to Congress. (3) The territory, after attaining a population of 60,000, could draft a constitution and apply for admission to the Union as a state equal in every respect to the older states. (4) Other provisions included a bill of rights which guaranteed freedom of worship and jury trial; another provision prohibited slavery.

English Influence in the Northwest.—After the conclusion of the Treaty of Independence the British maintained military posts immediately south of the international boundary. This was done to maintain control of the fur trade and to protect the settlements of Ontario by pacification of the Indians. Some English agents encouraged Indian attacks on the Americans while the fur trade enabled Indians to obtain weapons.

War with the Indians in the Northwest.—After American independence Congressional commissioners were sent out in the early 1780's to make peace treaties with the Indians north of the Ohio. White settlers subsequently moved into treaty territory reserved for the Indians. The commissioners now attempted to show their good faith with the Indians by sending out Colonel Joseph Harmar to remove the whites but he had too few men to do so. Harmar's ineffectiveness did more to encourage the Indians than to pacify them.

In 1789 Arthur St. Clair, governor of the Northwest Territory, tried to satisfy the natives by concluding a treaty with all the Indians he could bring together in January, 1789. On this occasion it was the Indians who made trouble by failing to observe their agreements.

In 1790 President Washington called out the militia of the states of Virginia, Kentucky, and Pennsylvania and placed them under General Harmar's command. The men were poorly equipped and included many who were unsatisfactory soldiers. After leaving Fort Washington, some of the men threatened mutiny, but they reached the present site of Fort Wayne, Indiana, and destroyed Indian towns and crops. Later a surprise attack by the Indians resulted in Harmar's retreat and loss of two hundred of his men. The disheartened troops returned to Fort Washington in early November. This retreat encouraged the Indians to attack more boldly than ever.

Washington next ordered Governor St. Clair himself to take command. In October, 1791, he led another poorly trained army of poorly qualified men into the Indian country along the Ohio-Indiana border. Again disaster struck when St. Clair and his men were attacked by surprise in early November; about half of the force were killed and wounded. The others straggled back to Cincinnati.

"Mad Anthony" Wayne in Command, 1792.—After St. Clair's disaster President Washington chose a man he hoped would not

repeat the previous debacles—a hero of the Revolutionary War, Anthony Wayne. He was given a similar army of the dregs of the frontier, but he set to work to prepare them thoroughly by discipline and drill. Before Wayne marched against the Indians another council was held with them, but they made such extravagant demands that no agreement was reached and Wayne advanced.

In the spring of 1794 he marched into the Indian country. Wayne took his time, marched deliberately, and watched for surprise attacks. The main Indian force was finally met in northern Ohio at Fallen Timbers within sight of the British Fort Miami. The British, who had led the Indians to expect support, permitted them to suffer defeat instead. Wayne proceeded to destroy Indian towns and built Fort Wayne, where he spent the winter in Indian country. In the spring, 1795, Wayne called the discouraged chiefs to a large conference and secured their acceptance of the Treaty of Greenville, which opened northern and western parts of Ohio and Indiana to the Americans.

The surrender of the British posts in the Northwest Territory, including Detroit, removed this source of encouragement to the Indians when the Jay Treaty was signed in 1794. Thus, the natives remained quiet for a time. But again the whites began to press into the Indian country. The federal government supported the whites and forced six new cessions from the Indians in the next ten years.

Difficulties with Spain in the Southwest.—In Washington's administration there were three sources of trouble from Spain on the Southwestern frontier. (1) There was the disputed ownership of the Yazoo strip paralleling the northern boundary of Florida. (2) The Spanish arbitrarily closed the mouth of the Mississippi River at New Orleans to American exports floated down river from the Ohio Valley. (3) The Spanish instigated Indian attacks on backwoods settlements in Tennessee and encouraged resistance to the advancing American frontier.

The disputed Yazoo strip was conceded to the United States by the terms of the Pinckney Treaty of 1795. Spain desired peace in America because of her involvement in war in Europe. The treaty opened the Mississippi to American shipping and gave the rights of deposit and of transshipment of goods free of customs at New Orleans for a three-year period. The unrest in Kentucky and Tennessee among the settlers quieted down after 1791 as the United States ended the war with the Creeks and as steps were being taken for the admission of the two new states. The Spanish gave up their plans to expand their holdings in the Mississippi Valley after a final attempt to win over Americans in the Southwest had failed.

In the Southwest as in the Northwest, the cessation of vexing foreign interference, was followed by an enormous migration of agricultural settlers eager to possess the fertile virgin soil.

New States Admitted After Independence.—Vermont, the fourteenth state, was the first admitted under the Constitution. It was admitted in 1791, having previously been claimed by the state of New York. The settlers of Vermont had asserted their independence of New York during the Revolution; they wrote their own constitution, refused to recognize the jurisdiction of New York, and persisted until finally admitted as a separate state.

Kentucky was admitted to statehood by the American Congress in 1792—after nine separate conventions in Kentucky had debated the provisions of their constitutions.

Tennessee was organized into a territory in 1790 by Congress, and William Blount, notable land speculator, was appointed governor. He filled offices with his friends, relatives, and associates, giving special consideration to those connected with the old State of Franklin. In 1796 statehood was granted and John Sevier became governor.

In Ohio the removal of the Indians in the 1790's and the promotional activities of the Ohio Company and of the Connecticut Land Company brought about such rapid settlement that the region was organized as a territory by 1798. In 1802 an enabling act was passed and in 1803 Ohio was admitted as a state under a liberal constitution influenced by the frontier environment.

The Frontier of the Eastern Mississippi Region

The defeat of the remaining Indians east of the Mississippi in the War of 1812 made possible the eventual opening of all this large region to American farmer-frontiersmen. As before, Indian opportunity to resist encroaching white farmers came when a European power needing Indian allies became involved in war against the United States.

The Frontier Origin of the War of 1812.—The War of 1812 against Great Britain was fought to protect American rights as a neutral nation to engage in shipping goods to Europe. The West, supposedly the section least interested in such commercial rights, and the South under the lead of Henry Clay and other young "War Hawks," prodded Congress into voting a declaration of war. New England, the commercial section, as a matter of expediency vigorously opposed the war, since she was profiting in spite of British refusal to recognize American rights. The West wanted war in the belief it would open markets to her depressed agriculture which had suffered from wartime interference with export trade. A second Western urge to war was the desire for the lands of Canada and Spanish Florida, Spain being an ally of Britain's. Even more important, in the event of war the Indians over the West could be thoroughly defeated and eliminated as a threat to the peace of the frontier. Western congressmen had much influence in Madison's decision to ask Congress for a declaration of war in June, 1812.

All attempts to take Canada failed; the Treaty of Ghent in concluding the war brought no territorial gains to either belligerent. Victories against Indians in the North and the South during the war removed the Indians as a source of danger to the frontier and eventually led to their complete removal.

Indian Warfare in the Northwest.—Well before the opening of the War of 1812 Indians in the Northwest began to stiffen their attitude to the whites. Causes of their resentment included the steady pressure upon their lands by Western expansion and the repeated cessions of territory forced upon them after earlier promises that they could keep the land. And Indian leaders resented the demoralization of their people by the evils of the white men.

Tecumseh and his brother, the Prophet, had assumed leadership of the Indians of the Northwest. Tecumseh, a patriot and able statesman, wished to save his people from white aggression and degradation. The Prophet, their religious leader, preached moral reformation; he particularly scorned drunkenness. He called for a return to the simple, old Indian virtues.

Tecumseh's plan called upon all Indians, north and south of the Ohio, to unite to resist encroachment upon their lands. When Tecumseh had gone south to enlist aid of those tribes, William Henry Harrison led a force to the Wabash and Tippecanoe rivers. The ensuing battle of Tippecanoe was hailed as a great victory, since the Indians withdrew from the site when their village was burned, but more whites than Indians were killed in the battle. Harrison lost no time in sending early dispatches announcing his "victory" against the Indians. This first news caused the battle to be remembered as a decisive victory.

As the Indian war continued, it merged into the War of 1812. The Indians, now as British allies, were encouraged to attack American settlements. Tecumseh and his Indian followers naturally took up an alliance with the British. At the Battle of the Thames River in Canada in October, 1813, Harrison won a decisive victory over a combined force of British and Indians; Tecumseh was killed.

Indian Fighting in the Southwest.—Tecumseh aroused the Creeks in the Alabama region in 1811, but they did not immediately take to the warpath. However, in 1813 they attacked a rude pioneer fortification at Fort Mims on the Alabama River and killed 250 settlers who had gathered there for safety. This was the occasion for sending Andrew Jackson against the savages. Jackson at the time was recovering from his shooting affair with the Bentons and should have remained in bed. At the head of Tennessee militiamen, in the spring and summer of 1814 he fought a series of engagements. The most important was at Horseshoe Bend, where at least 850 Indians were killed. After the

[46]

battle the Creeks gave up the fight, and Jackson forced them to cede about two-thirds of their territory.

THE RENEWED ADVANCE OF THE FRONTIER AFTER 1812

After the War of 1812 the Great Migration rapidly carried the frontier to the Mississippi. Soon filled by eager settlers were the Gulf Coastal Plains and the rolling country south of Tennessee as well as the area west of Ohio in the Northwest Territory. The vigorous movement, which was accomplished by about 1840, completed the occupation of most of this area. Migration into western Louisiana and Texas even carried the region of settlement well beyond the Mississippi. After 1825 most of the remaining Indians were removed from the north and south of the Ohio to reservations west of the Mississippi River.

Causes of the Rapid Settlement.—Factors responsible for this rapid settlement may be enumerated. (1) The Indians, after their defeat and removal both during and after the War of 1812, no longer resisted the advance of frontiersmen. (2) These level or rolling lands, with their great fertility, were ideal for agriculture. (3) The liberal land laws after 1800 made it relatively easy for small farmers to acquire land. (See Section 11.) (4) A large population of small farmers were ready for various reasons to move into the newly opened lands; exhaustion of soil fertility in New England and in the older states of the South drove many to seek the more productive soils of the West.

Settlement of Indiana and Illinois, Michigan and Wisconsin. —Pioneers from the South drifting down the Ohio in flatboats in the 1820's moved into the southern third of Indiana and Illinois. Lead mining in the region of northwestern Illinois brought a rush of population into that area. After 1825 the Sauk and Fox tribes were forced to abandon their lands to make way for pioneers. The Black Hawk War in 1832 was followed by further large cessions of fertile land. New England farmers, leaving their uneconomic farms, took advantage of the completed Erie Canal after 1825 to transport themselves into the northern Lake Plains. They settled in southern Michigan and northern Illinois. Extensive holdings of land in Indiana by Connecticut land companies caused pioneers to pass up that area for cheaper lands farther to the west and north in Illinois and Wisconsin. In the 1840's tens of thousands of immigrants from Germany and Scandinavia moved into Wisconsin.

West of the Mississippi River, the settlement of Iowa, after the Black Hawk War, came as a part of this rush to the fertile land of the Middle West.

Indiana in 1816 drafted its constitution and was admitted to the Union. Illinois followed in 1818. Michigan was admitted in 1834 and Wisconsin in 1848.

Settlement of Alabama, Mississippi, Louisiana, and Florida.— The occupation of the northern Lake Plains after the War of 1812 was paralleled by the settlement of the Gulf Coastal Plains and the rolling hills of the South. The wealth to be gained by growing cotton drew small farmers and large planters with slaves into the rich soils of the lower South. The invention of the cotton gin cleared the bottle-neck limiting increased production of upland cotton. The growing textile industry in New England and Europe provided a profitable and unlimited market for the fiber.

First to be cleared of Indian occupation were the lands of western Georgia. Whites overran their lands even before legal removal. President Adams in 1825 took steps to prepare for the eventual removal of the Creeks. The Cherokee tribe was removed in 1829 under President Jackson. Other tribes in the middle 1830's were escorted by the army to lands set aside west of the Mississippi River.

The Seminoles in Florida were the last of the Southern tribes to be removed. They were assigned to a reservation in the Oklahoma Indian Territory, except for those who escaped to take refuge in the Everglades of Florida. White settlers throughout the deep South came almost entirely from Georgia and the Carolinas; there was little migration into the slave-holding South by Europeans—they disapproved of slavery as such and of the political and social system of the South. Mississippi became a state in 1817 and Alabama in 1819.

The Frontier of the Eastern Mississippi Region

Florida.—After the Treaty of Paris of 1783 Britain returned Florida to Spain. The Florida panhandle to the west extended all the way along the Gulf Coast to the Mississippi River. Florida's proximity to New Orleans, Spanish control of the mouths of rivers flowing through Florida into the Gulf, and the soil itself made Florida coveted by Americans.

Parts of Florida were annexed in four separate moves. (1) The disputed Yazoo Strip, paralleling the border in the northwest, was conceded to the United States in the Pinckney Treaty. (2) West Florida, which extended eastwards from New Orleans to the Perdido River, came next into United States possession. American settlers, encouraged by American officials, revolted against Spanish authority in 1810 and President Madison proclaimed it as legally American territory. (3) In 1813 the occupation of West Florida was completed when General Wilkinson took Mobile as ordered. (4) In 1817 General Andrew Jackson on patrol on the Florida border invaded the main part of the province, known as East Florida, and captured Pensacola. This action and the problem of policing Florida caused the Spanish to cede East Florida to the United States in the Adams-Onis Treaty of 1819, finally ratified in 1821. An equally important provision of the treaty defined the boundary between the Louisiana Purchase and Spanish possessions to the southwest. In establishing the boundary along the 42nd parallel from the Rocky Mountains to the Pacific, Spain abandoned her claim to Oregon to the United States. Not until 1845 was Florida admitted as a state.

The Northern Boundary.—At approximately the same time as the Florida cession the boundaries Convention of 1818 with Britain extended the United States boundary westward from the Lake of the Woods across the northern part of Louisiana Territory along the 49th parallel and on to the crest of the Rockies. This left until later the settlement of the claims of Britain and the United States to the Oregon country.

6

FROM THE MISSISSIPPI TO THE 98TH MERIDIAN, 1800–1860

The settlement of the territory west of the Mississippi River up to the edge of the semi-arid plains, approximately at the 98th meridian, was the next geographical leap of the frontier after the settlement of the region east of the river. The advance into the southern part of this region, in Louisiana, Arkansas, Missouri, and Texas, coincides chronologically with much of the advance of the preceding regional frontier east of the Mississippi. In Texas, Spanish and then Mexican political control both encouraged and delayed the filling of the great vacant spaces there.

THE LOUISIANA TERRITORY

It was inevitable that Americans should occupy Louisiana, an area that lay in the path of the main direction of advance. The Louisiana Purchase in 1803 removed any potential political obstacles to the advance into this territory.

The Louisiana Purchase, 1803.—Up to 1800 the primary interest of the United States in Louisiana was in relation to the free use of the Mississippi River as an outlet for exports of produce. In 1800, Spain transferred Louisiana back to France in the Treaty of San Ildefonso. When Jefferson learned of this, he proposed purchase of the Isle of Orleans. The peace-loving, anti-British Jefferson felt so disturbed at the threat of Napoleon's control over this region that he suggested the United States ought to join Britain in an alliance. In 1802 the Spanish officials of Louisiana, who remained in charge pending the transfer to France, revoked the right of deposit at New Orleans. This renewed the anxiety of the American West, and Jefferson became acutely aware of Western need for free use of the Mississippi and the right of transshipment at New Orleans.

Napoleon's Decision To Sell Louisiana.—Napoleon's sudden willingness to part with his newly acquired empire of Louisiana may be attributed to several factors. (1) General Leclerc's disastrous failure to take Santo Domingo and establish the French base there demonstrated the hopelessness of re-establishing an extensive empire in America. (2) The opposition of American backwoodsmen to foreign control of the Mississippi and of the large territory lying across the path of the frontier movement could not be ignored by Napoleon as a real threat to his retention of Louisiana. (3) And there was the threat of the British fleet which could take Louisiana once Napoleon reopened the war with Britain as he planned to do.

In 1803 both the sale and the transfer of Louisiana to the United States was completed. The treaty did not define the boundaries of Louisiana and thus left unsettled the question of whether it included West Florida and Texas. In the same year the Lewis and Clark Expedition (see Section 19) began its westward journey of exploration of the northern portion of the territory.

Conspiracy in the West.—The Burr conspiracy, 1805–6, is symbolic of the political ferment and the uncertainty of loyalties in the West that had arisen from Western desperation over foreign control of the outlet for their exports. These conditions proved to be the appropriate setting for such unscrupulous and disloyal adventurers as General James Wilkinson and Aaron Burr.

After his disgrace following the death of Alexander Hamilton in the famous duel, Burr began entertaining various ideas of filibustering and adventure in the West. Like others whose future in the East had been doomed for one reason or another, Burr hoped to recoup his fortune in the West. In 1805 he traveled over the West and made contacts with many prominent persons, including General James Wilkinson, who commanded the United States army in the Mississippi Valley. He solicited support for whatever plans he may have considered for building an independent state in the West, possibly at the expense of both Spain and the United States. Although he failed to win much encouragement, he gathered an expedition and floated down the Ohio and into the Mississippi. He was too weak to create any military problem.

Wilkinson gave up hope of success for the venture and turned evidence against Burr. Burr was arrested and tried but could not be convicted of the treason charges. Jefferson's political rival, John Marshall, Chief Justice of the Supreme Court, conducted the trial at Richmond so as to favor Burr and frustrate Jefferson. The Burr conspiracy showed Britain and Spain that the West was more loyal than they had believed. The purchase of Louisiana had satisfied the West and insured its loyalty.

Admission of New States.—After annexation of the Louisiana Territory the west bank of the lower Mississippi filled rapidly with settlers and Congress organized the Territory of Orleans, which corresponded to the present state of Louisiana. When the census of 1810 made it clear that the population was over 60,000 and after New England opposition was overcome, Louisiana was granted statehood in 1812. With the westward surge of population during and immediately after the War of 1812 the population doubled within eight years after admission.

After Louisiana, Missouri became the next state to enter the Union from west of the Mississippi. Missouri was admitted in 1821 after the furor over the status of slavery there had precipitated angry debate in Congress. Missouri had been settled early, since it lay directly in the path of the westward-moving pioneers of Kentucky and Tennessee. A wide strip west of the Mississippi and up the valley of the Missouri filled rapidly after 1812 during the population advance of the Great Migration.

Arkansas, next to be admitted, attracted settlers more slowly. She entered the Union in 1836 and Michigan came in the next year.

The Black Hawk War, Iowa, and Minnesota.—The defeat of Chief Black Hawk and his followers the Sauk and the Fox in 1832 was followed by the opening in 1833 of a strip of land along the west bank of the Mississippi River known as the "Black Hawk Purchase." The area filled rapidly and more land was opened in 1837 and 1843. In 1846 Iowa was admitted to statehood after the slave state of Texas had been admitted earlier the same year.

Minnesota's first settlers were lumbermen along the Mississippi River. Then farmers moved in to grow foodstuffs for the logging towns. In 1851 Sioux chiefs gave up their claims to most of western Minnesota. Pioneers immediately rushed in. In 1858 statehood was granted.

THE ANNEXATION OF TEXAS

Texas now shares with Hawaii the distinction of having governed itself as an independent state before joining the Union.

The Colonization of Texas.—In 1821 Moses Austin, an enterprising frontiersman in Missouri, received a land grant from Mexico and permission to settle 300 colonists in eastern Texas. When he died, his son Stephen F. Austin proceeded to take the first immigrants into the grant. In 1823 Mexican officials sought to encourage further colonization to fill the vacuum in Texas and forestall the temptation of some other power to occupy it. As compared with American land laws, provisions of the Mexican laws were extremely liberal in both the size of the individual grants and in the price per acre. Liberal terms to promoters encouraged many other would-be colonizers to follow Austin's example and become *empresarios*. By 1825 Mexico opened all of Texas to colonizers and by 1830 about 10,000 had settled in the eastern part. The fertile soil of Texas offered opportunity for farmers and planters to raise cotton, and the depression in the United States beginning in 1819 caused many bankrupt Americans to look about for a new start.

Friction between Americans and Mexicans.—The presence of many aggressive frontier types among the colonists and the attitude of contempt for the Mexicans and for their institutions soon caused trouble. (1) The religious issue was one source of friction: settlers were required to accept Catholicism and were not permitted to attend their own churches. (2) Threats to abolish slavery and (3) moves to collect tariff duties on imports caused further restlessness and friction. (4) The absence of necessary services of government and political turmoil in Mexico caused persistent annoyance and antagonism. (5) When the Mexican government

[53]

realized the Americans were not sincere about becoming naturalized Mexicans, it prohibited further migration from the United
States. (6) The Texans were annoyed by the refusal of Mexico to
permit Texas statehood separate from the state of Coahuila. After
General Santa Anna made himself dictator in Mexico in 1834,
both Mexicans and Americans in Texas felt driven to resistance.
When Santa Anna marched to crush the Texans with a large
army, Texas declared its independence.

Texas Independence, 1836–1846.—As General Santa Anna
marched northeastward through Texas, the whole American
population fled before him in the direction of the Sabine River,
the American border. The 187 Texans who offered resistance to
Santa Anna's army at the Alamo carried out the delaying tactics
of the Texas leader, General Sam Houston, an old Tennessee
friend of Andrew Jackson's. None of the defenders of the Alamo
survived the slaughter by the self-styled "Napoleon of the West."
But in April, 1836, on the San Jacinto River near the present city
of Houston, the Battle of San Jacinto, an overwhelming victory
for Houston's army, won independence for the Republic of
Texas. In 1837 the United States recognized the new Republic.

In the ten years after independence the population of the
Republic of Texas grew to 142,000. The Texans were always
hopeful of joining the United States and steps to this end were
taken by President Andrew Jackson. The question of annexation,
however, became entangled with the slavery controversy in American politics, and it twice proved impossible to secure a two-thirds
vote in the United States Senate to ratify a treaty of annexation.

The Annexation of Texas, 1845.—In the election campaign of
1844 the Democratic nominee James K. Polk, a Jacksonian Demo-
crat from Tennessee, made the question of annexation the leading issue. The party platform demanded the "re-occupation of
Oregon and the re-annexation of Texas." Polk's victory with its
implied mandate for annexation was heeded promptly by the
outgoing President, John Tyler. The possibility that Britain
might establish a protectorate over Texas and the negotiations
between Texas and Britain spurred the American people in both

the North and South to act despite the slavery problem. The two-thirds majority requirement for Senate ratification was overcome by the passage of a joint resolution by a simple majority vote. The joint resolution was binding on both countries. On March 1, 1845, the annexation bill was approved by President Tyler only three days before Polk became President on March 4, 1845.

Early in 1846 Texas was formally admitted as a state. Settlement proceeded rapidly as far west as San Antonio and Austin; the semi-arid and Indian-infested western part of the state presented a different environment to that of east Texas. This part of the southern Great Plains had to await technological developments that would aid the conquest of that forbidding environment.

THE ADVANCE TO THE EDGE OF THE GREAT PLAINS

In the eastern parts of Kansas and Nebraska sufficient rainfall and favorable environmental conditions, not too different from those in the East, attracted farmers there before the opening of the Civil War.

The Opening of Kansas.—The immediate provisions for the organization of territorial government in Kansas came as a product of the slavery controversy and of the need for a transcontinental railroad. The Kansas-Nebraska Act was viewed by Westerners as simply an act permitting local residents to govern themselves through the principle of popular sovereignty or majority decision by local residents. The bill originated with Senator David R. Atchison, who was running for the United States Senate seat in Missouri. He made an appeal for the votes of land-hungry Missourians by promising to open to settlement the lands lying west of the Missouri River. Another purpose in organizing Kansas for settlement was to facilitate the construction of a transcontinental railroad that would connect Chicago with the West by way of a central route. The railroad connecting with the East at Chicago would enhance real estate holdings in the vicinity of Chicago in which Douglas and his friends were financially interested. The introduction of the Kansas-Nebraska Bill appealed to Senator Douglas, since it might elevate the ambitious "Little Giant" to the Presidency by winning him the nomination of the Democratic Party.

The politically disruptive consequences of the Kansas-Nebraska Act were not anticipated. It caused a complete realignment of political parties in the nation and provoked the bloody contest between pro- and anti-slavery forces for the control of the government of Kansas.

After the organization of territorial government in Kansas, Northern abolitionists initiated a movement to settle Kansas with the goal of planting an anti-slavery majority there to insure its admission as a free state. Societies were organized in New England to promote emigration of free-soilers, but they succeeded in sending in only a small percentage of those who actually settled Kansas. Instead, Kansas was populated largely by land-hungry settlers from adjacent states rather than by politically motivated idealists. Anti-slave elements, however, outnumbered immigrants from the slave-holding states, who would not risk taking their valuable slave property into communities where the propriety of slave-holding was so angrily contested. The violence of the "Border Ruffians," political chicanery, and the support of President James Buchanan prevented the anti-slavery majority from controlling the government of Kansas and its early admission as a free state. Kansas was admitted in 1861 after the Southern states had seceded.

The Settlement of Nebraska.—Treaties negotiated by federal agents with the Plains tribes, beginning in 1854, prepared the way for white settlers and helped bring the passage of the Kansas-Nebraska Act to open that territory to settlement. The factor of powerful railroad interests in building a line through the central route sped the territorial organization of Nebraska as well as of Kansas. Pioneer settlers proceeded with the occupation of the river valley lands of eastern Nebraska at the same time but at a less rapid pace than Kansas was being settled. The passage of the Homestead Act (1862) generously opened lands to settlement and

the ending of the Civil War released la'
who took up land in the plains areas
Union Pacific Railroad and the sale r
the federal government brought in ou.

Congressional leaders forced an enablu.
dents of Nebraska, in no hurry to assume expe
rejected the proposal. In 1867 Nebraska became a
bare majority of its citizens approved and the Republic
ity in Congress approved statehood over President Johnson's
Its population was adequate for statehood and by 1870 hac
reached 122,993 persons, concentrated in the eastern part.

Any further advance into the regions immediately west of the
line of the 98th meridian was postponed until more congenial
climates had been occupied. The settlement of the intermountain
region was neglected until after the Pacific Coast had been settled.
Westward-moving pioneers chose to cross over or pass around the
strange and difficult environment of the Great Plains—arid, treeless, and infested with the fiercest of the American Indian tribes.

7

THE PACIFIC FRONTIER (1769–1869)
AND THE MEXICAN WAR

On the Pacific Coast the earliest opening of the American
farmers' frontier occurred in the Oregon country. Bolder pioneers
migrated there at the same time the less venturesome were taking
up lands immediately west of the Mississippi River. There was
considerable overlap in the time span of this with other regional
frontiers.

CALIFORNIA

Although the American advance to the Pacific Coast occurred
first in Oregon for reasons of joint sovereignty, favorable climate,
and accessibility, European civilization was actually planted first
by the Spanish in California. The impetus of the Gold Rush

[57]

California to overtake within a year's time the head start
gon and to win statehood first. Of the three Pacific Coast
, Washington, at first a part of the Oregon Territory, was
last to achieve statehood.

Spanish Expansion Northwestward Toward California.—Beginning early with exploration under Cortes, New Spain extended its northwest frontier toward the Pacific Ocean and into Baja, or Lower, California. The primary activity in Baja California, until the establishment of the missions, was pearl fishing. Exploration of New Mexico, Arizona, and a part of the Great Plains was first carried out under Coronado, 1539–41. In conjunction with Coronado's exploration, two separate parties under Ulloa (1539) and Alarcon (1540) were sent out by sea to explore the Gulf of California.

Spanish Exploration of the California Coast.—In 1542 Juan Rodriguez Cabrillo and Bartolome Ferrelo explored the Pacific Coast as far north as Oregon. Interest in California then declined, but the mining frontier in northwestern Mexico continued to push Spanish control toward California.

The next explorations of the California coast were designed to locate suitable ports where Mexico-bound Manila galleons might replenish exhausted supplies and find protection against Pacific interlopers such as Sir Francis Drake (1579). Cermeno in 1595 and Vizcaino in 1596 both did considerable exploration of the California coast, but still no colony was established there.

The Missions in California.—The settlement of Baja California after 1696 was left to the Catholic missionaries, acting for the Church and the king. First, the Jesuits extended missions into northwestern Mexico and Baja California. Outstanding among the Jesuits was Father Eusebio Kino, who explored and established missions in southern Arizona. These settlements in Pimeria Alta were the beginnings of Spanish civilization there. By 1730 the Jesuits had established many missions in Baja California; the missions south of Alta California were to be indispensable to the ultimate success of the chain of missions beginning at San Diego and extending into northern California.

When the Jesuits were expelled in 1767, the Franciscans succeeded to the task of converting the Indians in the northwest region of Mexico. In the same decade the energetic viceroy, Jose de Galvez, began the extension of the missions into California. It was fear of Russian and British intrusion that spurred the establishment of the buffer settlements.

In 1769 four parties, two by land and two by sea, were sent out under Father Junipero Serra and Captain Gaspar de Portola; settlers remained at the mission sites of San Diego and, in 1770, at Monterey. Captain Juan Bautista de Anza, 1773–74, opened a necessary overland supply trail leading from Arizona to Monterey; this was vital because of the extreme difficulty of sailing against the prevailing northwesterlies which for a long time rendered California almost inaccessible from Mexico by sea. Eventually the Franciscans established 21 missions from San Diego in the south to Sonoma north of San Francisco Bay. At the missions the Spanish planted civilization in a remote and isolated area.

The Mexican Period in California, 1821–1847.—After Mexican independence in 1821, California, a province of Mexico, underwent important changes. During this time individual Californians received liberal land grants and established large ranchos. The missions were secularized following the decree of 1833, and their property passed into private ownership; the missions had established the cultivation of fruits and field crops and had stocked California with her largest and most valuable resource, cattle. Life in California under Mexico continued pastoral, easy-going, and primitive.

The Coming of Foreigners.—Intrusions of foreigners in California occurred in spite of Spanish prohibitions, but greater relaxation of restrictions in the early Mexican period permitted the entry of the foreigners. They came for various reasons. Beginning in 1800, American ships plied the coastal waters to catch the sea-otter and later the fur seal. These vessels also conducted a coastal trade that was welcome but illegal. Soon after 1820 and under Mexican rule, the whaling vessels began putting in at California ports to conduct a trade that had now been legalized.

[59]

American contact with California increased when the hide and tallow trade sprang up in the early 1820's. It came to be quite profitable for New Englanders and brought the flush of prosperity to the missions and ranchos.

American merchants soon settled in California and conducted a profitable trade with the Indians and Mexicans. One of these was an enterprising businessman from Massachusetts, Thomas O. Larkin. He went into business at Monterey in 1832 and in 1843 accepted the post of the American consul. Later he was directed to see what could be done to develop sentiment among the Californians to join the United States. Another naturalized American, John Sutter, gave aid to countless American immigrants who came in over the Sierra.

American Overland Traders.—Overland contacts of Americans with California were first made by the fur traders in the 1820's. Of these mountain men, Jedediah Smith was the first to enter. In 1826 Smith began blazing a path through unexplored territory southwest of the Great Salt Lake; his journeys took him across the Mojave Desert on to Mission San Gabriel at Los Angeles. After returning to St. Louis, Smith made a second journey to California in 1827. He traveled with his party to San Gabriel, but this time, instead of returning east, he went north through the Sacramento Valley to catch beaver. He explored the Northwest up to Fort Vancouver on the Columbia before returning to St. Louis. In 1827 the trapper, James O. Pattie opened the Gila River route to California. Other fur men followed in the succeeding years and improved these trails or opened new trails to California from Santa Fe and from Oregon. (See Chapter 18 for more details on trail-blazing and exploration in California.)

Immigration of Pioneer Settlers.—Most of the fur traders carried back glowing accounts of the Pacific Coast region to the East and thus attracted the first parties of American overland "pioneer settlers." Their migration, beginning in 1841, was a continuation of the migration that was crossing the Mississippi in the 1820's and 1830's and was settling up to the edge of the Great Plains. Actually some of the first Americans who came to California became permanent settlers, but they were single men who came by sea or came as fur men and married California women. In numbers these immigrants were relatively unimportant.

John Bidwell in 1841, with the guidance of fur men, led the first American emigrant party (also called Bidwell-Bartleson party), to California. From the Missouri frontier they took the Oregon Trail to Fort Hall and thence along the Humboldt River and over the Sierra into northern California. In 1843 and 1844 two more parties came in each year. Thereafter, a rapidly swelling overland stream of pioneer farmers and ranchers arrived annually from outfitting points in Missouri.

THE MEXICAN WAR, 1846–1848

The United States elected Polk and the Democrats in the national election of 1844. The Democrats' platform promised "Re-annexation of Texas" and the "Re-occupation of Oregon." In choosing the Democrats, the nation endorsed the goals of "Manifest Destiny."

Causes of the Mexican War.—The causes of the Mexican War grew out of the westward expansion of the United States. These causes were the annexation of Texas in 1845, the unpaid debt claims of American citizens against Mexico, the dispute over the boundary between Texas and Mexico, and American interference and intrusions into California. The clash of the Mexican troops with General Zachary Taylor's forces, sent by President James K. Polk into the disputed territory north of the Rio Grande, gave Polk the provocation that he had been awaiting.

Campaigns of the Mexican War.—Volunteers who made up the armies that invaded Mexican soil came predominantly from the South and the West. The first campaign, conducted under General Zachary Taylor of Louisiana, was the invasion of Mexico at the Rio Grande in 1846 and fought its way to a point west of Saltillo, where the Battle of Buena Vista was won over a much larger force under General Santa Anna. At this point the main effort of defeating Mexico was shifted to General Winfield Scott; he landed at Veracruz and fought a succession of hard-won battles which led him to Mexico City. These victories brought Mexican surrender and the Treaty of Guadalupe Hidalgo in February, 1848. The third main campaign of the war, headed by General Stephen W. Kearny, brought the American occupation of New Mexico. From Santa Fe Kearny marched along the Gila River route to San Diego and assumed command in California in 1846.

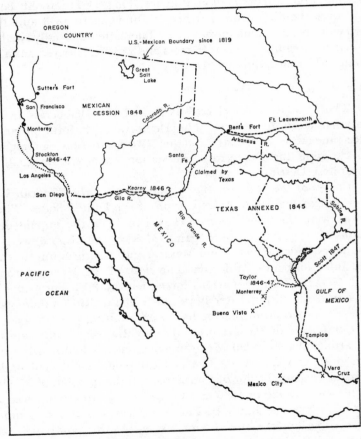

CAMPAIGNS OF THE MEXICAN WAR

Occupation of California.—Naval forces in the Pacific under Commodore Sloat and his successor, Commodore Stockton, took San Francisco, Monterey, and Los Angeles. Disgruntled and turbulent American settlers had begun the conquest of California earlier when they proclaimed the Bear Flag Republic at Sonoma. With the outbreak of the Mexican War Captain John C. Fremont continued the conquest begun by the Bear Flaggers and the independence movement thus merged into the American conquest as Fremont marched into southern California. When General Kearny arrived in San Diego, he assumed nominal command in all of California. Resistance to Americans by the Californians might have been avoided except for a lack of understanding and tact by American leaders, but this resistance movement too was soon overcome.

Peace with Mexico, 1848.—By the terms of the Treaty of Guadalupe Hidalgo, February 2, 1848, Mexico recognized the Rio Grande as the boundary of Texas. New Mexico and California were ceded to the United States.

Although a vast territory had been gained from Mexico, it was soon discovered that a railroad right-of-way was needed south of the Gila River. This strip, the Gadsden Purchase of 1853, completed the continental boundaries of the United States.

The Discovery of Gold, 1848.—The discovery of gold in California was made during the colonizing efforts of an enterprising Swiss immigrant, John A. Sutter. By 1848 he had built a fort at Sacramento on his Mexican land grant and was well on his way to founding a sizable feudality based on an economy of cattle ranching, wheat farming, and the fur trade. An employee of Sutter's, James W. Marshall, was supervising the digging of a tailrace for a sawmill when the flakes of gold were discovered. Other discoveries were made soon afterward. In a matter of months, not only Americans from the East, but Europeans, Chinese and other goldseekers flooded into the mining regions. (See Section 19 for further discussion of the gold rush and mining.)

California Statehood, 1850.—California in a few months had enough population for statehood. Instead of organizing as a territory, this stage was omitted and a state constitution was drawn up in 1849. The next year the free state of California was admitted as a part of the Compromise of 1850.

THE OREGON COUNTRY

Both Britain and the United States entered Oregon early for exploration and the fur trade. Their various interests and activities there became the basis of their respective claims to Oregon.

American and British Interests in Oregon.—The English navigator, Captain James Cook visited the Oregon coast in 1778, procured sea-otter furs there, and traded these profitably in China. The publicity he gave to his discovery soon stirred New England traders to engage in this fur trade and to obtain in return tea and other Chinese commodities. In this trade an American, Robert Gray, in 1792 re-discovered the Columbia River. The Americans soon came to monopolize the China trade. In 1793 the Canadian trading company, the North West Company, sent in Alexander Mackenzie and soon afterward David Thompson. These two explored much of the region. In 1812 the American, John Jacob Astor established his trading post, after much misfortune, at Astoria. When the War of 1812 broke out Astor sold out to the British North West Company just in time to avoid capture by the British navy. This greatly weakened American claims to Oregon and left the British fur companies in command. The Hudson's Bay Company in 1821, in order to end the severe competition, absorbed the rival North West Company and established new posts over the area. The Hudson's Bay Company under the command of Dr. John McLoughlin ruled the Oregon country until 1843, when American settlers took over the region south of the Columbia River.

Claims to the Oregon Country.—The Adams-Onis Treaty of 1819 established the boundaries between the Louisiana Purchase and Spanish territory to the southwest. In the treaty the United States relinquished her Texas claim to Spain, and Spain gave up her claim to Oregon north of the 42d parallel in favor of the United States. Russia abandoned her claim south of 54°40′ in

1824. This left the territory to the United States as joint but rival claimant with Great Britain. In the Treaty of Joint Occupation in 1818 it was agreed that both American and British nationals could freely enter Oregon. This treaty agreement was renewed in 1827 for an indefinite period. Actually, until the campaign of 1844, the disputed territory was that between the Columbia River and the 49th parallel, for each nation was ready to accept the claim of the other to territory outside these boundaries.

Activities of American Fur Trappers.—Parties of American fur men crossed the continental divide into Oregon in the 1820's. An almost fanatical agitator for the settlement of Oregon in the 1820's was Hall J. Kelley, a Boston schoolteacher who had never seen the region. He did much by speaking and writing to publicize Oregon; he petitioned Congress to provide aid to emigration societies so the region might be occupied by Americans. Kelley set out for Oregon in 1833 and accompanied Ewing Young's fur party to Fort Vancouver. Captain Benjamin L. E. Bonneville's party, sent out by New York capitalists, traveled as far as Walla Walla in 1832. Also in the year of 1832, a year of much activity in explorations and fur trading in the Far West, Nathaniel Wyeth, from Boston, led a party there to develop a fur trading business. After considerable activity in trading for furs, fishing for salmon, and cultivating crops, he found too severe the competition of the Hudson's Bay Company under the able management of Dr. John McLoughlin and returned to Boston. (See Section 18 for further discussion of the fur trade.)

Missionaries in Oregon.—In the 1830's missionaries entered Oregon to work among the Indians. In 1834 the Methodists sent Rev. Jason Lee with a group of settlers; he founded a mission in the Willamette Valley and became the most active of the missionaries in the praise of Oregon. Dr. Marcus Whitman set up a Presbyterian mission near the junction of the Columbia and Snake rivers in 1836. The Jesuits sent out missionaries in 1838, and in 1840 Father de Smet joined them in establishing several missions north of the Columbia River.

Migration to Oregon.—The first pioneer settlers began moving west over the long Oregon Trail in 1841. (See Section 19 on exploration and trails.) The first large migration, arriving late in 1843, numbered a thousand persons. A provisional government was created in May; another large migration came soon afterward. These provisions for government superseded the benevolent despotism of Dr. McLoughlin.

The Oregon Treaty, 1846.—The Democrats in the campaign of 1844 pledged to settle the Oregon question by taking all of the territory. After President Polk's inauguration he asked Congress for authority to terminate the joint occupation agreement and for a free hand to settle the Oregon question. The British previously had been willing to accept the 49th parallel. To demand more might involve the United States in war with Great Britain.

At this time Polk was following an aggressive Mexican policy that would certainly lead to war. The acquisition of New Mexico and California would bring the United States the two ideal harbors of San Diego and San Francisco. Under these circumstances the administration was willing to compromise on Oregon and thus avoid possible war with two nations at once. Britain's interests also dictated a conciliatory settlement at the time. Thus, in June, 1846, the two countries divided Oregon between them by extending the boundary along the 49th parallel from the continental divide westward to the Pacific Ocean. Territorial government was organized in 1848. Oregon became a state in 1858.

The Hudson's Bay Company had always sought to discourage Americans from settling north of the Columbia during the period of joint occupation. After 1846 the Americans were free to move into this region and began to engage in lumbering and cattle raising around Puget Sound. In 1853 the region was organized as Washington Territory but acquired population only gradually, and statehood was not realized until 1889.

8

THE INTERMOUNTAIN FRONTIER (1803–1890) AND THE ADMISSION OF THE LAST WESTERN STATES

The Spanish, the French, and the Americans were all responsible for opening the Rocky Mountain West. The fur trade, mining, and farming frontiers successively attracted Americans to this vast region.

FIRST PENETRATIONS OF THE WEST

Spanish colonists in New Mexico were the first to enter any part of the Rocky Mountain region. The fur trade became their greatest activity; the fur trade also brought in the French traders and later the American mountain men.

The Spanish Beginnings in New Mexico.—After Coronado's exploration of New Mexico no effort was made to colonize the upper Rio Grande until 1598. In that year Juan de Onate founded in New Mexico the first white colony in the trans-Mississippi West. The Franciscans set to work to convert the sedentary tribes. There was no great wealth of any kind to be gathered here, but tens of thousands of Indians were instructed and exploited. In the Pueblo Revolt of 1680 a sixth of the Spanish settlers were slaughtered and the rest fled to El Paso. Twelve years later the reconquest got underway but progressed only slowly.

The French in the Eastern Rockies.—The French explorers of the early eighteenth century were the first to explore the eastern limits of the Rocky Mountains. From the Mississippi River Valley the French traveled westward, winning friendship and opening trade with the Indians of the Plains and the eastern Rockies. The French generally came out best in the rivalry with the Spanish to the southwest, but in 1763 the Louisiana territory west of the Mississippi River was transferred to Spain.

When the Spanish at St. Louis and at other posts assumed

[67]

control of the fur trade, they conducted the business according to the pattern begun by the French. Indians from the west brought their furs to established posts; French personnel continued active under Spanish rule. British rivalry spurred the Spanish to advance and consolidate their friendship with tribes far up the Missouri River and its tributaries; nevertheless, the British from Canada made considerable progress in extending trade into the upper Missouri and Mississippi rivers. Following the American Revolution, and more so after the Pinckney Treaty in 1795, large numbers of Americans began settling west of the Mississippi in Louisiana and Missouri as the Spanish sought to fill these unoccupied areas.

The First American Explorations.—With the purchase of Louisiana, President Jefferson was able to dispatch the Lewis and Clark Expedition to satisfy his curiosity about the Rocky Mountain region and to open trading contacts with the remote tribes. Jefferson sent other exploring parties into the West, an important purpose being that of determining the boundaries of the Louisiana Purchase. Among the more significant of these expeditions was that of Zebulon M. Pike. In 1806, after returning from his successful expedition along the upper Mississippi to Leech Lake, Pike was chosen to lead a similar exploring party west from St. Louis into the southern Rockies. Although Pike's party was arrested in northern New Mexico and escorted to Chihuahua by Spanish troops, he was able to gather much information regarding the resources of the Southwest. Stephen H. Long in 1820 explored the present area of Colorado. (See Section 19 for more discussion of exploration and trails.)

The Beginnings of the American Fur Trade in the Far West.— The purchase of Louisiana made Americans heir to the fur trade already opened by the French and Spanish in the Far West. Favorable reports of Lewis and Clark regarding fur resources encouraged fur-gathering expeditions under Manuel Lisa and Pierre Chouteau to depart for the Rockies in 1807. The fur trade begun at this time continued year after year and took Americans into areas more and more remote. After Mexican independence, trade over the Santa Fe Trail was begun. From Santa Fe Americans now set out to trap in the regions of New Mexico and Arizona and along the Colorado and Green rivers and in western Colorado. They were the first explorers of this region. Among these earlier trapping parties were the mountain men who became the leaders in opening trails into California and Oregon. (See Sections 7 and 18.)

THE MORMON COLONIZATION OF UTAH

The settlement of the Great Basin region in the vicinity of the Great Salt Lake marked the beginning of the development of this region by agricultural settlers. This settlement brought eventual statehood for Utah. It was not the usual ruggedly individualistic American frontier settlers but a cooperative, religious denomination—the Church of Jesus Christ of Latter-Day Saints, or Mormons—who pioneered here. (In Section 14 the early history of the Mormons is discussed in detail in connection with frontier religious movements.)

Migration to Utah.—In 1847 Brigham Young arrived with the "Pioneer Band" at the Great Salt Lake and by the end of the year, 1,800 members had arrived there. Spreading out from their center at Salt Lake City in later years, they established hundreds of other settlements, not only in Utah but in present Nevada, southern California, and Idaho. Aggressive proselyting by the church, extending to the countries of northern Europe, brought a strong, steady flow of immigrants.

Political Developments in Utah.—In 1849 the Mormons organized the "Provisional Government of the State of Deseret" and gave it boundaries that included all of present Utah and Nevada and parts of several other future states. Many non-Mormons, or "Gentiles," moved into the region during the Civil War and others came in with the building of the transcontinental railroads.

In 1850 Congress organized territorial government and changed the political designation to the Territory of Utah. The appointment of Gentiles to some territorial offices brought friction and defiance of federal authority. This trouble culminated

[69]

in the "Utah War" of 1857 when General W. S. Harney, later succeeded by Colonel Albert Sidney Johnston, led 2,500 troops to Utah. Related to this invasion by federal troops and because of resentment against suffering the Mormons had endured earlier in Missouri and Illinois, was the "Mountain Meadows Massacre" in 1857. A combined force of Indians and Mormons secured the surrender under truce of a California-bound party of 140 emigrants coming from Missouri and Arkansas. Members of the party, while passing through Mormon settlements earlier, had been guilty of the most provocative insults and outrages. All but 17 small children were shot and killed in this episode.

Statehood, although desired by the Mormons, was long delayed. Polygamy, publicly advocated by the Mormons beginning in 1852 but practiced earlier, was the reason. In 1882 Congress by the Edmunds Act created a commission government for Utah and by a later enactment provided fines and imprisonment for those guilty of polygamy. After much resistance, successful enforcement eventually brought capitulation by the Mormons, and in 1890 plural marriage was banned by a church convocation. Utah was admitted in 1896 under a constitution that repudiated polygamy.

STATE-MAKING WEST OF THE MISSISSIPPI

Most of the economic developments peculiar to the Far West are discussed separately in the sections dealing with the types of frontiers. Population and political developments leading to statehood are discussed in the remainder of this section. Population attracted by mineral deposits usually brought the organization of territorial government, but the further growth of these states was due to developments in ranching, farming, and railroad building.

Nevada.—The first settlers in Nevada were Mormons, who settled there from 1851 to 1853; others came in later in the same decade. Nevada, at first a part of the Utah Territory, was organized as a county under Utah in 1854. When the "Utah War" broke out in 1857 Nevada lost her Mormon settlers, who were called back to Salt Lake City by Brigham Young.

Nevada's significant population boom came in 1859 with discovery of the Comstock lode. This discovery, like most of the others in the West, was a sequel to the Gold Rush in California. As the crowded mining population in California quickly claimed and exhausted the surface gold there, prospectors began searching throughout the Western mountain areas. Miners started working gold deposits in Nevada soon after the discoveries in California. But it was in June, 1859, before prospectors stumbled on the rich mineral vein that came to be known as the Comstock lode. The publicity given the rich find set off a great boom in the organization of silver mining companies to operate in the vicinity of Mount Davidson. Virginia City soon grew into a typical mining settlement but with an unusually large population.

In 1861 Congress organized the Nevada Territory. Legal confusion in mining claims created a need for state government so that the confusion could be untangled locally. The needs of the Lincoln administration for Republican votes in Congress during the Civil War and for ratification of the Thirteenth Amendment brought eastern support for statehood even though Nevada had only 20,000 population. Nevada became a state in 1864.

The Mining Frontier in Colorado.—The existence of gold deposits in small quantities in Colorado was confirmed by California-bound miners in 1850. In the summer, 1858, a number of small gold discoveries were made in the eastern part of the state. They were sufficient, however, to stimulate a great deal of publicity in Missouri. By the end of the summer, 1859, there were 100,000 miners in the Pike's Peak rush in camps at Denver, Pueblo, Canon City, Boulder, and in other towns. Strikes were so disappointing that half of the immigrants returned to their homes in the East in the same year.

Colorado Statehood.—Even before the rush of the fifty-niners, the prospectors met and demanded, in November, 1858, that Colorado be organized as the Territory of Jefferson. Congress refused and a meeting of delegates from six mining camps held at Denver in 1859 asked the people if they wished to draft a constitution. A convention assembled, drew up a constitution, and

THE TERRITORIES AND STATES, 1860

organized local government pending action by Congress. The temporary government had no legal basis and did not function well. After the slave states left the Union, Congress was able to organize the Territory of Colorado in 1861.

During the 1860's the attraction of mining brought more people in. As the mining shafts were dug deeper, heavy machinery had to be used. Farmers came in to raise foodstuffs for the mining population. In the 1870's new mines were opened when prospectors found beds of silver ore near Leadville and deposits of gold later at Cripple Creek.

In 1876 Colorado entered the Union after it had already progressed well beyond the frontier mining stage.

Idaho Territory.—In Idaho spectacular strikes were made in the several years beginning in 1860 and these brought in the first permanent settlers. As the stampedes of miners developed in these districts near the Snake River and its tributaries, Fort Boise was built to protect the miners against Indians. Walla Walla developed as a market center to service the mining regions of the Inland Empire, but other towns, strategically located for trade, grew up. The mines attracted farmers into this northwest region. In 1863 Congress established the Territory of Idaho which included not only Idaho, but all of Montana and much of Wyoming.

Organization of the Territories of Montana and Wyoming.— In 1862 a small population boom of about 400 occurred near Bannack when gold discoveries were made there. The opening of a military highway and the inauguration of steamboat navigation on the Missouri River brought a stampede into southwestern Montana in 1863. At Alder Gulch a population of 4,000 rushed in after a rich find. Helena arose as a mining camp in 1864 when a Georgian made an unusually rich discovery. Helena's central location soon gave her preeminence as a commercial center as farmers and merchants joined the mining population.

In 1863, after mining with heavy machinery and agriculture had been introduced, Congress recognized the permanence of the new population by creating the Territory of Idaho for this region. In 1864 Congress separated Montana from Idaho Territory and organized her too as a separate territory. In 1864 further subdivision of Idaho came with the organization of Wyoming Territory.

The Black Hills Gold Rush.— In South Dakota settlers avoided the Black Hills region on account of the fierce Sioux and because the army was pledged to keep Americans out. But persistent rumors of gold caused thousands of prospectors in 1874 to force their way past the soldiers. The army, trying to disprove the rumor, investigated and found the district rich with gold. In 1875, six hundred miners panned for gold, were ousted, and returned again. The military now tried to get the Sioux to concede, but after a long conference they failed, and the army decided to let the miners go in at their own risk. The big rush began then. In the fall of 1875, fifteen thousand entered. In April of the next year Deadwood was founded. Deadwood became the last and the roughest of the Western mining, boom towns. It was the most lawless town in the nation during its early years. This was the last of the fabulous discoveries by prospectors. Future mining would be conducted by large, highly capitalized companies using heavy machinery and hired labor.

South Dakota and North Dakota.—The Dakotas were opened to ranching and farming in the 1870's and 1880's. Except for the Black Hills mining boom, these states were populated by ranchers and farmers whose movement into these areas is a part of the larger story of the cattle kingdom, the building of the railroads, and Great Plains agriculture.

North Dakota was organized as a part of the original Dakota Territory in 1861. When the Omnibus States were admitted in 1889, the territory was divided into two states in recognition of their divergent interests. North Dakota's first sizable population came when the Northern Pacific Railroad entered the state in 1872. A large farming population moved in during the 1870's. To the north the building of the Great Northern Railroad in the 1880's brought in more farmers. Wheat was their main crop.

The Omnibus States.—North Dakota, South Dakota, Montana, and Washington were admitted as states in 1889 under the so-called Omnibus Bill; Idaho and Wyoming were admitted in 1890 —all together known as the Omnibus States. During the early 1880's Democratic strength in Washington, D.C., had prevented admission of these states since they would likely elect Republicans to Congress. The complete victory of the Republicans in Harrison's election in 1888 assured the admission of the Omnibus States.

Wyoming.—Two fur trading posts and a Mormon colony in 1853 were the beginnings of the settlement of Wyoming. Wyoming did not share the West's mining boom population inrush until 1867 when gold was found near South Pass. The gold findings were disappointing and most of the population drifted out. The significant beginning of Wyoming's settlement is due to the

Union Pacific Railroad which brought in the construction gangs and an attendant criminal element similar to that of the mining towns. Wyoming had been a part of various other territories before it was organized as a separate territory in 1868 with the same boundaries it would retain as a state. The railroads were the main economic base during this time, but by 1873 the cattle industry became the predominant economic base. In the eighties, farmers began irrigation; dry farming came later. Wyoming was admitted to statehood in 1890.

Oklahoma.—Oklahoma had its beginnings as a governmental entity in 1825, when President Monroe requested Congress to set aside this part of the unorganized Louisiana Territory as an Indian reservation. In the following decade the Five Civilized Tribes were removed to reservations west of the Arkansas Territory and this region became known as the Indian Territory. At the end of the Civil War the Five Tribes were punished for aiding the Confederacy by having to surrender a large part of the western half of the Indian Territory which now became the Oklahoma District. By 1889, 22 tribes formerly dwelling east of the Mississippi River and in the south Plains had been relocated in the Indian Territory. In 1889 part of the Oklahoma District was opened in the famous and spectacular "run." Overnight about 50,000 settlers had staked homestead claims. In 1890 it was organized as the Territory of Oklahoma. In the succeeding years more Indian lands were opened to settlement in similar "runs" recurring until 1895. Additional openings of land were made until all of western Oklahoma had been added to the Oklahoma Territory. Population approached 60,000 by 1890. The pressure to open this land came from the "Boomers," pioneers who wanted the rich land, and the railroads who wanted traffic built up along their ways.

The Indian Territory (eastern Oklahoma) grew rapidly at the same time, as the railroads and white settlers came in. In 1900 there were more than 500,000 whites in the Indian Territory! The whites there had no political rights, however, and consequently demanded statehood for all of Oklahoma. But the Indians asked for separate statehood for their Indian Territory. Congress refused the Indian's request.

In 1906 Congress passed an enabling act and in 1907 both parts of Oklahoma entered the Union as a single state. Oklahoma's admission had been long delayed because of conflict of Indian and white interests, the need to prohibit sale of liquor to the Indian population, and because of the differences between the Oklahoma and the Indian territories.

Arizona and New Mexico.—In 1858 gold dust was discovered along the Gila River. A new strike in 1862 in the vicinity of the Colorado River brought a stampede from California and in the course of this rush into Arizona, the city of Tucson sprang up and soon attracted a large criminal population. Demand for orderly government forced Congress to create the Territory of Arizona in February, 1863; previously it had been a part of the Territory of New Mexico, created in 1850.

The increase in population in Arizona and New Mexico came only slowly because of the aridity and isolation of the regions. Population grew more rapidly with the construction of the railroads and, later, irrigation projects attracted other settlers. By 1893 Arizona had over 70,000, more than enough for statehood.

New Mexico, with a much larger population than Arizona, might have entered earlier, but its population and culture were predominantly Spanish-American and differed from that of Arizona, which was Anglo-American. Both territories had a high percentage of Indian population. Each wanted separate statehood. In 1905 a plan was proposed in Congress for making a single state of New Mexico and Arizona, but both opposed it strongly. The political fact that the new state would send Democrats to Congress and, if organized into two states, would send twice as many Democratic Senators, delayed admission during the years of Republican supremacy.

Finally in 1912, New Mexico (January 6) and Arizona (February 14) were admitted to statehood. Their admission finally completed the organization of the entire mainland of the nation into state governments.

THE GREAT PLAINS, 1865-1890

America's last large mainland frontier, that of the Great Plains,[1] does not readily coincide with well delineated physiographic boundaries and much less so does it coincide with any political boundaries. Nevertheless, in its most limited sense, it may be roughly defined as the region between the 98th (sometimes 100th) meridian on the east and the Rocky Mountains on the west and extending from southern Texas up to the forested area in northwestern Canada. It is primarily a climatic environment characterized by such uncongenial weather phenomena as low rainfall, high wind velocity, and extreme seasonal and abruptly sudden changes in temperatures. Topographically it is a region characterized by a land surface varying from almost level to one of broad undulations.

Examination of a political map of the United States will show no exact correspondence of the geographic area of the Great Plains to the boundaries of any state or group of states. Instead the Great Plains straddles the western portion of a row of states from the Canadian boundary southward to the Rio Grande and the eastern portion of the row of states from Montana to New Mexico. But the Great Plains environment, or at least certain features of it are also present in all the states found in the western half of the United States. Therefore, the settlement and organization of this region, state by state, is not outlined here. (Other features of the Great Plains frontier are dealt with in the sections covering the various types of frontiers, particularly the cattleman's frontier and the farmers' frontier in the Far West, Sections 21 and 22, respectively.)

The western states entered the Union before those portions

[1] Section 22, "The Farmers' Frontier in the Far West," is largely concerned with the problems of the farmer in the Great Plains; the student may wish to read it in connection with this topic; Section 21, on the cattle industry, should be considered in this connection also.

of their land characterized by the Great Plains environment were settled. They attracted enough settlers for statehood by reason of mining booms or humid agricultural lands in their eastern portions and not because of economic attractions of their dry plains portions. Chronologically the settlement of the Great Plains occurred from the end of the Civil War to approximately 1890.

The Great Plains Environment.—The area of the Great Plains at first was considered a desert because of its semi-arid conditions. The fallacy of the Great American Desert was perpetuated in school geographies, and originated with reports of United States Government explorers (e.g., Major Long) and other observers. Even though much of it has proved to be highly productive in wet years and under dry farming practices, the fact remains that the Plains constituted a different environment from that the Eastern frontier farmer had been accustomed to. For this reason pioneers completely passed over it by taking the long Oregon Trail or other routes to the Pacific Coast, where they found a more familiar environment of timber and rainfall.

Walter Prescott Webb, in *The Great Plains,* vividly describes its distinct features. The institutions by which the frontier had advanced up to the Plains had to be modified, and technological advances had to be made before the Great Plains could be occupied. The frontier in the East traveled on three legs: wood, water, and fertile soil. It was the absence of sufficient wood and water that made the Plains so forbidding to the Eastern farmer. In addition were the presence of two other outstanding features, the buffalo and the most formidable of North American Indians.

The Plains Indians.—The Indians of the Great Plains offered the worst threat to the advance of the white men in that area; they were a more formidable foe than the Indians of the woodlands. What made them so fearful was their adoption of the horse and their original ferocity. Originally nomadic, these Indians became still more mobile when they acquired horses from the Spanish.

As mounted warriors they could raid and run, or, under pur-

[78]

suit, were such expert horsemen they could hang by a heel on one side of a horse running at full speed and at the same time shoot arrows rapidly at their white foes. The bows and arrows thus used gave them more fire-power than the Anglo-American had with his single-shot long-rifle or with any other weapon used on horseback. Not until the Colt six-shooter was invented and used by the Texas Rangers did the American have a weapon that enabled him to pursue mounted Indians effectively.

As nomads these tribesmen were more difficult to control since they took their homes with them and lived off the land. They almost never spared men as prisoners of war. They were referred to as "wild Indians" to distinguish them from the "civilized" or Eastern Indians. The Comanches were probably the fiercest of all: they stopped the Spanish advance into the plains of west Texas and for generations raided ranches in northern Mexico at will. It was especially the Indians of the southern Plains that delayed the advance of cattlemen and farmers. (See Section 10, which discusses the Indian wars.)

The Buffalo.—Basic to the livelihood of the Western Indians and uniquely associated with North America were the millions of buffalo, or bison, that dominated the Great Plains. Buffalo were also present in the wooded East. The Great Plains Indians followed the herds north in the summer and south in the winter and were so much a part of the biological complex that they were designated the "buffalo Indians." From these beasts the Indians obtained their "beef"; from their hides they fashioned clothing, lariats, bowstrings, and shields; their bones provided knives, hoes, and small utensils. When the buffalo were exterminated, the Indians faced starvation and were forced to stay on the reservations designated by the white man, where they were dependent upon government doles of beef.

At the close of the Civil War, it is estimated there were about 15,000,000 buffalo grazing the Plains. The herds, stretching as far as one could see, constituted an obstacle to trains and precluded cattle grazing. The buffalo were first utilized economically by the white man to supply meat for railroad construction gangs;

hunters like William F. "Buffalo Bill" Cody were hired to bring them down. Passengers aboard trains shot them for amusement. Professional hunters systematically killed them for their hides, used for fashionable buffalo robes in the East. For meat many were shot, but only the tongue and choice cuts were taken. Thus, they were rapidly killed in the late sixties and early seventies. Soon afterward their whitened bones were gathered in wagons from the plains and ground into fertilizer or used in sugar refining. By 1885 fewer than a thousand remained alive.

The Six-shooter.—The familiar long rifle of the woodlands hunter and Indian fighter proved inadequate in fighting the Plains Indians. It was a single-shot gun that took too much time and procedure to reload. The barrel alone was about 44 inches long; it was obviously a weapon meant to be used on the ground or rested on a tree trunk, not designed for use on horseback. When the Americans struck the Plains, they too had to fight on horseback to pursue Indian raiders and had to develop a rapid-fire weapon to offset the fire-power of the bow and arrow. The Colt six-shooter was invented before the Plains were settled but did not bring financial success to its inventor until the settlement of the Plains began in western Texas. The old horse pistols were single-shot weapons. The Texas Rangers first tried Colt pistols, and to their delight found, they could pursue Indians on horseback and match the Indians' fire-power. They were popularized in the Mexican War. With the annexation of Texas and the acquisition of the Mexican Cession, much territory was added where the weapon was needed, and the six-shooter quickly found its place among American weapons.

Lack of Timber.—Wood was a basic resource of the pioneer in the East. The settlers used it to build their log cabins and fences to protect their crops and for fuel in the winter. They made tools and implements from it. In the East the pioneer had so much timber he had to burn most of it to clear the land for his crops. But the Great Plains supported no trees because of recurring drouths. Having been at home in a wooded environment, the Plains pioneer was forced to adjust himself to the absence of timber.

Housing and Fuel in the Absence of Timber.—Construction in these timberless regions was of two types. Dugouts were hollowed out of the sides of hills, and sod houses were built. The sod houses were made of turf cut in large blocks, stacked for walls, and supported on poles for roofing. Such houses were warm in the winter and cool in the summer but were damp and wet; soil fell loose inside them. As soon as the pioneers had earned enough money from their crops, they replaced these abodes with frame dwellings.

Fencing Without a Timber Supply.—In the East the traditional fence was made of split logs or rails laid in a straight line, or in zig-zag "worm" fashion. The necessary timber was close at hand. Importing wood to the treeless Plains, however, was too expensive and it was, therefore, impractical to use wood for fencing the hundreds or thousands of acres necessary for making a living at dry-farming or ranching.

Stone was sometimes used, as in parts of Texas. At first, live plants, such as the osage orange, were tried for hedges, but many plants would not survive. Mud fences were tried. Smooth wire, available for fences, proved unsatisfactory.

The solution of the fencing problem came with the invention of a suitable kind of barbed wire, perfected in 1874 by Joseph F. Glidden. There followed an amazing growth in the manufacture of barbed wire, a growth that paralleled the settlement of the Plains. Barbed wire proved ideal because livestock learned to be afraid of the sharp points set into double strands of twisted smooth wire. Livestock would not press against it or crawl through it. It required just a few posts, spaced about twenty feet apart, to support from three to seven strings of barbed wire; the number of strings of wire depended upon the kind of livestock it was intended to enclose. Suitable posts had to be shipped in.

The use of barbed wire revolutionized ranching on the Plains. The rancher found it necessary to buy or homestead the grassland he used and set up permanent improvements. Otherwise he would find himself dispossessed of his government-owned grazing ranges by legitimate homesteaders, called nesters by the open-range cattlemen. The farmer acquired his small holding legally and fenced cattle out of his crops; or, in fencing his own claim, he enclosed waterholes in the creeks.

The Lack of Water.—The worst difficulty on the Great Plains was the lack of water from any source. Back East the settler was accustomed to an abundance of water. He could ordinarily depend upon rainfall during the growing season for his crops. Running streams maintained their flow throughout the year on the farm. For household use he could dig by hand one of the so-called "dug wells" and find water at a depth of 10 to 40 feet. But on the Plains the average rainfall was from 10 to 20 inches a year; a minimum of 20 inches is needed for growing crops under ordinary farm practices. The water level of streams varied from raging floods to bare trickles and might go completely dry almost every summer and fall. The Plains pioneer had to learn to dig deep wells by drilling them. He might have to go two or three hundred feet deep and had to build derricks to support windmills to provide power to pump from such depths. The familiar hand pumps in eastern kitchens or just out-of-doors could not be used. For his crops he had to learn a new method of farming, known as dry-farming. Dry-farming required the use of new tools and techniques for working the crops, or it required the introduction of new crops or varieties of the old crops that were adapted to thrive in semi-arid conditions. Irrigation could be used only to a limited extent. (These foregoing agricultural adjustments are discussed in Section 22 dealing with agriculture in the Far West.)

The Windmill.—The steel windmill in the United States was developed after the settlement of the Great Plains; it was another of the necessary technological developments accompanying the opening of the Plains. It was invented soon after barbed wire. It was used by the small farmer, the rancher, by railroads, and by small-town dwellers. The windmill appeared after waterholes had been isolated by barbed wire fences. The windmill could not supply enough water for irrigated agriculture; its use was limited to supplying water for human use, for livestock, small gardens, and for limited decorative plantings.

The Transportation Problem and the Railroads.—Without the railroads the Great Plains could not have been settled; the railroads were as essential as any other technological development to the settlement of this vast area of the Far West which lacked deep streams affording water transportation. It is true that the railroads were not developed in response to the challenge of the Plains environment as were other technological advances, but this does not alter the fact of their essential role. Had the railroad not been developed earlier, it probably would have been developed to meet the challenge of the trickling water courses of the West, where the steamboats of eastern streams could never find enough water to float them.

The Railroad Frontier.—The cattle kingdom could never have attained its great proportions except for the railroads that provided access to eastern markets for western beef. The industry did not thrive until after the railroads had built numerous lines into the eastern edge of the grazing lands.

The farmers' frontier in the Far West followed the penetration of the railroads. The railroads provided speedy transportation over great distances at lower rates than available wagon freighting could offer. Just as the mining boom attracted some permanent settlers into isolated areas, the railroads brought in workmen and others who saw the possibilities of opening agricultural settlements. The railroads moved ahead of the farmers and induced them to buy railroad lands or other lands offered by speculative land companies. The railroads afforded transportation for bulky grain, cattle, and other produce. There was no satisfactory solution to the fuel problem until the railroads brought coal into the Plains towns.

The population booms that filled many areas in the Far Western states in the 1880's were more a product of railroad promotion than of anything else. The history of innumerable settlements of towns and larger areas in the West began with the railroads. The population booms in Kansas, Nebraska, the Dakotas, Wyoming, parts of Montana, and other states began with the railroads. The so-called farmers' frontier followed the newly laid tracks.

Where the Plains' Settlers Came From.—The American-born migrants who occupied the Plains states in the two decades of the seventies and the eighties came from the next tier of states to the East, all of which either suffered a net loss in population or remained static. Some immigrants came from Canada. From Europe came many Irish; Germans came in by the tens of thousands. It was in the upper Great Plains that the immigrants from Norway, Sweden, and Denmark settled. Minnesota became noted as a Swedish state and the Dakotas for their Norwegian population.

An aggressive campaign was conducted by railroad and steamship companies to induce migration from northern Europe. The campaign took the form of advertising and the establishment of immigration bureaus in the East and in Europe. Agents were hired to make personal appeals to Europeans: The railroads offered land for sale on credit, reduced the price of tickets to prospective buyers of land, and provided free shipment for household goods. Exaggerated advertising lured many by promising early wealth from the prairie soil, and a great many farmers did prosper from the expanding markets for food crops.

PROBLEMS AND FEATURES OF THE FRONTIER

Problems and Features of the Frontier

10

THE PACIFICATION OF THE INDIANS

On the leading edge of the frontier the greatest threat to the well-being of the settlers was the Indian. Life and property were in jeopardy from Indian resentment of the pioneer's intrusions and because of the Indian's way of life; they were oftentimes predatory or their customs regarding the ownership of property differed from those of the European. The central government had jurisdiction over Indian policy and had to face the problem of opening the thinly occupied land to settlers and protecting those settlers from the Indians. The corresponding problem of enforcing treaties to prevent whites from intruding on Indian lands and violating their rights had to be met.

CONFLICT BETWEEN INDIANS AND WHITES

Indian Concepts of Property.—The Indians were, in theory, recognized by both government and some land speculators as owners of the land, since the aborigines occupied it originally. But the frontiersmen, except in colonial times, never recognized such ownership and considered the Indian a nuisance to be eradicated.

Indian tribes occupied the land as tribal property, but it was not owned privately. Federal agreements, or treaties, were made with the tribes as if they were foreign powers. Theoretically, territorial ownership by the tribes was recognized, and the whites were supposed to stay out. But intrusions could not be prevented. Pioneers, and statesmen too, could not accept the right of a few savages to occupy thinly and leave undeveloped vast territories rich in natural resources of soil, game, and minerals when "Christion men" lived in want. In spite of theory, the tribes were actu-

[87]

ally no longer independent nations and were not so recognized by foreign powers when they transferred such Indian-occupied territories among themselves. Settlers and other intruders paid little attention to agreements recognizing Indian ownership, and the national government found it physically and politically impossible to enforce obedience to its own laws, much less enforce agreements made with Indians.

In selling land, the Indians never realized they were giving it up permanently but expected to continue to share it to some extent as "Indian givers." To them it seemed a kind of lease or sharing arrangement. In chattels too, Indians did not share European ideas of private property. They shared their meager food and belongings with the whites in expression of hospitality. But when they appropriated property of the whites without permission, such as livestock (!), this was regarded as thievery and was drastically punished. A common experience of Europeans when in contact with the natives all over America was the need to guard their possessions, large and small, with watchful eye upon the aborigines. Moreover, many tribes were in a more or less continual state of warfare with their neighbors or lived largely by predatory raids on others. Settlers' livestock and belongings were natural objects of their cupidity. Conversion to Christianity did not always quickly or with certainty eradicate the urge to share the white man's jealously owned property.

Indian Treaties.—When conflicts arose because of white occupancy of Indian lands, the usual action of the government was to secure title to the land in dispute by purchase or forced cession and then formally open it to settlers. In this procedure the Indians would be called to a council. Government agents would arrange a cession of land from Indian chiefs. The agents used a combination of threats, a show of friendship, and gifts of various articles, food, and liquor. Gifts might include blankets, cloth, weapons, jewelry, and annuities of some kind. Most likely the treaty would be with a minority of the chiefs of a tribe or with some dissenting faction.

When the Indians, who never really understood the concept

of buying and selling land, tried to reenter it, this was considered a violation of the treaty. The violation was usually committed by one or more small groups acting on their own who often did not know of or understand the agreement. But the United States did not take account of this, held the whole tribe responsible, and sent military forces to punish any Indians that could be found. Further cessions might then be forced from the tribe as the cycle repeated itself.

Responsibility for Conflicts.—From an objective viewpoint one should not attempt to pass judgment or blame either red man or white man for these conflicts. It was easy for those whites located far from the frontier to pity the Indians, the victims of aggressive white men. Once the land had been won, it was magnanimous to sympathize with the victim and it seemed mean not to do so. It seems out of place to recall that the tribes were also victims of each other's aggression. Whatever the justification for Indian attacks on white frontiersmen, individuals who lived in danger of such retaliation could not be expected to sacrifice themselves to expiate the sins of others. On the other hand, it should be noted that when Indians did accept defeat, Americans were too slow to extend adequate humanitarian stewardship.

It is fairer, perhaps, to stand aside and view the conflict as one of two radically different cultures that were almost impossible to reconcile. As usual in such conflicts, the culture possessing the more advanced military and economic technology won the contest.

AMERICAN INDIAN WARS AND INDIAN POLICY

Generally the formulation of Indian policy by the national government was undertaken because it was necessary to prevent friction between Americans and Indians. After the subjection of the Indians, policy was shaped by the goals of making Indians adapt themselves to American institutions or by humanitarian considerations. Almost continuous conflict, whatever caused it, demonstrated the failure of government policy.

Indian Relations at the End of the American Revolution.—

After the American Revolution white settlers began moving rapidly into the West. The fears of the Indians were aroused as their hunting grounds were occupied and as incidents of violence occurred. The Spanish in the South and the British in the North encouraged Indian attacks as a means of stopping the advance of the Americans and maintaining control over trade with the Indians. At this time two large Indian confederations were organized, one in Ohio by Joseph Brant and the other in Georgia by Alexander McGillivray.

The Indians in the Southwest were eventually pacified in a series of treaties in the 1780's. Treaties were made in the Northwest also, but the treaties did not prevent Indian raids or other reentry into the lands that had been vacated. Failure of the treaty agreements with the Northwest Indians brought on a succession of military expeditions during Washington's administration. After the fiascoes of Harmar and St. Clair, Anthony Wayne defeated the tribes in Ohio and Indiana (as discussed earlier, pp. 42–43). As already noted, further land cessions were made and the Northwest Indians forced farther and farther to the West.

Indian Troubles in the War of 1812.—In the War of 1812 Indians in both the Northwest and the Southwest took advantage of the embroilment of their leading adversary, the mass of land-hungry pioneer farmers moving westward from the Atlantic seaboard. Indian leaders aroused their people to make war when the United States found itself at war with another nation. It should be observed that this pattern was repeated from the time of the British colonial wars with the French to the American Civil War. The sequel to these wars likewise followed a pattern: defeated tribes made further land cessions and were removed farther to the west. (For further discussion of the Indian problem during the War of 1812, see Section 5, pp. 45–47.)

Indian Policy After 1820.—The first treaty providing for the relocation of Indian tribes to the remote regions west of the Mississippi River was forced in 1817 under President Monroe. The belief that these lands were too dry and sterile for white occupancy was growing in the national mind at this time. But it was thought that this region would be suitable for the thin occupancy of Indians. Secretary of War John C. Calhoun made a survey of the Indian population and reported to Congress in 1823. He recommended the removal of all eastern Indians into the region west of the Mississippi. President Monroe announced the policy and his successors pursued it, mainly President Jackson. To protect this arrangement, the Indian country was policed to keep out white trespassers. These new western homes were expected to be permanent and were promised to them forever. Likewise, treaties were made with the tribes north of the Ohio, and they were moved beyond the Mississippi in the next two decades.

The Black Hawk War, 1832.—This campaign against the Sauk and the Fox tribes under the leadership of Black Hawk resulted from the removals. Black Hawk disagreed in the interpretation of an earlier treaty, harried white settlers, and in 1832 led his people across the Mississippi east into Illinois, believing he could raise a crop of corn and not be disturbed. In an early clash Black Hawk frightened the raw militia, who fled in disorder. This weakness encouraged other Indians to attack. In the campaign against Black Hawk that followed, he was pursued down the Wisconsin River and all except 150 of his 1,000 followers were killed. He was forced to cede a strip of land just west of the Mississippi in Iowa.

Removal of the Five Civilized Tribes in the Southwest.—The Choctaws, Creeks, Chickasaws, Cherokees, and Seminoles in the old Southwest, known as the Five Civilized Tribes, presented a more difficult problem of removal, since they numbered about 60,000 and had adopted the white man's ways of settling in fixed residences and of cultivating the land and raising livestock. Nevertheless these tribes were each in turn forced to cede their lands.

First, the state of Georgia deprived the Creeks and the Cherokees of their lands by fraud and violence. Three cases involving the Cherokee lands reached the Supreme Court under President Jackson's administration. The Court judged the action of Georgia as in violation of previous agreements and of property rights.

But President Jackson refused to support the Court decisions and Georgia ignored them. Jackson is reported to have said in this matter: "John Marshall has made his decision—now let him enforce it!" From 1835 to 1838 the last of the Cherokees were driven into Oklahoma Territory by the United States Army. In the winter of 1838 the last remnant of the Cherokees lost a quarter of their number owing to the hardships of the journey. In 1830 the Choctaws surrendered their lands and the Creeks from 1832 to 1835; both were forced to migrate beyond the Mississippi.

Government Policy in the Permanent Indian Country.—About 1830 the lands to be permanently occupied by Indians were designated by a definite boundary on the east. Beginning in the north, this boundary was drawn from Lake Michigan across northern Wisconsin to the Mississippi River, which it followed to the

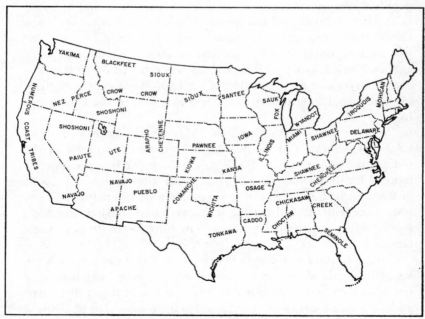

INDIAN TRIBES IN AMERICA

boundary of Missouri. From there it followed the northern boundary of Missouri westward to the Missouri River and from there to the present western boundaries of Missouri and Arkansas on to the Red River.

The Commissioner of Indian Affairs in the War Department was given supervision of this Indian reserve. The territory was divided into three superintendencies with agents appointed to deal directly with the tribes, distribute annuities, and preserve peace. The Indian Intercourse Act of 1834 tightened regulations for licensing Indian traders and provided for the exclusion of whisky. Unauthorized whites were expected to stay out of the Territory. The government's policy of aiding the educational and religious work of missionaries was enlarged and became permanent. It was intended that ultimately the Indian would settle down and farm a limited number of acres and adopt the white man's ways. This would lessen the land requirements of the Indian and open more land for white settlers.

The Role of the Army in the Indian Country.—The necessary police role of the army in preserving peace in the West gave the army a share in the control of Indian affairs. The whole region was organized as the western department of the army and guarded by a few thousand soldiers. Forts were built along the Indian frontier and within the Indian country. In addition to police work the army sent out important exploring expeditions.

The army was inadequate for the task of preserving peace among the Indians. Even working together the Indian agents and the army were unable to keep unauthorized whites out. Traders and white residents in large numbers moved into the Indian country. The attempt to prevent friction by separation of the races failed; the frontier line did not hold, and the federal government failed to keep its treaty agreements.

Breakdown of Indian Isolation.—The resettled Indians were not left to themselves. Parties of fur traders accelerated their activities and were generally welcomed for the goods they brought. Exploring parties and military expeditions made the Indians uneasy. Caravans of immigrant farmers constituted a real threat for the future as pioneer settlers moved across Indian lands to Oregon and California. With the coming of the mining booms all over the West, great numbers of whites crossed into and many settled within Indian lands; no real or long-lasting attempt was made by the army to hold them back. These intruders killed game, occupied lands, aggressively took advantage of the Indians in many ways, and became involved in violence with them. With the construction of the railroads in the 1850's and 1860's, large areas were stripped of wild game to feed construction gangs. Later, professional hunters came in to shoot the last of the buffalo and other game.

Indian Relations After 1850.—Effective control of Indian affairs was to be delayed until well after the Civil War. Troops in the West were insufficient and widely scattered but under able leaders. In the event of Indian violence, the army took charge. When peace prevailed, the Indian Bureau—placed in the Department of Interior in 1849—was in control. Disagreements over policy between the Indian Bureau and the army led to conflicting actions. The Indian Bureau followed a policy of kindness while the army favored one of severity and fairness. The Indian Bureau distributed guns to the red men for shooting game, but these were sometimes used against white troops. Some corrupt and inefficient Indian agents caused Indian resentment by distributing shoddy clothing and spoiled provisions.

On the other hand, dictatorial army officers led expeditions that incited Indian retaliation and lost the good will won by earlier agents. Eastern humanitarians, whose soft-heartedness was sometimes unrealistic, made the army's job more difficult. The humanitarians were quick to criticize severity. The confusion and resulting ineffectual policy encouraged Indians to take matters into their own hands to protect themselves. The movement of whites into the West in the 1850's forced abandonment of the idea of "One Big Reservation" for one of "Concentration"; the need to extinguish Indian titles in order to open land for a central transportation route was responsible.

The Pacification of the Indians

A series of Indian outbreaks flared up over the Far West just before the Civil War and continued until well after. Almost continuous campaigns and wars raged into the late 1870's, by which time the Indians had all been defeated and confined to relatively small reservations.

Indian Campaigns Beyond the Rockies.—Conflicts between miners and Indians in the intermountain areas brought the defeat of many tribes throughout that part of the nation. In California the "Diggers," exceedingly primitive and backward Indians, and others were, for the most part, easily exterminated by a series of campaigns conducted against them by miners during the 1850's and 1860's. More warlike Indians in Oregon, Nevada, Idaho, and Utah were forced into reservations. In the Southwestern deserts and mountains, the Navahoes and Apaches, fierce plundering tribes, required innumerable campaigns and cost many lives, many years, and much money before they were finally confined.

The Civilized Tribes During the Civil War.—Slave ownership among the Civilized Tribes caused all of them, either as whole tribes or factions of tribes, to make alliances with the Confederacy during the Civil War. Apparently their decision was not easy, for some Indians fought on the Union side. As a consequence of the alliances with the Confederacy, the Civilized Tribes were forced to surrender the western half of the Indian Territory, which was organized as the Oklahoma District.

The Plains Indians.—The most warlike and difficult to conquer of all American Indians were the mounted tribes on the Great Plains. Among them were the Sioux in the north and the fierce Comanche in the south. These nomadic tribesmen were aroused by the pioneer migrations, the stagecoaches, and railroad-building across the central plains of Kansas and Nebraska. When, in 1851, the government began the new policy of opening the wide, central transportation route, these tribes were assigned to smaller areas. They were forced into well-defined hunting grounds fixed to separate the various tribes.

[95]

In 1859 a hundred thousand miners invaded the areas just assigned the Cheyennes and Arapahoes. War broke out in 1861; it reached a climax in the fall of 1864, when most of eastern Colorado had been devastated by the natives. It was at this time that Colonel Chivington led Colorado militiamen in the massacre of over 450 sleeping Cheyennes and Arapahoes—men, women, and children—at their camp on Sand Creek. The massacre of these Indians, who had just sued for peace, brought further savagery by other tribes. The Sioux War of 1865–67 was opened when the United States took steps to build the Powder River Road through Sioux hunting grounds. During the war the massacre to the last man of the Fetterman party occurred in December, 1866, east of the Big Horn Mountains.

The "Small Reservation" System; Renewed Warfare.—The Sand Creek Massacre brought a storm of protest in Congress against the army's conduct in the West. Congress sent out the Peace Commission in 1867 to stop the Sioux War and introduce a new policy of "small reservations" to isolate Indians in remote places. It began the policy of segregation of the Indians from contact with whites and of making the Indians wards of the government (instead of treating them as independent nations). Plans were made to teach them to adopt the settled agricultural life and ultimately become American citizens without special status. This policy would please both land-hungry Westerners and humanitarian Easterners.

At a great council on Medicine Lodge Creek several Plains tribes agreed to accept reservations in Oklahoma. At another conference the Sioux agreed to accept a reservation in Dakota Territory. In August, 1868, war broke out again over the southern Plains as the younger warriors of the Cheyenne, Arapaho, Comanche, Kiowa, and Apache refused to accept reservations. By March, 1869, General Sheridan and Colonel Custer had decisively defeated them and corralled these tribes in the Indian Territory. In 1871 these Indians rebelled once more and started a war that lasted into 1875. General Sherman, now in charge of the Western Army, finally pacified the Indians of the southern Plains. The last major Indian war occurred in 1876, when the Sioux in the Black Hills rebelled due to the invasion of gold miners. It was in this engagement that the massacre of Custer's 265 men occurred on the Little Big Horn River in Montana. Before the year was over the defeated Sioux were ready to return to their reservation. Subsequent Indian fighting took the form of Apache raids under Geronimo and lasted until 1885. The final sizable Indian "war" occurred in 1890. The massacre of about 200 Dakota Indians occurred in the "Battle" of Wounded Knee in the Badlands of South Dakota.

New Indian Policy, 1871.—Congress reaffirmed the new Indian policy inaugurated by the Peace Commission. Now the Indians were no longer recognized legally as sovereign nations. Their tribal governments were to be ignored. They became only dependent social groups and individuals without rights under the federal Constitution. The new policy of the Indian Office was to help the tribes organize councils to exercise governmental powers and thereby undermine the powers of the chiefs. One step after another was taken to break down tribal organization and treat them as individuals. In 1879, as a part of the program to absorb Indians into the main stream of national life, federal schools began to provide more than the equivalent of a public school education. Higher education stressing agriculture and mechanical training was provided in special schools. In 1883 the Indian Office relieved the chiefs of their judicial powers by providing the Indians with systems of federal courts.

The Dawes Severalty Act, 1887.—The Dawes Act climaxed the new Indian policy originating with the Peace Commission in 1867. The purposes of the Dawes Act were supported by both humanitarians and by interests hungering for their lands. Several groups organized themselves about 1880 to assist the Indian. Helen Hunt Jackson in 1881 published *A Century of Dishonor* and in 1884 *Ramona*. The humanitarians exerted considerable influence in Congress.

One outcome of the reshuffling of Indian policy was the Dawes Act. This law provided for individual ownership of land with the natives eventually acquiring title to farms and ranches with the full rights of ownership that such fee simple title gives. First, however, the divided tribal lands had to be held in trust for 25 years from the government. This would give the Indians time to realize the full meaning of ownership and prevent their selling the land or being cheated out of it. In 1902, 1907, and 1908 steps were taken to shorten the trust period and subsequently many lost their land after they had acquired the power to transfer it.

In 1924 all Indians were given full citizenship. In 1934 Indian policy was reversed by the New Deal in the Wheeler-Howard Act. Since Indians had been acquiring some of the worst traits of the whites, this reversal of policy sought, not to replace, but to conserve Indian tribal culture. It provided that land allotments were to cease and tribal ownership under incorporation was encouraged.

11

THE DISTRIBUTION OF THE PUBLIC DOMAIN

Another problem that greatly concerned the West was the political problem of legislating provisions for the transfer of the lands of the public domain to private ownership. With Indian claims removed, pioneers and land jobbers were concerned next with the terms by which they might acquire government land.

The Ordinance of 1785.—The national government under the Articles of Confederation fell heir to the states' claims to the Western lands. At Maryland's insistence the states surrendered their claims; therefore, it became the duty of Congress to legislate terms by which land would be sold.

Colonial precedents were considered in providing for the survey and sale of these lands. The New England and the Southern states each had distinct and sharply contrasting systems for individuals to establish claims to land. In the South, individuals were allowed the greater freedom: the settler could go out and locate his land and describe his claim according to irregular natural boundaries. In New England the process was quite orderly: the land was first set aside as townsites, then surveyed, and farms were allotted to individuals in a systematic manner.

It was the New England system that was adopted in the Ordinance of 1785. (1) The system of rectangular land surveys was established. (2) Careful surveys of townships six miles square, divided into 36 sections, were to be made before lands could be put up for sale. Each section of "one square mile" contained 640 acres. (3) The land was to be sold at auction with a minimum price of $1 an acre and a minimum purchase of 640 acres. (4) One section in each township was set aside for the support of schools.

Provisions of the law favored land jobbers, of whom there were many in Congress. Small farmers on the frontier did not have the necessary minimum of $640 in cash and could not cultivate an entire section even if they could purchase it. Only moneyed men could afford to buy the land, subdivide it, and extend credit to buyers. One intent of the law was to provide revenue to the national government; this purpose overruled the policy of developing the land more rapidly by selling it to small farmers.

The Land Law of 1796.—An impractical revision of the original land law of 1787 was passed by Congress in 1796; the intent was to promote sales of land to smaller buyers. The credit system was introduced: the purchase price was raised to $2 per acre and the buyer had one year to pay half the purchase price of his land. The law proved impractical because it retained the minimum unit of 640 acres and because no frontier farmer could expect to earn $640 in one year to pay his debt.

The Land Law of 1800 (Harrison Act).—William Henry Harrison, elected as a delegate from the Northwest Territory to Congress in 1800, secured the passage of a more liberal land law. This law represented the desires and the influence of the West in the disposal of land. The terms provided (*a*) that land might be bought at local land offices in minimum tracts of a half-section (320 acres); (*b*) that it would be first offered at auction to the highest bidder but if not sold could be bought at a minimum price of $2 an acre and (c) under terms of credit extending to four years when the full amount became due. Heretofore, buyers bought land at offices located in the East; provisions for land offices in the West served the convenience of frontier farmers.

Under the Harrison Act a great many settlers took up lands in Ohio, Indiana, Illinois, Alabama, Mississippi, Louisiana, and in Missouri. The Great Migration and the eventual admission of six new border states occurred while the Harrison Act was in effect.

The Land Law of 1804.—In modifying the terms of the law of 1800, this act reduced the minimum purchase to a quarter-section (160 acres); otherwise it did not importantly change the basic law. But it was still almost impossible for the settler to pay for the land out of the produce he raised on it, as the theory of the law assumed.

In the long run, nearly a third of the buyers on credit did not finish payments and gave up their land. In 1809 Congress began passing annual relief acts extending time for making payments. After a while this developed into a scandalous situation. The Harrison Act made it possible for the federal government to foreclose on land not paid for, but political considerations made it difficult to do so. The act created a large number of debtors who owed money to the government and who voted their own interests above all else. The more numerous they were, the less willing they were to pay, since everyone else was in the same situation. Congress repeatedly postponed foreclosure and the collection of these debts. After a while the small settler began to feel that the land should be distributed free of charge. The original intent was that land sales should be a source of revenue, but the revenues barely paid administrative costs. Western congressmen began to lay stress upon the public service of the men who settled the land. The spokesman for a liberal policy came to be Thomas Hart Benton of Missouri; he entered the Senate in 1821. The East opposed liberal terms and maintained more restrictive terms as long as they had the votes to do so. The East desired revenue from the land and opposed the expansion of the West, since it would bring a corresponding decline in the political power of the East.

Land Law of 1820.—The minimum purchase was further reduced to 80 acres, but the credit provisions were abolished. The minimum price was reduced to $1.25 per acre. Those who still owed money were given the choice of surrendering an amount of land equal in value to the unpaid debt. This law proved successful and, unlike earlier land laws, disclosed no special weakness in its provisions.

"Squatters' Rights."—It was always difficult to administer the land laws and survey land as rapidly as people occupied it; this was especially true when migration again accelerated after 1830. Thus developed the problem of squatters who took up land and proceeded to make improvements and clear the soil before the surveys could be run. Later the government surveyors would catch up with the frontier and the tracts would be put up for sale at auction to the highest bidder. The squatter had to face the risk of having his land bought by another, or he had to outbid some more pecunious Easterner who coveted his improvements. To protect themselves, squatters began to demand the first right to buy the land—preemption, or "squatters' rights."

In the absence of squatters' rights farmers in the West resorted to direct action through extralegal "claims associations" of squatters. These associations wrote constitutions, adopted by-laws, elected officers, and recorded claims of members. Squatters bid the land at the minimum price at the government auctions. If anyone raised the bid, he might be whipped or tarred and feathered; competitive bidding was often prevented. The claims associations also settled disputes between their own members. Numerous claims associations were organized in Iowa, where many squatters slipped in after the Black Hawk War, before the land was offered for sale.

The Preemption Act, 1842.—Limited rights of preemption had been granted by legislation since 1830, but these acts were assumed to be temporary expedients and did not recognize the principle of preemption. The Whigs promised a better preemption law in "the log cabin and hard cider" campaign of 1840.

After the Whigs had resorted to much evasive maneuvering in Congress, Benton and the Democrats forced them to make good their campaign promise. The Act gave anyone who had cultivated the land the right to buy 160 acres at the minimum price. It was a great victory for the West, for by it Congress established the principle that the person who actually occupied the land had special rights; it also established the policy of giving priority to the settlement of land over the production of revenue from its sales. After the preemption victory the West began agitating for free homesteads. The Preemption Act was repealed in 1891.

The Graduation Act, 1854.—A favorite plan of Benton's to help the poorer settlers to buy land was that of graduation. Graduation provided for successive reductions in the price at which unsold public land would be offered. The East opposed such measures because it was believed it would drain away industrial workers to the West and would reduce federal revenues. In 1854 the Graduation Act was finally passed; it provided that lands not sold should be reduced in price over a period of 30 years. Land sales increased under its provisions, but it was repealed and the Homestead Act took its place.

The Homestead Act, 1862.—The West had long agitated vigorously for donation of land to actual settlers. After 1850 the East and the South reversed their political positions on land policy. The East came to favor liberal policies. Because the East was receiving an increasing labor supply from the Irish immigration of the forties and fifties, it now began to favor an expanding West as a market for manufactures. This development was a part of the shifting political realignment of the sections as the North and East became economically allied with the West preceding the Civil War. Sentiment for free homesteads grew as reformers in the labor movement argued that free homesteads would provide an escape for oppressed workers; others argued that free land would promote the growth of the country.

The first homestead act to pass Congress was vetoed by President Buchanan who sided with the South. After the Republican victory of 1860 and the secession of the South, the Homestead Act was passed in 1862. Its terms provided that any citizen over 21 years of age could claim 160 acres from the surveyed public domain after five years residence by payment of a reasonable registration fee. It did not replace the Preemption Act, which still functioned to permit settlers to claim unsurveyed lands.

In its operation the Homestead Act was not as instrumental as commonly thought in the distribution of public lands. Furthermore, its provisions were perverted by large land companies in one way or another. Railroad land grants, other land grants, and other subsequent land legislation providing for public entry account to a greater extent for the distribution of public lands. Enormous fraud occurred in the establishment of claims under the Homestead Act. Ranchers, for example, acquired large holdings through their cowboy employees who transferred the land to their bosses. Land speculators practiced fraud to acquire lands or bought blocks running to tens of thousands of acres at $1.25 per acre and resold it to pioneers at several times that figure.

Land warrants, issued not only to veterans of the Civil War but warrants originating with the American Revolution, were bought by speculators as they engrossed the public lands. Indian lands, when the tribes were removed to smaller reservations, were acquired by speculators, not homesteaders. Lands granted to the states under the Morrill Land Grant College Act of 1862 as endowments for agricultural and mechanical colleges were sold by the states to land jobbers. Land that could be homesteaded was located so far from transportation that, more often than not, it was more practical for a settler to buy land instead of homesteading it.

The Homestead Act was passed as the frontier was reaching the semi-arid country, but it did not increase the 160-acre unit, and thus it kept farms too small to enable farmers and ranchers to make an adequate living in the dry lands of the Far West. The Homestead Act did not provide the boon to farmers as popularly assumed.

The Timber Culture Act, 1873.—The need for larger farm units in the West was recognized by the Timber Culture Act, which permitted a homesteader to acquire an additional 160 acres by planting a fourth of it in trees within four years. Under the act ten million acres were taken, mostly by genuine homesteaders who were enabled to increase their holdings to more economic units. The act failed to promote reforestation as much as intended.

The Desert Land Act, 1877.—This act, passed under pressure from wealthy ranchers, permitted the purchase of 640 acres at a price of $1.25 per acre. It required proof that a part of the land had been irrigated. Under this law a relatively small amount of land was taken, much of it fraudulently, by large ranchers and irrigation companies.

The Timber and Stone Act, 1878.—Individuals were permitted to buy 160 acres of land "unfit for cultivation" for its timber or stone. Lumber companies used this measure to appropriate fraudulently valuable timber lands at an iota of their value.

12

FINANCIAL PROBLEMS OF FRONTIER AREAS

Frontier regions often suffered from financial difficulties. A large proportion of settlers were poor, but all needed to spend heavily to pay for improvements, public and private. Borrowing was necessary to import capital. Money shortages were therefore chronic. Frontier communities were ready to resort to radical solutions and were quick to blame Eastern creditors and government classes for their difficulties. Sometimes their complaints were against the fiscal measures of the government. Much of the time they complained of broad economic forces, but most often they complained of money and banking policies of the government. Their dissatisfaction gave rise to radical and third party political movements.

EARLY FINANCIAL DIFFICULTIES

In colonial times the lack of money in the colonies, and especially on the frontier, caused friction between the colonies and Great Britain and between debtors in the West and creditors in the East. Favorable fiscal policies of government and debtor relief measures were among the demands of the West.

The Basis of Frontier Financial Problems.—Individuals on the frontier needed money or credit to pay for land and to make improvements on farms; communities needed facilities such as roads, bridges and other transportation facilities, schools, churches, and public buildings. They had to borrow money before they were able to generate their own savings out of which to finance these needs. Capital savings are accumulated in older communities. The frontier became a borrowing region, first from England or the eastern seaboard and later from all over Europe. The West was usually in debt. The resulting differences of interests between debtor and creditor classes and sections gave rise to political differences.

In the British American colonies, and later on the national frontier, new regions suffered from a "drain of specie," or hard money, because they had to spend what specie they possessed. The lack of specie made it difficult to support an exchange economy, and when specie was not present, inconvenient barter had to serve in its place. Furthermore, the lack of specie made it difficult to provide a reserve to support issues of paper money that might have provided a medium of exchange.

In the colonies there were loud complaints that England's mercantilistic policies drained specie and that the colonies were not permitted to legislate to provide any system of paper money, such as bills of credit, to meet their needs for a circulating currency. Various foreign coins were used in the colonies, the Spanish being the most common. The Spanish dollar was cut into eight pieces to provide fractional currency. Tobacco, furs, gold dust, and whisky were used as money, particularly on the frontier. Anything of relatively high value in relation to its bulk, that was easily divisible, that would store well, and was universally desired was likely to take the place of specie or paper. Much of the shortage of money on the frontier was a result of the normal operation of economic forces and was not necessarily due to exploitation, but Westerners blamed the ruling and creditor classes.

Financial Issues in Frontier Uprisings.—Of five prominent frontier uprisings up to 1800, financial grievances were present in all except one. Bacon's Rebellion was caused partly by low prices for tobacco and the refusal of the governing aristocracy to prevent overproduction by law; poll taxes were another complaint. In the uprisings of the Regulators in North Carolina and South Carolina complaints of poll taxes, tax sales of land, and corruption were prominent. The uprising of the Paxton Boys, the exception, was directed against Indian policy. In Shays' Rebellion the farmers of western Massachusetts revolted against the tax system, debt foreclosures, and demanded paper money. In the Whisky Rebellion farmers in western Pennsylvania protested against the burdensome excise tax on whisky, a commodity that took the place of money. Whisky was an important export of backwoods communities, because it provided a means for reducing the bulkiness of their grain crops into a form that could be more easily transported. In the American Revolution the West as a debtor region supported the Patriot (rebel) cause more strongly than did the East.

The Money Problem During the Confederation.—With the outbreak of the American Revolution and the accompanying uncertainty and insecurity, people hoarded whatever specie they possessed. The state legislatures and the Continental Congress were forced to resort to the issuance of paper money in the form of bills of credit (continental currency) to finance the war. At the end of the war this inflated currency had lost nearly all its value and ceased to circulate. People had to depend upon specie or bills of credit in the few states that still used them. This scarcity of a circulating medium and the letdown from a war-stimulated economy caused falling prices and depression in the 1780's. Western farmers who had contracted debts when prices were high were hard hit. Foreclosures for taxes and debts resulted. In seven states the demand for paper money was met by

the legislatures. But in others the Eastern creditor interests dominated politics and refused to authorize paper money issues.

In 1786 the most prominent protest of the debtor class occurred among the farmers of western Massachusetts in Shays'
Rebellion. The uprising illustrates significantly the conflict between the West and the East over the regulation of currency and
credit. The rebellion hastened action by the frightened creditor
classes to establish a stronger national government to prevent the
states from issuing paper money in response to such movements.

THE BANK OF THE UNITED STATES

The regulation of the nation's currency by the Bank of the
United States was resented by the agrarians and speculative Westerners. The Bank became the leading issue in the administration
of Andrew Jackson. His opposition and that of the West killed
the Bank.

Attitude of the West to the Bank of the United States.—Leading opposition to the national bank came from the South and the
West. It was opposed because it exercised monopoly powers, justly
or unjustly, to restrain the issuance of excessive paper money;
this tended both to limit the supply of money and to raise interest rates. The West knew the Bank was under the control of the
Eastern creditor class.

The West wanted to operate its own banks free of domination
by a central bank. The states had their own banking laws under
which banks could be chartered; also individuals and groups
engaged in banking and could even issue their own paper money.
To the Westerner the most important service a bank could render
was to issue large quantities of bank notes and lend them freely.
He was optimistic and did not realize the need to limit issuance
of paper money to some reasonable reserve of specie on deposit.
The Westerner, not having much respect for experts, thought any
man of common sense could and ought to be permitted to operate
a bank. These views, tolerating loose banking practices, conflicted
with sound money views.

Many banks were opened in the West after 1800. Restrictions

on the conduct of early Western banks were insufficient to insure safety of the paper currency issued by them. The Bank of the United States discounted the bank notes of such institutions according to their lack of soundness and frequently challenged them to prove their solvency by gathering stacks of their currency and presenting it for specie payment. This disciplinary action forced Western wildcat banks to follow more conservative practices; many of the Westerners resented this, since they desired easy money which would support rising prices.

Banking After 1811.—When the charter of the first Bank of the United States expired in 1811 the Jeffersonians refused to recharter it. The small banks saw their opportunity and multiplied indiscriminately. A flood of paper money was issued, each bank being able to print its own banknotes. The War of 1812 forced the suspension of specie payment; this left the door wide open for easy banking and the issuance of paper money backed by little or no specie. It was difficult for banks to achieve liquidity on short notice, since most loans were long term and could not be called quickly.

In addition to loose banking the Western system made frauds possible. Banks were not expected to maintain ornate buildings; an imposter might ride into town with a large amount of new paper money and make loans from an office to farmers on easy terms in return for promissory notes. He would then sell the notes at a discount to a local merchant and skip town. Another fraud was counterfeiting—made possible by the large variety of paper money with which no one could be familiar. Because of these opportunities for fraud and the uncertainty of the soundness of the issuing bank, state bank notes were not accepted far from the bank of origin and would be discounted more or less in proportion to the distance from the bank of issue.

The Second Bank of the United States.—The anarchy in money and banking caused even the Jeffersonians to agree to charter a new Bank of the United States in 1816. This second Bank of the United States resumed its policing of banking practices, established branches in the states, and issued its own banknotes. It worked to decrease issues of paper by less stable banks, with the result that the West found its currency and credit shrinking. Any money contraction causes pain and this one seemed unreasonable to the West. Western and Southern banks secured legislation to tax branches of the Bank of the United States out of existence. The case of *McCulloch* v. *Maryland* ruled such laws to be unconstitutional.

In 1819 there occurred a money panic and business crash accompanied by bank failures and widespread insolvency of individuals and firms. The panic was precipitated when the Bank of the United States resumed specie payment and forced other banks to do the same. State banks had to call in loans. The credit crisis proved to be severe because of the preceding loose lending practices and widespread borrowing for the purchase of land.

Jackson and the Bank.—The second Bank of the United States was terminated by the veto of Andrew Jackson, who dramatized Western hostility to the "Monster," as it was called. Jackson did not like banks because their issues of paper money led to speculative excesses. He especially disliked the Bank of the United States because he remembered how it had ruthlessly resumed specie payment and caused the panic of 1819.

It was known that President Jackson was opposed to the renewal of the Bank's charter, due to expire in 1836. Henry Clay and the other opponents of Jackson decided to make an issue of the Bank in the presidential election campaign of 1832. Clay, ambitious to become president, believed he could win on the Bank issue. Clay, from Kentucky, represented one of the older, more conservative states of the West where the Bank was favored. Clay thought the nation would support his stand on the Bank and elect him in preference to Jackson.

When the bill to recharter the Bank passed Congress, Jackson vetoed it as expected. In the election campaign that followed he criticized the Bank as a monopoly and as a source of corruption. Jackson was thoroughly angered by the Bank for its use of financial power to make loans and bribes to attempt to influence politics and win the election for Clay. He could not wait for it to expire in 1836, but began to work immediately to destroy it. This he did by withdrawing deposits to pay government obligations and by depositing revenues in the "pet banks," i.e., state banks.

The destruction of the power of the Bank of the United States left state banks free once more to resume freely the issuance and lending of paper money. This set off a boom in land speculation and canal-building, a great surge of westward migration, and the founding of wildcat banks. Prices rose rapidly although they had been stable during the twenties. The stage was set for boom and collapse.

The Distribution Bill, 1836.—One result of the boom in credit and land values was to bring huge revenues into the federal treasury from land sales. These revenues, combined with those from the Compromise Tariff of 1833, embarrassed the government with more money than it needed. Various suggestions were made for spending it; the West wanted it spent for internal improvements. The outcome was the passage of the Distribution Bill in 1836 providing that the treasury would divide the surplus funds among the states according to population. In theory these payments were made as loans, but no one expected the federal government ever to ask for repayment and it never did. When the treasury asked the "pet banks" to return the funds that had been deposited with them, they had difficulty in doing so. They ceased to make new loans and outstanding loans could not be renewed. Debtors were forced into bankruptcy by the resulting credit stringency.

Panic of 1837.—Another factor that ended the plentiful supply of money in circulation was the Specie Circular of 1836. Jackson and the Westerners did not like to see Easterners speculate in Western lands as they were doing in the boom of the early thirties. The speculators were using state bank notes to purchase federal lands. Jackson had tried earlier to prevent so much speculation and now decided to issue the presidential order. The Specie Circular, sent to federal land offices in the West, directed them to accept only specie in payment for land. Since there was not enough gold and silver to support the land boom, the effect of the directive was to take millions of dollars out of circulation that had been used to purchase land. Severe panic followed from this money contraction and prices of commodities fell sharply. Bankruptcy spread to all kinds of businesses and to the booming canal companies. The West was long in recovering from its effects; the panic turned into a depression that was resumed in 1839 and lasted into the middle 1840's. Western farmers were hard hit, and many lost their property. Some states had to stop payments on their bonds. The West came to distrust banks of issue and drafted new state constitutions with severe regulations of banking. A faction of the Democratic party in the West, known as the Loco-Focos, arose to oppose all banks of issue.

THE MONEY QUESTION AFTER THE CIVIL WAR

The next general furor in the West over the money issue came as a consequence of the Civil War.

Effect of the Civil War on the Monetary System.—During the Civil War the national currency was forced to go off a specie basis because people took gold and silver out of banks and hoarded it. There was not enough specie to redeem national bank notes on demand. The Union, like the Confederacy, had to resort to issues of irredeemable paper money. Those issued by the federal government were called "greenbacks." These issues created a plentiful supply of money and prices rose. Debtors now found it much easier to repay loans. Although greenbacks could be purchased at discount with gold dollars, they were legal tender for the payment of debt and for other payments. Debtors naturally paid their obligations with the cheaper greenbacks.

After the war was over the treasury ceased issuing greenbacks, but the expansion of the country increased its monetary needs. In fact greenbacks were withdrawn from circulation in an effort to contract the money supply in preparation for a return to redeemability in gold. Prices for farm products fell, partly because of increased production from new lands opened in the West. A movement to expand the currency swept the whole nation but was strongest in the West. As usual those who had money or had made loans or owned bonds benefited with deflation and opposed inflation.

The Greenback Movement, 1868.—The debtor status of the West produced the Greenback movement. The "Ohio Idea" was first written into the Democratic platform of 1868. In the same year Congress repealed the law providing for the withdrawal of greenbacks, but after that the hard money advocates of the Republican party, for the most part, had their way in Grant's administrations and the country underwent steady deflation with ever falling farm prices. The Greenback party arose in the Middle West in protest and demanded a regulated paper currency that would prevent debtors from suffering from falling prices.

The Movement for Silver Coinage.—Another remedy demanded to counteract deflation was the use of more silver in the nation's currency system. But in 1873 Congress passed the coinage act, on the recommendation of the treasury, to discontinue the minting of silver dollars. The measure happened to coincide with the rising output of silver by the Western mines and the partial discontinuance of silver currency in various countries of Europe. To the inflationists this law seemed a deliberate measure to forestall any flow of the more abundant silver into the monetary system. It was soon branded as the "Crime of '73" by the inflationists and Western silver mining interests. The agitation for free (unlimited) coinage of silver bore meager fruit in the Bland-Allison Act of 1878; the silver coinage it permitted was a mere trickle and brought no relief. The abiding distrust of creditors, banks, and corporations increased in the Western mind.

Boom Times in the Eighties.—Plentiful rainfall and increased crops over the West in the early eighties brought a limited degree of prosperity. Railroad construction was resumed and agriculture expanded in the Plains and in the Far West. Population grew over the whole West. The East welcomed opportunities to lend money in the West by investing in farm mortgages. Interest rates were high, but money was easy to borrow; land booms developed all over the West. Farm mortgages were increased by the greater need for capital to finance farm improvements and to buy the agricultural machinery then coming into use.

The Sherman Silver Purchase Act, 1890.—The large number of new senators coming in from the newly admitted states of the West in 1889–1890 helped the inflationists win a victory in the passage of the Sherman Silver Purchase Act. The measure was passed in conjunction with the Tariff of 1890 to help gain support for the higher tariff rates. The silver law required large purchases of silver with treasury notes and made both redeemable in gold. When the notes were redeemed in large quantities during the Panic of 1893, the gold reserve set up for this purpose fell below the figure of $100,000,000, long regarded by the conservatives as the minimum reserve necessary for the maintenance of the gold standard. The measures taken by Cleveland to replenish the gold reserve and thereby preserve the gold standard antagonized the inflationists who did not wish to maintain it. The silverites and inflationists now abandoned the Democratic party and turned to the Populists.

Populism.—As the favorable rainfall cycle came to an end and the land booms subsided in the last years of the 1880's, hard times returned to the West. Now the Farmers Alliance became the spokesman of the farmers' protest. Farmers in the Great Plains suffered the most and protested the loudest. They complained of monopoly by railroads and other corporations, of unsympathetic government when in the hands of either major party, of high interest rates, and of the money shortage. By 1890 the Alliance movement was converting itself into the Populist movement, which centered in the Plains states but was strongly supported all over the West and in the South. The movement grew rapidly until 1896 and developed into a strong third party. In 1892 the Populists elected over 50 representatives to Congress.

In the campaign of 1896 the Populist movement came to a climax. They demanded various political and economic reforms, but they emphasized the need for inflation through free silver and paper money. The Populist party nominated the great orator and silver advocate from Nebraska, William Jennings Bryan. The

[113]

Democrats also adopted the free silver platform and nominated Bryan. The campaign was the hardest fought in American political history. Fear of radicalism lost the election for Bryan and the Democrats. As prosperity returned and the output of gold mines increased at the turn of the century, demands for monetary reform lost their former appeal.

13

THE SOLUTION
OF TRANSPORTATION PROBLEMS

Another of the greatest needs of a newly settled area is transportation. The need is fundamental, yet new communities found it difficult to finance such costly improvements.

EARLY PROGRESS IN TRANSPORTATION

In contrast with colonial times, rapid improvements were made in transportation after the establishment of the national government in 1789. New forms of transportation quickly succeeded each other in the West—the macadamized roads, the steamboats, the canals, and large scale operators of various forms of overland communication to the Pacific.

Colonial Transportation.—When the colonies were founded, the first settlements were located near sheltered rivers or harbors where anchorages were available and wharves could be constructed. The many waterways and the rough coastline of the Atlantic provided travelways and shelter for boats. The rivers, especially in the South, penetrated far inland. They were deep enough for a considerable distance for the ships of that time and made accessible to transportation the inland areas up to the first rapids. Ocean-going ships served farms and plantations along the banks of the rivers. Thus, waterways served as roads within and between the colonies. Shipping and shipbuilding were major industries. The lack of roads and the expense and difficulty of building them greatly limited intercolonial communications by land.

[114]

The Solution of Transportation Problems

Transportation for Frontier Communities.—New settlements located at a distance from navigable waterways depended almost for their very life and certainly for their growth upon some form of transportation. They needed a means of sending their produce to market cheaply and quickly and a means of bringing in goods and news from the East and Europe. The lack of capital in the West was felt especially in this matter; for this reason "internal improvements" became a leading political issue there.

In the interior, the river valleys were settled first because they afforded transportation. The Mississippi became a great funnel through which the produce of the West was poured into New Orleans for reloading on ocean-going ships destined for the East Coast, the West Indies, and Europe. Exports from the region west of the Appalachians therefore moved west and south because transportation floated on the rivers. Flatboats were used by westward-moving pioneers on the Ohio. They could be constructed inexpensively and a whole family with its livestock could float down river. From any given point a great many flatboats could be counted floating down the Ohio during the period of the Great Migration. They were large enough to permit fairly normal life aboard. When the destination was reached, they were broken up and the timber used for building homes. And they were used to float agricultural produce down to New Orleans, where they were taken apart and sold for lumber.

On land the first ways were mere paths or traces opened up for pack animals. Next they were widened by cutting trees and became wagon roads. Stumps had to be left; no roadbed was constructed. Swampy sections were made passable by laying logs transverse to the direction of the road. Streams were forded or ferries provided by some enterprising individual. These early roads were extremely unpleasant to travel and even dangerous. Deep mudholes and stumps made coach travel exhausting.

Construction of Improved Roads.—The construction of roads was revolutionized in England about 1790 by McAdam and Telford. Macadamized roads were all-weather roads made of crushed rock, with the sides sloping to a ditch that provided drainage.

[115]

The turnpikes first applied new engineering techniques in roadbuilding, but they were privately financed and built. The first one built, the Philadelphia-Lancaster Turnpike, in Pennsylvania, was opened in 1794. Its success touched off a wave of such building. In construction the turnpikes were underlaid with heavier stones and smaller stones were used toward the surface. The surface would be finished with gravel and packed so as to become almost solid; but no binder, such as tar, was used. Freight on these roads was carried in the covered, or Conestoga, wagon, developed early in Pennsylvania.

Counties and towns built most of the publicly financed roads, and citizens worked on them instead of paying taxes. The states and the federal government often subsidized roads. Zane's Trace from Wheeling to Maysville was subsidized by a land grant in 1796 from Congress. An act of Congress in 1802 provided that 5 per cent of revenues from public land sales should be set aside for road-building; this act was continued in force and through it a fund was accumulated in the United States Treasury.

The National Road.—Provision for the National Road (also referred to as the Cumberland Road) was made by Congress in 1806, when the general route was chosen between Cumberland in western Maryland and Wheeling in Virginia. It was 1815 before construction was begun, but by 1818 the United States mail was being carried over it all the way to Wheeling. Bridges were built of stone. Stones for the roadbed were broken with hammer by manual labor. Traffic passing over the surface packed the stones solid.

The road fell into disrepair very quickly and for ten years Congress wrangled over whether the federal government could constitutionally charge tolls or should be responsible for repairs. Repairs were finally left to the states; they set up toll stations to collect funds for repairs.

The National Road was supported politically by both the East and the West; it helped attract traffic to the East and divert some of it from New Orleans. From the start it proved to be an extremely busy road for commercial and immigrant travel. Freighting and coach companies were set up to provide service. Taverns built along the whole route were an integral part of transportation service. The National Road for a generation remained the only hard-surfaced road in the West; in moderately remote frontier regions hard-surfaced roads were never built until the day of the automobile.

River Traffic.—For the earliest inland river traffic, the canoe provided an important means of transportation for furs in the trade with the Indians. The flatboat on the larger rivers for downstream freight has already been described. Somewhat later than the flatboat came the keelboat, essential for upstream freight but necessarily used for downstream freight too. This long, narrow boat, about 50 feet long and 8 feet wide and of shallow draft, could be moved upstream against the current. The keelboat could carry 20 to 40 tons of freight and had a roof to protect the cargo against the weather. The keelboat was rowed with three to six oars on each side, and a sail was provided for use with favorable wind. It might be towed at times by 20 to 30 men scrambling through the water dragging it upstream. In shallow water it might be pushed forward with poles. Only valuable goods without excessive bulk could stand the expense of such arduous exertion and use of manpower.

Mississippi River traffic provided a livelihood for a rough and hardy population on the boats and waterfronts. These men called themselves half-horse and half-alligator; only the stronger, restless element could stand this life and they formed a lawless, wild lot, outrageously coarse in talk and crude in behavior.

Another special-purpose river boat was the Far West's bullboat; its round willow frame was covered with buffalo hides and the seams were calked. The bullboat, used in the fur trade, was easily built, could carry as much as six tons, and was moved with poles or paddled from the front.

The Steamboat.—In 1807 Robert Fulton proved the steamboat to be practical and only two years later the Fulton-Livingston monopoly sent Nicholas Roosevelt out to the Ohio to determine the possibility of operating steamboats on the Western rivers. He traveled by flatboat from Pittsburgh, stopping at towns along the way to promote the company's plans. From New Orleans he returned to the East by ocean vessel and reported favorably for the project. The "New Orleans" was built at Pittsburgh and launched in 1811.

When, after the Fulton-Livingston monopoly was broken in a long court fight, competition arose. Boats were built larger and decks added; they were fitted out to carry passengers and were elaborately decorated. In 1817 the record run from New Orleans to Louisville was made in 25 days, but in 1853 that same trip was cut to four days and nine hours. Efforts to exceed speed records caused many accidents. Old wreckage was treacherous in flood-time, and during low water boats were sometimes caught on sandbars. Using wood for fuel, the boats were propelled by paddle-wheels. After the Civil War the colorful steamboats gave way to railroads, which could carry passengers faster and more directly.

Canals.—The era of canal-building extended from about 1800 to 1837 and reached its peak during the business boom of the early 1830's. The end of canal-building days was foretold by the coming of the railroads. The promotion and construction of canals contributed to the boom times of the early 1830's. Canals were dug first in the East to connect the seaboard cities with the back country.

The Erie Canal is the classic example of such transportation. Because of the magnitude of the project and its phenomenal success, it set off a boom in canal construction. Governor De Witt Clinton was its chief advocate. Construction started in 1817, and the canal was opened to traffic for its entire length in 1825. It extended from Albany to Buffalo and connected the Hudson River with Lake Erie; numerous branches were added to it. The canal was vital to the early development of New York state and it strengthened New York City as the metropolis of the East. The canal became the chief route for emigrants from New England to the Great Lakes states and helped develop an agricultural boom in the West.

[118]

Philadelphia's envy and alarm at the growth of New York City caused Pennsylvania to build a marvelous system combining canals and a railroad through the mountains, an engineering wonder in its 363 miles. It connected Philadelphia with Pittsburgh on the Ohio; the Pennsylvania Railroad took its place in the 1840's.

Many other canals were constructed and proved successful. Several connected the Great Lakes with the tributaries of the Ohio and Mississippi rivers.

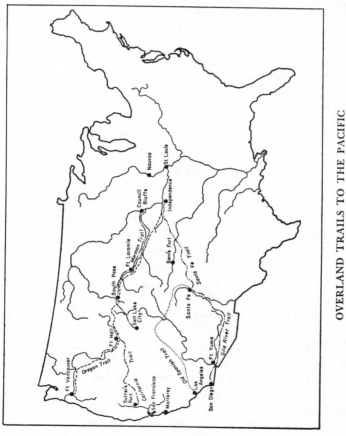

OVERLAND TRAILS TO THE PACIFIC

Overland Transportation to the Pacific Before the Railroads.—
The hordes of people who came to California in the years following the Gold Rush caused Congress to seek means of delivering
the United States mail by overland transport.

In 1857 Congress authorized the establishment of the first
transcontinental mail route, from the Mississippi to San Francisco. Under this contract, James Birch, of the California Stage
Company, ran monthly mail stages from San Antonio to San
Diego. In the same year a contract was signed with John Butterfield to follow a southern route; Butterfield put stages into operation in 1858; they followed a route from St. Louis through Little
Rock, El Paso, and Fort Yuma to San Francisco. Concord coaches
and wagons were used to carry passengers and mail. Stations were
set up every ten to fifteen miles; the service was expensive to
operate. At the same time the national government contracted
also with two other firms to run the central route, one east from
Salt Lake City and the other west.

In 1861 Russell, Majors, and Waddell became the chief stage
line and its operation had to be shifted from the southern to the
central route. In 1862, bankruptcy of the company brought its
transfer to Ben Holladay, a coarse, domineering tycoon of pro-
digious managerial and financial ability. In 1866 a further transfer took place when Holladay, foreseeing the completion of the
transcontinental railroad, shrewdly sold his company to the
Wells, Fargo management. Wells, Fargo itself had been organized
in 1852 to conduct the Western business in express carried on by
the American Express Company in the East.

*The Pony Express.—*The lack of speed of the overland mail
and the desire to demonstrate the feasibility of a central transportation route brought about the establishment of the Pony Express. The Pony Express was made up of hard-riding, wiry men
who dashed relays to speed light mail and letters across the Plains
in about ten days. It was a pet project of William Russell of the
firm of Russell, Majors, and Waddell; it began operation in
April, 1860, from St. Joseph, Missouri, to San Francisco. The service was maintained for only eighteen months and then discon-

tinued after the Pacific Telegraph was completed in October, 1861. The spectacular Pony Express brought losses to its operators and was chiefly responsible for their bankruptcy.

THE RAILROADS

The first railroads were not built until after most of the region east of the Mississippi River had passed beyond the frontier stage. But railroads were soon advocated as a solution to the transportation problem in frontier regions. The railroads opened the whole West to the frontier farmer; otherwise, settlement would have proceeded much more slowly. Rails were extended into the Plains states before the settlers came in; railroad advertising and land promotion attracted settlers. The railroads built into the West after the Civil War under the encouragement of the business-oriented Republican administrations. Construction was halted by the Panic of 1873 but resumed in a few years. The peak of railroad construction occurred in the prosperous early 1880's.

Early Land Grant Railroads.—Since the national government had made land grants in the western states for canal-building, it was quite natural that land grants should be made for another internal improvement, the railroads.

About 1850 the agitation for a railroad from southern Illinois northward was begun by businessmen in Cairo, Illinois. Stephen A. Douglas took up the project and expanded the proposed railroad into the South to secure their support for a land grant from Congress. Thus began in 1851 the first important land grant railroad. Douglas proposed that the railroad in southern Illinois be connected with Chicago in the North and in the South linked with another line already started from Mobile to Cairo. The result was the passage of an act making a huge grant of land for the Illinois Central Railroad. The act established the precedent for federal land grants for railroad construction which was to cost the public domain 132 million acres in the next 20 years. The Illinois Central was completed in 1856.

Railroads in the Rivalry of the Sections.—The railroads had

the effect of overcoming the political alliance between the South
and the West. The effect of Mississippi River transportation had
been to tie the West to the South economically. The railroads
built trunk lines in an east-west direction and thus overcame the
water transportation link of West to South. Closer ties, economic
and political, developed between the West and the Northeast during the 1850's. The South gave too much attention to tying various parts of its own section together.

Early Efforts To Launch a Transcontinental Railroad.—Asa
Whitney, during the 1840's, worked diligently for many years
publicizing and lobbying for a railroad that would carry goods
from Asia eastward to the Atlantic Coast. The need for a transcontinental railroad to link the nation together was obvious to
all after the Mexican War. In the years before the Civil War it
was assumed that only one transcontinental line would ever be
built. Where it would be located, therefore, became a subject of
controversy between the North and the South. Jefferson Davis of
the South favored a route such as the Southern Pacific follows
today, whereas Douglas favored a northerly route connecting San
Francisco with Chicago.

Before the Civil War the South dominated the national government and used its influence to advance a southern route for
the railroad. The acquisition of the Mexican Cession and the
Gold Rush created an immediate need for transportation. In 1853
the Gadsden Purchase was made to provide more suitable terrain
for a southern route and strengthen the case of the South. When
Jefferson Davis became Secretary of War in 1853 he sent out
parties to survey five possible routes for a Pacific railroad.

Davis reported to Congress in 1855 favoring the southernmost
route, that of the 32nd parallel, as the shortest, most practical,
and most economical. It was thought that Davis was prejudiced
in favor of this route and no railroad was authorized as a result
of his surveys. The next ten years were experimental years in providing transportation between the Mississippi Valley and the
Pacific Coast. The overland mail went by stagecoach and freight
by wagon while the Pony Express and the telegraph provided

quicker communications before the railroad was completed.

While Davis was urging a southern route, Douglas and the North were working for a central route that would run west from Chicago. The leading motive of Douglas in the introduction of the Kansas-Nebraska Bill was to organize that territory to help open the way for a railroad through the central route.

The First Transcontinental Railroad.—After the South seceded, the opposition in Congress to building a railroad through the central route was overcome. Two companies were authorized in 1862 to build the road: the Central Pacific was to build eastward from the Pacific and the Union Pacific to build westward from Nebraska. The founders of the Central Pacific started the action in Congress resulting in this legislation. A gifted young engineer, Theodore D. Judah, lobbied energetically in Washington for the Central Pacific. Other leading founders of the company, who came to be known as the Big Four, were Leland Stanford, Collis P. Huntington, Mark Hopkins, and Charles Crocker.

The subsidy provided a 400-foot right-of-way and ten alternate sections of land on both sides of the right-of-way for each mile of track laid. Later further lobbying in Congress brought additional subsidies in the form of a federal loan. This loan provided $16,000 for each mile built through level country, $32,000 through foothills, and $48,000 in the mountains.

Construction was slow in getting started during the Civil War: labor, capital, and materials were scarce. After 1867 construction went forward rapidly. As the crews gained experience, the work came to be expertly organized. Irish labor predominated in the eastern part and after a time Chinese coolies were imported to build through the Sierra Nevada in California. Indians had to be subdued in the Plains. The builders lived in tent cities that were moved up each time a stretch of line was completed.

The actual building was contracted to construction companies. But these companies were owned by the same men who owned the railroad operating companies. The construction companies were more significant as devices for exploiting the smaller stockholders and the government. In this way some of the great railroad builders obtained their enormous fortunes. In May, 1869, the Union Pacific and the Central Pacific met at Promontory Summit, Utah, northwest of Ogden, to complete the first transcontinental line. The road had been thrown down so hastily

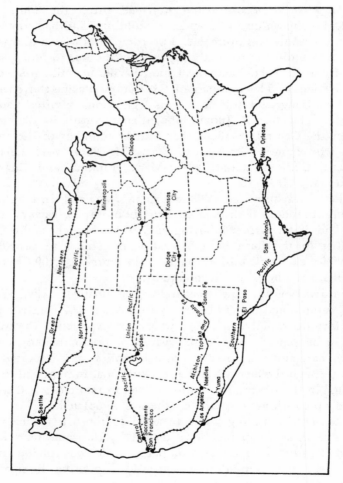

EARLY TRANSCONTINENTAL RAILROADS

in order to earn the subsidies that soon after "completion" much of it had to be rebuilt.

Other Transcontinental Railroads.—The next railroad to be completed across the Far West to the Pacific was the Southern Pacific; this road followed the 32nd parallel route from California to El Paso. In 1882 the Southern Pacific, now owned by the controllers of the Central Pacific, completed connections east of El Paso with Eastern lines.

Two more transcontinentals were completed in 1883. The Northern Pacific secured a federal land grant but received no loans; instead it was financed by Jay Cooke. The burden of financing the railroad brought Jay Cooke and Company into bankruptcy in 1873. In 1881 Henry Villard secured control and reorganized the Northern Pacific and in 1883 completed connections between Lake Superior and Portland, Oregon. The Atchison, Topeka and Santa Fe also completed its line in 1883; it built along the 35th parallel route. This company, organized before the Civil War, received a land grant from Congress in 1863. The Santa Fe bought out the Atlantic and Pacific Railroad with its lines in Oklahoma leading directly to St. Louis and with the purchase of the Atlantic and Pacific secured rights to federal land grants in New Mexico and Arizona. In 1883 the Santa Fe completed connections all the way from Chicago to Los Angeles.

In 1893 the Great Northern was completed from St. Paul to Tacoma and later to Seattle. Hill was a railroad and financial genius who saw the profit possibilities of opening up the country north of the Northern Pacific and south of the Canadian boundary. He built without government subsidy but had J. P. Morgan's financial support. He built the line slowly so as to settle the country as he went and thus finance the railroad by creating traffic. Feeder lines were built, immigrants brought from Europe, model farms laid out, blooded cattle imported, money loaned to farmers, wheat farming introduced, and free transportation offered to homeseekers. It was a great colonization program that settled thousands of pioneers in the northern Great Plains.

Granger Opposition to the Railroads.—Railroad builders for a long time enjoyed great favors and various forms of subsidy from the national and local governments. This aid came as land grants and free rights-of-way, as outright money grants by towns and counties, as loans in the form of mortgage bonds, and various exemptions from taxation. These liberal rewards were offered to enterprising individuals who organized the railroad companies. Although the railroads were "natural monopolies" and public utilities, their managers, abusing their power and privileges, operated them as any other private property.

In the 1870's the public, particularly the Grangers, accused the railroads of various evils and abuses. They were often guilty of granting rebates to large, favored shippers. They were accused of charging more for a short haul where there was no competition than for a long haul where competition existed, of cutting rates where competition existed and making it up by overcharging where there was none, of forming pools and other monopoly devices, of selling watered stock, and of various forms of corruption in politics.

In 1869, O. H. Kelley organized the Farmers' Grange under the official name Patrons of Husbandry. It originated as a social and educational movement for farmers in isolated communities in the West, but in the hard times of the early 1870's it was transformed into a political movement and came to be directed against what seemed to be the greatest exploiter of the Western farmer, the railroads. State legislatures over the West came under control of the Grangers and railroad commissions were established to regulate the railroads, particularly their rates. When state regulation of interstate railroads was forbidden by the Supreme Court in the Wabash Decision of 1886, the Court pointed out the need for federal regulation. After investigation, Congress created, in 1887, the Interstate Commerce Commission. Effective regulation was achieved in time as the powers of the Commission were increased.

14

GOVERNMENT AND POLITICS
ON THE FRONTIER

The nature of government and politics on the American frontier is exemplified by the tableau of events and activities in the various territories and states, but there are certain conditions, characteristics, and patterns of government that need to be specifically delineated or described. (References to related topics elsewhere in this guide are too numerous to be pointed out and illustrations are too extensive to be repeated here. The student is reminded to use the index as he may wish.)

Political Characteristics of the West.—The influence of the frontier environment was to accelerate and augment the existing trends toward democracy in the western world. Since every man was valued for his labor in the thinly populated West, class distinctions were minimized and equality was conceded in the early years of each frontier. Common poverty and discontent bred democracy. Since the West faced unique problems which were not understood by the East, the West rebelled against outside control or interference. It is granted that the West was not really inventive in producing new political devices or reforms, but it did adopt the most liberal examples and ideas more readily than older communities did. In his political beliefs the Westerner was practical; he was no theorist or idealist. The West was inconsistent in that it resented outside interference but sought federal aid for roads, canals, railroads, and other needs.

Political reforms or changes prominently associated with the West are numerous. Some of these are an outgrowth of Jacksonian democracy. Jackson himself was the personification of frontier politics. (1) Religious and property qualifications for voting were abolished early. (2) The West gave legislatures greater powers and kept them responsive to their constituents by requiring annual or frequent elections. (3) New state constitutions both made

[127]

more offices elective instead of appointive and shortened terms of office. (4) The frontier deprecated the value of education and experience. Rotation in office was considered desirable. (5) Any ordinary person of good intentions and common sense was held capable of performing the duties of public office. (6) Toward the end of the frontier, the West took the lead in adopting widely such democratic devices as the initiative, referendum, recall, and secret ballot.

Western communities kept in touch with politics in several ways. The local weekly newspapers brought political news to frontier settlers and exerted much influence upon avid readers. These newspapers dealt with practical local and state issues. Western editors were famous for their vigorous partisanship and unrestrained personal denunciations that brought frequent physical encounters and duels. Stump orators impressed the yokelry with high-flown speeches and appealed to them in forceful language. Speakers often displayed their agility by replying in kind to hecklers. Holidays, barbecues, and picnics brought crowds together to hear politicians, or the attraction of the speakers themselves were the occasion for mass meetings.

Provisional Governments.—American pioneers showed their genius for self-government in the organization of numerous compacts. Americans everywhere expected to take the initiative in organizing local government if none existed. There were nearly always a large number of lawyers, land speculators, and petty politicians ready to step forward and assume the leadership role. The Mayflower Compact was the first of these settlers' agreements to provide temporary self-government when settlement had occurred outside the bounds of established jurisdictions and law-enforcing agencies. The Watauga settlement in eastern Tennessee in 1773 offers another such case. There settlers met in convention and signed the Articles of Association by which they promised to obey five commissioners who were to preserve order and perform the usual functions of county and territorial officials pending the establishment of regular government. At least two other similar compacts were formed in Tennessee. In 1842 Oregon settlers took

[128]

steps to organize a provisional government and the next year adopted laws for "Oregon Territory." They reformed the government in 1844 as more able leaders furnished better guidance for improvement of the framework of government. The Mormons in Utah organized their own theocratic civil government.

Extralegal Government.—In several of the economic types of frontiers, Americans organized to protect and regulate themselves. Traders in the wagon caravans on the Santa Fe Trail agreed to obey their elected lieutenants, and companies of emigrants on Western trails likewise chose their leaders. Peaceable early miners and prospectors needed no formal organization, but when strikes were made and lawless elements were attracted, temporary measures had to be taken to preserve life and property and to protect mining claims. Mass meetings were called and laws passed to regulate the staking of claims, holding claims, the settlement of disputes, and suppression of crime. In the early fifties, vigilante committees were formed when criminal elements became so numerous and strong as to require drastic countermeasures. Leading law-abiding citizens, first in San Francisco, met secretly to draw up a constitution and pledge their cooperation. After becoming strongly organized, the vigilantes rounded up leading criminals and gave them a brief trial before assembled citizens. The vigilantes quickly spread to mining camps everywhere in the West. Claim clubs were organized by squatters and performed various functions of government outside their primary purpose of registering settlers' land claims. Cattlemen on the open ranges organized "cattlemen's associations" to regulate the use of the free range, register brands, cooperate for protection against rustlers, and perform other functions of government.

Political Elements in the West.—As frontier conditions receded, so did equalitarianism. Differences in wealth and education caused the formation, with the passage of years, of the upper stratum in Western communities. Merchants, lawyers, bankers, well-to-do farmers and planters, land speculators, and town builders drew apart from the ordinary run of folk. These wealthier groups expressed their own interests by voting for the Federal

Constitution and by voting for Federalists after 1790. Later, they voted Whig and, still later, Republican. In 1896 there were many Republican votes cast by conservative elements over the West. Special local interests in particular projects, issues, or personalities often affected the political alignment of different areas. The origin of the settlers, whether New England, Southern, or foreign, strongly affected local politics.

County Government.—Frontiersmen were all cognizant of the need for political order. Local militia needed to be organized to give protection against Indians. Records had to be made of land titles, marriages, births, and the descent of estates, and wills had to be probated. These routine, practical functions touched the lives of every individual. The most important function of the counties was the administration of justice through law-enforcement officials and the county courts. Road-building and, in some states, the operation of schools were county functions. For the performance of the county functions officeholders with titles such as sheriff, judge, county surveyor, lieutenant, overseer, magistrate, coroner, supervisor, clerk, recorder, constable, and tax collector might be chosen, usually by election.

The organization and functions of county governments were determined by state constitutions or state legislatures. Most political issues affecting counties were settled on the state level. Counties served as the administrative unit in government between state governments and towns. In most of the North, counties were subdivided into townships. In the South and in much of the West, the county was the smallest unit of government, except for chartered towns, and it was a geographical area of state administration. In such states, county governments represented the rural areas, since incorporated towns were permitted by state law to perform certain functions for themselves. It has been claimed that county governments in the Southeast were modeled upon Southern tidewater county governments, which in turn were transferred from England.

Some counties were organized in every territory before statehood came. Counties were sometimes organized to cover as much

as a whole future state. Most of Kentucky was first o.
Fincastle County. Such large counties were later sub
new counties split away from the parent county. Cou.
organized partly to satisfy the hunger for offices. Count
found opportunities to profit from their participatior
ernment.

County seats with their "courthouse rings" served as centers
for political activities. These rings were made up of officials and
local citizens who made themselves conversant with political
issues and candidates. These local men gave advice and explained
political issues to county residents. They exerted considerable
influence over elections—local, state, and national. They kept in
close contact with the people. Much rivalry sprang up between
towns for the location of the county seat, for the county government brought customers into town, assured its permanence, and
profited speculative town builders.

Territorial Governments.—The Northwest Ordinance provided, among other provisions, for a two-house legislature for
organized territories and for a delegate to the Federal Congress.
The organization of territorial governments provided numerous
political jobs which became the spoils of politicians in power
locally and in Washington. Territorial governments required
governors, judges, law-enforcement officials, surveyors, revenue
collectors, and clerks. The organization of counties and the location of county seats was the source of much controversy in the
territories.

Frontier State-Making.—The experiences of state-making, if
recounted for all the states admitted after 1800, becomes so
monotonously repetitive that it is better to observe some of the
common elements in their creation. During the Revolution, frontiersmen living west of the mountains, conscious of their unique
problems and interests and rankling from earlier neglect by colonial governments, demanded freedom to deal with local matters.
Many separate statehood movements arose among Western settlements during the war. These demands spurred the Confederation
Congress to enact the Ordinances of 1784 and 1787 in order to

provide a regular procedure for the creation of new states. Instead of being treated as colonies, new states were given equality in the Union with the original states. Undoubtedly if demands for equality had not been met, new independent governments would have been erected just as the thirteen colonies had declared independence from Great Britain. General Wilkinson's schemes to secure Spanish support for a separate nation of Kentucky, and other such intrigues in the West, arose from nascent movements for self-government. The Ordinance of 1787, by making provisions for the admission of new states, made possible the expansion of the United States to the West.

Enabling acts passed by Congress permitted states to proceed with drafting constitutions but placed certain restrictions upon them. Ohio was the first state to become the subject of an enabling act, but these acts were required for most other states thereafter. Ohio is another of the early states which set the pattern for state-making. It was the procedure by which she was admitted that set the precedent for states carved out of the Northwest Territory and for other states. In the determination of state boundary lines the residents often took the initiative. The inclusion of any uncongenial population element by boundaries drawn by Congress brought protests. But Congress usually had a hand in the determination of boundaries and defined them in the enabling acts. Accessibility of the capital was considered and tended to limit the size of states. The original states exerted an influence in the direction of creating large states to minimize the political strength of the West in the federal government; at least this was true in the Old Northwest. Texas is noteworthy as a state that was granted permission to divide herself into as many as five states, but Texas did not divide herself because of sentiment and the practical advantages of voting as a unit, as at political conventions and in the electoral college.

Constitution Drafting.—New states usually followed the precedents of earlier states and used them as models in drafting their own constitutions and statutes. Kentucky adopted her Bill of Rights verbatim from Pennsylvania's constitution and followed it in other respects. Kentucky's revised constitution served as a model for many states. Tennessee revised the North Carolina constitution to suit her needs. California's first constitution, like those of some other states, showed the strong influence of Iowa and New York constitutions. State constitutions followed the traditional pattern of creating the three branches of government—legislative, executive, and judicial. Qualifications for voting and officeholding were prescribed. Local political leaders ambitious to go to Washington or serve in state offices helped organize state governments in hope of winning election or appointment to office. These leaders had the census taken to prove the qualification of a territory for statehood and issued calls for the election of delegates to state conventions to draft constitutions. Early state constitutions were drafted by elected delegates but were not submitted to voters for approval until Mississippi did so in 1817. Thereafter, most of the states followed the precedent of Mississippi.

After the Civil War, farmers' protest movements influenced the provisions of constitutions drafted in the new states, which, of course, were settled mainly by farmers. The railroads and other business corporations had to be regulated. During the last decades of the nineteenth century, the Western states drafted new or revised constitutions of great length. These later constitutions dealt with such special problems of the Far West as water rights and mining and grazing regulations. Many matters were covered which should have been left to statutory laws. These instruments, with their provisions to prevent political radicals from making hasty changes, reflect a distrust of legislatures.

Admission of States.—Admission of new states by Congress was strongly affected by the effect upon the balance of power among political parties. When Tennessee applied for admission, the lines were being drawn between Federalists and Republicans. Federalists debated her admission, since it was assumed the state was Republican in its politics. Tennessee was organized as the Southwest Territory and was also the first state to pass through the territorial stage of government.

The slavery issue delayed the admission of Missouri and led to the famous struggle in Congress. But before 1820 the slavery issue was not brought forward, but probably would have been if there had been any threat of an extended imbalance of the states. After 1820 the slavery question came up in Congress and delayed the approval of statehood in every case until the Civil War. In at least two states, Iowa and Nebraska, statehood was delayed by a reluctance of residents to assume the tax load to support the expenses of state government. There was never much adherence to the population standard of 60,000 required for admission by the Ordinance of 1787. The admission of the "omnibus states" and subsequent states was delayed by political factors, chiefly the opposition of Democrats or Republicans in Congress. (Section 8 discusses the organization of territories and states in the Far West.) Population varied from 20,000 for Nevada to over 600,000 for Oklahoma. Rapid increases in population occurred before action could be taken, and political struggles in Congress delayed admission.

After admission, state legislatures in most cases adopted the statutes of earlier states or their own territorial statutes or wrote original statutes. Statutes dealt with local problems and implemented provisions of the state constitution.

15

PEOPLE AND RELIGION OF THE FRONTIER

People behaved differently on the frontier than in the old communities. To study these differences in the multiple aspects of frontier life helps to understand the frontier phenomenon.

CHARACTER OF WESTWARD MIGRANTS AND THEIR ACTIVITIES

What kinds of people undertook to settle in the West? How did they go about settling? What were the leading businesses and other activities?

Characteristics of Westward Migrants.—It is difficult to generalize about the migrants to the frontier. However, a large proportion of them had not found success in older communities. Generally a successful person would not undertake the hardships of readjustment to an undeveloped region. The migrants were either poor or unusually ambitious and hopeful. They were mostly farmers, and they moved much more in times of boom and prosperity than in depression. The notable exception was the land speculator who was necessarily well-to-do. Previous lack of success is not necessarily a reflection upon the migrants. Poor men from the poor soils of New England moved out. Southerners were crowded out by slave plantations, and immigrants came from over-populated parts of Europe. There were also adventurous persons who hoped to prosper from the various resources on the frontier; others came as carefree adventurers. Some were criminals escaping the grasp of the law. Some were able persons whose careers had been blighted in the East; among them were such men as Aaron Burr, Sam Houston, and David Crockett. Some succeeded notably as did Houston. Some pioneer farmers were simply a shiftless lot; some were anti-social and felt crowded when they could hear a neighbor's rooster crowing.

Well-to-do adventuresome persons moved West to take advantage of unusually lush opportunities to acquire large land holdings, to carve out a career in law, politics, or merchandising. Advance might be more rapid where there was less competition. Opportunities in the West appealed to young men who could endure the hardships and who were still adjustable. For example, the average age of men in the Gold Rush was in the twenties; a great many were under twenty and a person in his forties was looked upon as a little out of place.

Sources and Direction of Frontier Migration.—Pioneer migrants generally followed parallel lines of latitude in migrating; they tended to relocate directly west of the place of their origin. An important variation of this tendency was caused by the attraction of waterways. Settlers in the earlier decades remained close to waterways to avail themselves of a transportation outlet for their produce. They followed the banks of streams, lakes, or canals in whatever direction they led. When the railroads were built, they freed settlers from dependence on waterways; the first settlements then began following the railroads.

The states of New York, Michigan, and Wisconsin were occupied predominantly by pioneers from New England. They followed the Erie Canal and filled the regions south of the Great Lakes. Virginians moved west into Kentucky and North Carolinians directly west into Tennessee. Kentuckians and Tennesseans in turn moved due west into Missouri and then settled a thin line westward up the Missouri River. The southern parts of the states of the Ohio Valley were settled largely by migrants moving northwestward from the older state of Kentucky. A large part of the early wagons that crossed the Plains to pioneer in Oregon and California were filled with Missourians. In the deep South emigrants from the old states of the Southeast took up the lands in western Georgia, Alabama, and Mississippi. Southern Louisiana, an early center of population, furnished much of the population that moved up streams northwestward into Arkansas. Texas received its colonists from the states to its east and northeast and in turn provided some of the settlers who occupied New Mexico, Arizona, and southern California.

Locating a Farm.—The greatest single group of migrants were young unmarried farmers twenty-one years or older; they often located a tract of land in the West and then returned East to take a bride back. The head of the household scouted out the land by himself at first to find a likely homestead or he might depend upon reports of friends or relatives who had moved earlier. Usually they chose a definite location, but some just moved on until they found what appeared to be a suitable farm site.

The most important factor in locating a farm was the soil; pioneers sought deep, friable, fertile soil. This could be determined best by observing the vegetation it produced; land densely wooded with hardwoods was more likely to be preferred. The prospector might be guided by the color of the soil but he was sometimes misled by this rule of the thumb.

Acquiring the Land.—Title to the land might be acquired by squatting on it or by purchase from a squatter. Land might be bought from a land company, or the government, or, toward the end of the frontier period, by claim under the Homestead and subsequent laws. War veterans were rewarded with warrants to land they might locate on the public domain. Much land was purchased at government land auctions.

Shelter.—Until a log cabin could be constructed, the family made a three-sided shelter of poles and small branches. A fire would be maintained on the open side. The construction of this log home would most likely be a community project because of the heavy lifting required. After being cut, logs would be rolled into place, notched, and then lifted into position. Openings would be cut for the door and a fireplace, after the structure was completed. The floor would be hard-packed earth until wooden floors could be laid. Clapboards were used for roofing; spaces between logs were chinked with clay.

The Land Speculator.[1]—As private enterprise land speculation was freer to develop and promote land sales than government was. Accordingly, it was instrumental in distributing much of the un-occupied land to settlers. Large speculators might buy land from the federal government or the states or buy land warrants from war veterans. Speculators were interested not only in good land but in town sites; they caused new towns and communities to boom on the early frontiers. Every farmer was more than a culti-vator, he was part speculator. The land would be partially cleared and improved until later settlers with more money would come in and buy it at a higher price.

Merchandising.—Although the frontiersman was unusually self-sufficient, a few necessities had to be procured from a store-keeper. Usually these were obtained by barter. Corn, pigs, furs, and whisky were traded for salt, spices, iron or iron implements, glass, gunpowder, lead, and cloth. On the Eastern frontier, mer-

[1] The term "speculator" is commonly used to designate those who acquired land for the profits to be made by reselling it later; the term does not neces-sarily carry an invidious connotation. Though these activities were often harmful, they also provided an important public service.

[137]

chandise was brought in by wagon from such cities as Philadelphia, Baltimore, or Richmond. Western produce was loaded on flatboats and floated down to New Orleans; the flatboatmen returned overland. Bulky western produce could not stand the expense of moving eastward over land, except for furs and whisky, and goods of high value in relation to weight.

Frontier Industries.—Industries typical of frontier settlements included grist mills, distilleries, tanneries, sawmills, textile mills, and iron works; these were located in the larger settlements. In frontier cities there were also glass factories, paper mills, shoe factories, and factories for processing tobacco. Iron works developed in Pittsburgh and pork packing in Cincinnati.

Sports.—Horse-racing was a popular sport and race tracks were operated in the towns of both the North and the South. There was much gambling and betting in connection with racing. Other sports included shooting matches, foot races, and wrestling. There were shooting contests for exercising and demonstrating this practical skill. Turkey shoots were prominent in frontier settlements. Wrestling and fist fighting were brutal. Opponents kicked, bit, and gouged each other's eyes; often an eye, ear, finger, or nose might be lost in such encounters.

Foreign Immigrants to the Frontier.—The importance of the German and Scotch-Irish in settling the Old West has been noted earlier. After them an Americanized population carried the frontier westward during the years of the Great Migration and for three decades thereafter. In the late 1840's a large immigration of the Irish occurred; many found their way to Western farm lands, especially in the Northwest, but they were more likely, if they got beyond the Atlantic seaboard cities, to settle in the cities of the Midwest. The Germans made the largest contribution of any immigrant group in peopling the West. After 1848 they moved in large numbers, especially into the Northwest and almost made Wisconsin a German state. Other large centers of German settlement were in Missouri and Texas. Farther to the northwest, during the period following the Civil War, large numbers of Scandinavians pionereed in the northern tier of states from Wisconsin to Washington. In the California mining boom a lively mixture of Germanic, oriental, Latin, and other types gave a more thoroughly cosmopolitan flavor to that frontier than was ever experienced by any other.

FRONTIER RELIGION

From the very beginning of the Puritan migrations, people moved to the frontier for freedom to follow the practices of their own religion. (Other cultural developments on the frontier are discussed in Section 16.)

Splintering of Religious Bodies.—Many groups or sects who sought to isolate themselves so that they could practice their religion without interference migrated to the American colonies. Many groups left Boston as religious dissenters. Various German sects settled in Pennsylvania. The Scotch-Irish added a large number of independent-minded Presbyterians to the back country. Throughout the settlement of America further splintering of Protestant bodies occurred and new denominations arose.

The Great Awakening.—A series of religious revivals over the English colonies began in the 1730's and in some denominations lasted until after the American Revolution. An evangelical movement marked by vigorous preaching, its various manifestations flourished on the frontier. The Great Awakening was concerned with the common man and appealed to him as a kind of spiritual democracy, since it was critical of formalism and conservatism.

In its effects the movement strengthened the more radical Protestant denominations and sects; this protest against Anglicanism was democratic in its political and economic implications. Baptists, Methodists, and Presbyterians strengthened themselves. Religious leaders preached liberty of conscience and thus helped prepare the way for the separation of church and state. Itinerant preachers carried the message into the back country. The movement provided frontier folk with social life and improved their manners and morals.

A similar religious upheaval began on the frontier in 1797. This Great Revival was characterized by camp meetings, to which backwoods people came from great distances. The greatest of the camp meetings occurred at Cane Ridge, Kentucky, in August, 1801.

Religion in the West After 1800.—At about 1800 less than half the people in the West were affiliated with any church. Ministers were hard to find, and it cost too much to build and maintain churches. There were so many sects that it was difficult in small communities to support a separate church for each. Among the larger denominations were the Methodists, Baptists, Presbyterians, Congregationalists, Roman Catholics, Episcopalians, and Lutherans. But there were such smaller groups as the Moravians, Dunkards, United Brethren, Anabaptists, and Quakers.

In addition to providing the usual moral and emotional values, religion had a special significance in the West. It helped men to bear the dangers of the wilderness and of the Indians if they felt God was taking care of them. Since the Indian was not a believer, his destruction was a victory over the devil. At church meetings people exchanged news of other people, of politics and crops, and they realized emotional release from monotonous work. Successful religions in the West stressed the importance of the individual and provided social and emotional content. Effective ministers were those who could speak the language of the people in their vocabulary and manner. Sophisticated Eastern ministers left simple frontiersmen cold. The East concerned itself with the lack of support for religion in the West. Groups were formed and societies organized to send missionaries on tour or to provide pastors for churches.

Methodists.—The Methodists were the most active and numerous of any group on the early frontier. They were only a sect or school within the Anglican Church both in England and in the colonies until the American branch made itself independent during the American Revolution. Francis Asbury organized the American Methodists as a separate denomination and did more than anyone else to spread Methodism in the United States. He traveled and preached widely. Methodism crossed the Appalachians in the 1780's and quickly spread over Kentucky, Tennessee, Ohio, and into Missouri.

The Methodists' organization was well adapted to the West. A minister rode a circuit instead of giving all his time to one congregation; in his absence lay preachers conducted services for the congregations. The Methodists used forceful men, regardless of education, who could talk the strong and colorful language of the frontier. They could describe Hell in realistic terms and used vigor and pathos to bring sinners to repent and join. The Methodist circuit riders worked to civilize and provide culture where few such opportunities existed; they brought contact with the outside world and carried books for lending.

Baptists.—The leading rival of the Methodists were the Baptists. The Baptists were distinguished by their belief in immersion, close communion, and freedom for local congregations. They, too, made emotional pleas and practiced religion as the frontier liked it. From the Baptists emerged the Disciples of Christ, commonly known as Christians, or Campbellites, from their founder, Thomas Campbell and his son, Alexander Campbell. They favored a purer, more primitive, and simple Christianity intended to combine true believers of all churches.

Presbyterians.—Third in size among the Western Protestants were the Presbyterians. They were handicapped by the more gloomy doctrines of Calvin, the use of an educated clergy, and the lack of organization on the frontier. This denomination tried to meet the need for ministers by founding many small colleges in the backwoods settlements. Dissatisfaction over the issue of educated ministers led to the secession of the Cumberland Presbyterian Church in 1810. This latter church stressed piety in preference to book learning. Calvinism expressed itself most prominently in the South through the Presbyterians and in the North through the Congregationalists.

Roman Catholics.—Catholicism was introduced by the Spanish and French in their colonies, by the English in Maryland, and by individual immigrants in various colonies. It expanded on the frontier as did other churches. Early American Protestants looked upon Catholicism with a certain degree of horror.

Camp Meetings.—Camp meetings were not frontier in origin, but they were held oftener in the West than elsewhere and were reshaped by the West. These meetings served to give a sense of common purpose and weld people together emotionally. In modern community life, where people have ample opportunity for emotional release through association with others and through various forms of art and literature, it is difficult to understand the religious emotionalism characteristic of the camp meetings. Under the high emotional pitch of these meetings people reacted by jumping, singing, sobbing, shouting, and swooning; they would get the "jerks," have trances and visions. The greater these manifestations by the worshipper, the greater was his sanctification.

When meetings were held at small churches, tents and cabins had to be brought into use to care for the large crowds. The greatest of all the camp meetings, the meeting at Cane Ridge, Kentucky, in August, 1801, was attended by between 10,000 and 20,000 people. Whole families traveled as much as a hundred miles to go to a camp meeting and brought housekeeping articles with them and raised tents. The Methodists were most prominent at these meetings. Preaching was the main organized activity. There was much singing and praying. The audience took part in the services with spontaneous responses and in their exclamations gave support to the minister.

The meetings were also the occasion for more normal social life among people who had few occasions to visit others. Sometimes rowdy elements would be attracted by the large gatherings. Of course, it was an occasion for courtship and marriages resulted. Many were led into more socially desirable patterns of life.

THE MORMONS; UTOPIAN COLONIES

The Mormons stand out as the most prominent instance in America of a religious body developing under frontier conditions and utilizing those conditions to avoid friction by isolating themselves.

Social Background of the Rise of Mormonism.—During the 1820's, when the frontier was advancing vigorously, a great deal of new, unconventional thinking was being done in the ferment of ideas of that time. Novel political, social, and religious ideas were being advanced for the improvement of the lot of the common man. During this time of revolt against established patterns, scores of new movements appeared, among them were transcendentalism, Anti-Masonry, and Jacksonian democracy. In social reform movements, communitarian and utopian colonies were organized by the score. In religion an equally large number of new sects developed; strong preachers, aggressive men, took their congregations with them and founded personal churches to fulfil their ambitions for leadership, power, and the uplift of man. At that time the disintegrating effect of the frontier was most active against established institutions.

Founding of the Mormons by Smith.—Joseph Smith, the founder of the Mormons, came of New England pioneer stock. His father, who came from a group of backwoodsmen from Vermont, moved to Palmyra, New York, about 1817. Young Joseph began to have visions in the early 1820's, and in 1827, according to his account, certain gold plates were revealed to him. These he translated and issued as the Book of Mormon; the book bore a strong similarity to the Old Testament.

Early History of the Church.—Joseph Smith formally organized the followers of his faith in 1830 following a revelation that made him a divine intermediary; their correct name was the Church of Jesus Christ of Latter-Day Saints. Smith kept a firm hold on the faithful, made tithing effective, and thereby accumulated a fund for promoting the church. His leadership rested on his strong personality and the claim of direct revelation. In 1831 the church moved to Kirtland, Ohio, near Cleveland, where the Ohio Canal was about to open the country to agriculture. There were about a thousand converts then and a steady stream was coming in from the missionaries active elsewhere. But the Mormon community was unpopular among other settlers. The Mormons gained a reputation of strict control over both the thoughts and the votes of the members of the community; they were thought of as clannish and out of sympathy with the individualism of the frontier. Tense relations and the panic of 1837 caused them to move to their previously chosen Zion at Independence, Missouri.

Independence also proved to be unsuitable; it came to be a gathering place for traders and other individuals who derided the Mormons and found ways of annoying them. There was retaliation and violence on both sides. In 1833 they relocated at Far West, also in western Missouri. Again the cohesiveness of the Mormons antagonized their gentile neighbors. In 1838 they bought a deserted communitarian village in Illinois, renamed it Nauvoo, and moved there in 1839.

The Mormons at Nauvoo.—Here again the Mormons could not avoid antagonizing their frontier neighbors, who claimed the causes of friction were the intolerable manners and corrupt political influences of the Mormons. It was whispered that personal immorality was prevalent and that leaders had numerous wives.

Joseph Smith became active in Illinois politics and secured special privileges for the colony at Nauvoo. In Illinois, leaders of both Whig and Democratic parties began to distrust Smith. In 1844 Smith announced his candidacy for President of the United States. Now antagonism flared up against the Mormons and both parties, Whigs and Democrats, turned against them. As the Mormons became overconfident, their neighbors became jealous of the power of the church.

With this background, internal dissension broke out among the Mormons at Nauvoo. The cause of this new trouble for Smith was his announcement of a new revelation sanctioning plural marriages. Many Mormons refused to follow Smith in this doctrine and set up a newspaper to oppose him. When Smith persuaded the city council to order the destruction of the rival newspaper, his rivals precipitated the arrest and jailing of him and his brother. Both were killed in a mob attack upon the jail.

The leadership of the church was soon assumed by Brigham Young; he saw that the Mormons could never live in peace at Nauvoo while angry mobs demanded their removal. Young managed to stay off the mob for a year but was forced to cross the Mississippi in a cold February in 1846. Later in the year the colony moved to Council Bluffs. Young had decided they would have to move outside the United States and now made plans to migrate. The migration of the 12,000 followers was carefully planned: cabins were built and crops planted by advance parties along the trail they were to follow. In 1847 they began the march, with hundreds of wagons and large herds of livestock, paralleling the Oregon Trail.

Mormon Society at the Great Salt Lake.—At some point in the migration, Young conceived the idea that the Mormons could succeed in a cooperative effort of irrigating the desert and at the same time settle where the typical individualistic farmer could not live. Thus, in 1847 they came to settle near the Great Salt Lake.

The society that Young guided at the Great Salt Lake turned out to be a well-planned and benevolent autocracy. With cooperation and cohesion facilitated by a common faith, hard work brought success. Their new society may be described as an experiment in state socialism. Young did not tolerate any rival leader and dissenting members were silenced or evicted. Missionaries in the East and in northern Europe brought in a steady stream of converts. New communities away from the main center were opened, and eventually Mormon communities came to be scattered in adjoining states in the intermountain region. (See Section 8 for political developments in Utah.)

Utopian Colonies on the Frontier.—Like dissenting religious groups, Utopian societies availed themselves of vacant lands on the frontier to isolate themselves, get a new start, realize their ideals, and create a way of life that others would wish to join. Utopian societies were both religious-economic and philosophic-economic communities.

[145]

The Shakers, a Protestant monastic group, organized under the teachings of Mother Ann Lee, became most active after the Great Revival of 1801. They organized communistic colonies in the Ohio Valley and in New York. They carried on a flourishing agriculture but attracted no great number of converts; they had to recruit new members from the outside, since they practiced celibacy.

The Rappites were a celibate, authoritarian sect organized among German pietists in Pennsylvania. In 1815 they founded New Harmony, Indiana, but in 1824 sold the property to Robert Owen and relocated near Pittsburgh. The society declined after Rapp's death; more aggressive members left the community for opportunities outside and not enough new converts were drawn in.

The New Harmony colony founded by Robert Owen lasted only two years. Lack of common sense, laziness, antagonism to the ideas of Owen, and the attractions outside the colony brought its downfall.

The most successful of all communistic religious societies was the Amana Society of German pietists who came to New York in 1843. In 1855 they moved to Iowa on the frontier and soon had established six villages. They operated as a communistic society until 1932, when they became a profit-sharing cooperative organization.

16

CULTURE AND THE FRONTIER

While many frontiersmen were preoccupied with the scramble for furs, minerals, and land, there were others in the agricultural and urban frontiers either seeking to enrich their cultural heritage or engaged in its perpetuation and propagation. In its cultural life the West always borrowed heavily from the East. The frontier attracted a great many illiterates and underprivileged persons who had neither the leisure nor money to support cultural interests, but some frontiers also attracted a large number of educated persons. And among the families of plain people who moved into the frontier settlements there were always varying numbers of responsible persons concerned with the support of the civilizing influences of school and church and who paid some attention to literature and the arts. The cities provided the cultural as well as the business centers of the frontier. The frontier attracted scientists, artists, and writers who studied and recorded its life and features. Not to be forgotten is the wealth of natural resources of the frontier that came to be used in the support of educational, scientific, and cultural pursuits. (Religion and other cultural features of the frontier are discussed in Section 15; Section 23 deals specifically with urban developments.)

Education on the Frontier.—Educational developments on the frontier in America corresponded to earlier developments in the East. As the frontiersmen moved into the backwoods, Eastern models were usually introduced, with some lag in time and quality. Puritan regard for schooling and the more concentrated community life brought more rapid educational progress in the North than in the South. When the Far West was settled, educational progress proceeded more rapidly than on earlier frontiers, because evolving educational institutions of the East were soon adopted.

One of the early concerns of the English colonizers on the Atlantic seaboard was the establishment of schools and churches. When pioneers settled widely separated farms in the wilderness, it became more difficult to provide schooling for their children. Nevertheless, some of the most typical frontier folk, the Scotch Presbyterians, exhibited considerable zeal in the founding of schools in the backwoods. Most of the farmer settlers on the early nineteenth-century frontiers beyond the Appalachians were suspicious of any schooling beyond the most elementary instruction in reading, writing, and arithmetic and felt they could not afford the expense of providing teachers and schools; yet there were many settlers who held a high regard for education. At first elementary schooling was provided privately by interested parents who hired the teacher. Land set aside for the support of public schools was usually inadequate, even under the Northwest Ordinance of 1787. Teachers usually had little preparation, were poorly paid, and used teaching as a steppingstone to some more profitable and more esteemed calling. There was much illiteracy on the frontier, for many children never received any schooling at all. But secondary education was provided by a few seminaries and "colleges" that were established even before the danger of Indians had vanished from the Ohio Valley frontier.[1]

Public schools were established in the cities of the Ohio Valley in the 1830's and were greatly increased in number in the 1840's. Public school teaching was then becoming a profession. However, teachers received no special training anywhere in the West in the 1830's. Not until 1839 was the first normal school opened in the United States (in Massachusetts). Hundreds of private academies had been established in the West by 1840. These academies offered the only educational opportunity approaching that of the public high schools, which began to flourish only after the Civil War.

For many years elementary schools were handicapped by the lack of textbooks or suitable books. The most famous of early American schoolbooks was the McGuffey reader. The first of these was published in the late 1830s, but the readers continued in use until about 1900. To meet Western tastes, William Holmes McGuffey, a Presbyterian preacher educated in the West, wrote his first reader in 1836. His textbooks, made up of selections from good literature, stressed morality and patriotism and exerted an enormous influence in America. Noah Webster's "blue-back speller" was an early widely used text designed to eliminate English forms and promote American patriotism. A geography by Jedidiah Morse and a grammar by Lindley Murray were both

---

[1] The outstanding work dealing with the subject of this section and most used in its preparation is Louis B. Wright's *Culture on the Moving Frontier* (Bloomington: Indiana University Press, 1955).

written before 1800 and were widely used. In general it should be noted that these early textbooks nourished the spirit of nationalism and helped stabilize the American language.

The lyceum, a kind of adult education society, had become a feature of education all over the United States by 1830. At these meetings, lectures and discussions were conducted on important problems and popular subjects. At other public gatherings topics of politics, religion, and the current reforms were enthusiastically discussed at length before patient audiences.

Another popular and entertaining educational institution in the Ohio Valley was the museum. Larger towns established collections of animals, plants, relics, coins, curiosities and freaks, wax figures, and the like. Traveling shows provided entertainment similar to that of the local museums. P. T. Barnum, who entered the show business as a museum operator in New York, made tours with his shows in frontier towns.

Higher Education in the Ohio Valley.—Transylvania University, the first college on the frontier west of the Appalachians, was opened in 1788 at Lexington, Kentucky, the "Athens of the West." Other colleges were established in Kentucky, Ohio, and Tennessee after 1800. After Horace Holley became head of Transylvania in 1818, it became the most famous of the early colleges in the West; it attracted many well-known men to its faculty and developed its medical school as its strongest department. The number of colleges north of the Ohio increased rapidly after 1825.

Many church colleges were established for the training of ministers and teachers. Presbyterians were outstanding in the founding of these frontier colleges. Other denominations active in higher education were the Congregationalists, Methodists, and Baptists. Some outstanding men, many of whom were ministers, served on the faculties of these early colleges. Faculty members were generally poorly paid but also poorly prepared. The colleges were small, and many of their students did not pursue studies of college level. Professional schools of law, medicine, and theology were established early in the West. Oberlin College (1834), near Cleveland, was outstanding for its advocacy of advanced ideas;

it was the first coeducational college established in the United States.

The Fine Arts on the Frontier.—Musical expression in the West was primarily vocal, but cultivated young ladies practiced on the pianoforte and drunken fiddlers played the violin for country dances. Singing classes were popular; church singing was unaccompanied.

The graphic arts enjoyed relative importance before the days of photography. Outstanding as a Western artist and author was George Catlin (1796–1872), who studied North American Indians between 1832 and 1838. His sketches, full-length portraits, and paintings of Indian scenes are preserved in the National Museum in Washington, D.C., and in the American Museum of Natural History in New York City. George Caleb Bingham (1811–1879), painter of typical scenes of life in Missouri during frontier times, did paintings of artistic merit and of documentary value. Two outstanding painters who dealt with subjects of the Far West on the last frontiers were Charles Russel, who painted ranching scenes, and Frederick Remington, who painted Indians.

In sculpture Hiram Powers' *Slave Girl* stands out most prominently. He found funds to pursue his study of art in Europe and produced much work of merit afterward, mainly statues and busts. Powers began his career in Cincinnati, where he made wax figures for Dorfeuille's dime museum.

Theaters were first built in Pittsburgh and Cincinnati, but in most towns they were nonexistent and vacant rooms had to serve for theaters. Public opinion over much of the country looked upon the theater and actors as basically immoral. Larger cities produced amateur theatricals. When theatrical companies, with their professional actors, began to come in after about 1810, many towns tried to discourage them by levying special taxes against them. Audiences were mostly men, often with a large number of rowdies present. The greatest theatrical town in the West was New Orleans and second to it was Cincinnati. By 1840 other cities of the trans-Allegheny region had built theaters. Shakespeare's plays were shown more frequently than any others.

Journalism.—Newspapers served important needs of pioneer communities and printing presses were established in most new frontier towns west of the Appalachians soon after 1800. Many were established during the 1820's and 1830's. Optimistic speculations of newspapers helped promote the growth of pioneer towns. Early frontier newspapers appeared first in Pittsburgh, Lexington, and Cincinnati. These newspapers were issued weekly but became dailies in larger cities by the 1830's; they depended heavily upon Eastern papers for clippings and in their content were more or less magazines as well as newspapers. Newspaper printing offices also published almanacs, pamphlets, sermons, law books, and a miscellany of other materials.

Almanacs circulated widely on the early frontiers and carried the kinds of information characteristic of this type of publication: the calendar and weather forecasts, advice on planting crops, miscellaneous bits of information and advice.

Monthly magazines increased sharply in America after 1800. They published literary, religious, or scientific materials. From 1827 to 1833 Timothy Flint in Cincinnati published original Western material in his *Western Magazine and Review,* possibly the most successful of the magazines.

Formative Books on the Frontier.—The most common and influential book on the whole American frontier was the Bible. It was not only a book of religion but was assumed to be the sum of wisdom on other subjects. Puritans, Presbyterians, and other Protestants thought children should have at least enough education to be able to read the Bible. In many households it was read aloud and quoted. Study of the Bible was considered a requisite for a general education and especially helpful to persons in public life.

Bunyan's *Pilgrim's Progress* and the poems of Milton were often to be found in pioneer homes. General merchants imported quantities of books from the East and advertised them. Among them were school books, books on law, medicine, religion, and works of ancient writers as well as of the famous English classicists and romanticists. Sir William Blackstone's *Commentaries on the*

Laws of England was indispensable to lawyers everywhere and supplied Americans with the doctrines of the common law of England.

Science on the Frontier.—Much important work in various fields of the natural sciences was pursued in the West by qualified scientists, including many European specialists. Geologists and mineralogists were employed by the federal government and the states to conduct surveys. Many scientists independently studied anthropology and archeology on the frontier. The biological scientists in particular obviously found much to observe and report in plant and animal life. William Bartram, son of the pioneer botanist John Bartram of Philadelphia, toured much of the frontier in the South during the Revolutionary era and gathered seeds and specimens. He observed birds and published a fascinating book of his *Travels* in 1791. André and Francois Michaux made botanical studies. In the Far West, John Bradbury, an English botanist, made scientific observations on the Missouri River in 1809–1811 and published his findings. Best known of the botanist-explorers of the Far West is Thomas Nuttall; he accompanied various scientific expeditions from 1815–1835. The artist-ornithologist John James Audubon published his famous *Birds of America* in 1826. One of the most industrious of frontier scientists was the eccentric C. S. Rafinesque, a professor at Transylvania University. He worked in almost every field of science, and his interests and publications during the 1820's and 1830's were almost boundless. He recognized biological evolution, without developing the theory, twenty-five years before Darwin published *The Origin of Species.*

Books on the Trans-Appalachian Frontier.—First, Pittsburgh and, after 1820, Lexington and Cincinnati became early centers of writing and publishing. Many early books and pamphlets published in the Ohio Valley dealt with religion and politics. Booksellers did not flourish in the frontier towns, but subscription libraries offered reading matter in the larger towns. Zadock Cramer, an active Pittsburgh publisher, in 1801 wrote *The Navigator,* a practical book that provided much information about the early Ohio River towns. A very early, notable historical work was John Filson's *Discovery, Settlement, and Present State of Kentucke* (1784). The reputation of Daniel Boone was launched in this book: Boone's *Autobiography* was published in the appendix.

Timothy Flint (1780–1840) and James Hall (1793–1868) stand out prominently as Western writers in the Ohio Valley frontier. Beginning in 1815 Flint traveled in the West for eight years, became familiar with frontier life, and spent his later years in writing about the West. His writings, affected too much by imagination and melodrama, lack reliability. James Hall worked as a newspaperman and magazine editor in Illinois and Ohio. A voluminous writer about the West, he has provided authentic descriptions of the frontier.

The humanity of early Georgia is described with genuine local flavor by the lawyer A. B. Longstreet in his book *Georgia Scenes* (1835). Another lawyer, J. G. Baldwin in *Flush Times in Alabama and Mississippi* (1853) used local dialect also and demonstrated a sharp understanding of backwoods society. Daniel Drake (1785–1852), a physician of many talents and an early settler who organized the medical department of Cincinnati College, left much first-hand information in his *Pioneer Life in Kentucky, 1785–1800*, as well as in several other important books. Clergymen often produced books of observations on frontier life. Outstanding among these is the *Autobiography of Peter Cartwright, the Backwoods Preacher* (1856).

Travelers' Accounts of the West.—Foreign travelers, curious about America and its democratic institutions, and other travelers recorded a wealth of information about the West throughout the frontier movement. An early visitor to the Ohio Valley (1802), Andre Michaux, analyzed frontier society in his *Travels*. One of the most solid, accurate accounts of the early Mississippi Valley frontier is Timothy Flint's *Recollections of the Last Ten Years*. Mrs. Frances Trollope, possibly the most successful English critic of frontier society, wrote her observations in *Domestic Manners of the Americans*. From 1827 to 1830 she observed the faults of frontier Americans until her department store in Cincinnati failed and she returned to England.

Many valuable accounts of life in the Far West were produced by travelers after 1815. Among them were the naturalist Thomas Nuttall, the mountain man James Pattie, the Jesuit missionary Father De Smet, and the Santa Fe trader Josiah Gregg. Among early works about the West that have become classics are three books by the leading literary figure of this time, Washington Irving, *Astoria, Captain Bonneville,* and *Tour of the Prairies.* In the latter book Irving describes his own tour of the West. R. H. Dana's *Two Years Before the Mast* is not only a classic of the sea but is a source of information about California under Mexico and of the hide and tallow trade.

Fiction and the West.—In the years before Western cowboy stories appeared to entertain the reading public in the nineteenth century, the public demanded books about Indians. Writers responded with books either romanticizing the Indian or making him the devil of the frontier. Dealing with the Indian theme were such early writers as Philip Freneau, Charles Brockden Brown, Henry W. Longfellow, William Gilmore Simms, and James Fenimore Cooper.

Of course, an enormous quantity of fiction has been written under the classification of Western stories. This type of popular fiction began mainly with the dime novels of the Civil War period and afterward. Owen Wister's *The Virginian* is frequently mentioned by critics as an early and reasonably authentic novel. Emerson Hough has received some praise for his books about the cowboy. Rated as of distinct literary quality because of their authenticity are the writings of two one-time cowboys, Will James and Andy Adams. The most popular of all Western fiction writers was Zane Grey. Like many other popular Western writers, he produced after the frontier had been pronounced closed, but Grey, regardless of a lack of realism, succeeded above all others in producing absorbing stories exploiting Western themes, mainly the cowboy.

The last frontier, that of the farmer in the West, supplied the themes of a number of realistic novels. Hamlin Garland, who was familiar with farming conditions on the edge of the Great Plains, describes in several of his novels the hardships of life on the farmer's frontier. Frank Norris, a Californian, in *The Octopus* dealt with the problem of wheat farmers and railroad domination in the Central Valley of California. Willa Cather and Ole Rölvaag wrote about the struggle of pioneer farmers on the plains. Mari Sandoz's *Old Jules* is a moving account of the life of an immigrant farmer in western Nebraska.

The Gold Rush and Culture in California.—In California the civilizing influence of schools, churches, and of literary outpourings experienced probably their most rapid growth on any American frontier. The gold rush attracted not only a large population but a large proportion of educated persons with cultural interests. The mineral wealth of gold, and later silver in Nevada, provided financial support. California benefited also from the advanced state of cultural institutions introduced from east of the Mississippi. In one respect progress was slower than it should have been: the state's obsession with its material blessings delayed the provisions for an adequate public school system until 1866. If the state government was slow, the various churches lost little time in establishing many private schools, academies, and colleges. Catholic competition stirred leading Protestant churches into greater activity.

California was particularly active in supporting literary activities. Leading early literary periodicals, the *Pioneer*, the *Golden Era*, the *Hesperian*, the *Californian*, and the *Overland Monthly* were the equal of any in the nation. Among well-known writers who received their apprenticeship in early California journals, Samuel Clemens (Mark Twain) is outstanding. His book *Roughing It* (1872) dealt mainly with the mining boom in Nevada. Bret Harte became editor of California's *Overland Monthly* and in it published some of his stories about the mining frontier, such as "The Outcasts of Poker Flat." Ambrose Bierce and Joaquin Miller were among these early California writers.

LEADING TYPES OF FRONTIERS

17

EARLY AGRICULTURAL FRONTIERS

Agriculture was usually the last of the economic stages of the frontier. Not until agriculture came was there a large enough settled population over an area for adequate and satisfactory community life. Many of the first wave of pioneer farmers moved West to build a simple home and live by a self-sufficient, or subsistence, agriculture in a small clearing. They were likely to be extremely poor and not overly ambitious or progressive. These woodsmen-farmers were succeeded by "equipped farmers," a more progressive type from the East who bought out the first settlers and proceeded to make great improvements in clearing and fencing the land and in building larger dwellings. They produced livestock and crops to be sold to pay for a few refinements and improvements. Thus, the bulk of permanent population on the frontier settled the land to make a living or to produce crops and livestock for the market.

Expansion of Tobacco Farming in Virginia.—Almost ideal conditions for agriculture in Virginia gave an early impetus to farming after John Rolfe succeeded in growing an improved type of tobacco there. Soon private ownership of land and grants of one-hundred acre tracts to settlers motivated individual industry. The profitable market in England for tobacco and a liberal land policy brought rapid expansion of tobacco cultivation. Maryland prospered from tobacco growing, too. Planters moved westward to occupy the fertile valley lands. An exploitative type of agriculture soon depleted the fertility of the older lands and forced farmers out at an accelerating rate to clear new fields in the wilderness. The easy availability of land and a large supply of indentured labor aided this agricultural expansion in the tidewater region.

Frontier Farming in New England.—New England never discovered any agricultural crop with sufficient market in the mother country to give that region a profitable export crop. Even if she had done so, the thin soil and the limited area of tillable land would not have permitted any great expansion. Her agriculture, therefore, remained of a subsistence type. Cattle raising became the most profitable farm industry on the frontier and proved a stimulus to expansion to the West into the Connecticut Valley. The fur trade, fishing, and shipping, instead of farming, became the leading industries. New England's old world system of land distribution whereby separate strips of tillable land were allotted to individuals would undoubtedly have given way more rapidly to unified plantations with more freedom of individual enterprise if a profitable export market had developed for any staple crop.

The rugged hill country of New England was settled by farmers who secured land from speculators in the East. These back country farmers produced grain for sale in the East but self-sufficient farming predominated.

Agricultural Development in Carolina.—Tobacco did not thrive in the swampy lands occupied at first by settlers in the Carolinas. Agricultural prosperity came later when rice was introduced in the tidelands and after the frontier had passed to the West. Early settlers turned to the fur trade and to subsistence farming.

Agriculture in the Middle Colonies.—After 1710 German Palatines were attracted to the western valleys in New York and Pennsylvania, where the Germans began an industrious mixed farming of livestock, grain, and fruits. Land speculators encouraged them to settle on the frontier. Following the Germans there soon came a large stream of Scotch-Irish who moved into more remote western valleys and followed a subsistence agriculture to supplement their hunting.

Early Southern Livestock Production.—The upland regions

west of the fall line were occupied by land-hungry settlers from 1700 to 1763. Prominently at the front of this movement were the cattle ranchers, who fenced "cow-pens" to raise corn and also to manage their livestock. Thousands of small farmers moved into this "Old West," after they had been crowded out by the expansion of plantations in the tidewater region. Land speculators helped promote settlement in some parts but held it back in others.

Techniques of Frontier Farmers.—The primitive tools and methods over the whole frontier showed no important improvement until the inventions of the 1830's. The most important tool, the plow, was made of a forked or straight stick, sometimes tipped with iron; it was drawn by oxen.

Grain was planted by hand and when ripe was harvested with a scythe. One of the earliest farm improvements was the cradle scythe developed before 1800. The grain was "threshed" by driving horses over it or by beating it with a hand flail, a device made of two sticks fastened to a long handle. It was winnowed in the breeze. Manure was not used and chemical fertilizers were unknown. Wheat was the most common cash crop on the Western and Northern frontier farm.

The first and leading frontier crop was Indian corn. All of the work of harvesting was done by hand. Some of it was sold off the farm, but it was also fed to livestock and used in making whisky, both of which were marketed in the East. Much tobacco, hemp, and flax were grown south of the Ohio.

Since fences were built only to protect crops from neighborhood livestock, the poor quality of frontier livestock deteriorated through uncontrolled breeding. Under open-range conditions, fields had to be fenced to protect crops. Cattle and hogs were driven over the mountains from the Ohio Valley to Pennsylvania to be marketed. In Kentucky, however, the breeding of blooded horses became a special industry.

Agricultural Expansion in the North After 1800.—Removal of the natives from the Lake Plains north of the Ohio after the American Revolution and during the War of 1812 opened much of the richest land in the nation to American farmers. From 1795 to 1850 an agricultural population from the worn out soils of New England and from the states to the east and southeast rapidly took up the lands from Ohio northwestward to Wisconsin. The movement continued, after the Black Hawk War, across the Mississippi into the rich lands of Iowa and into the eastern part of the Great Plains states.

Between 1815 and 1830 small farmers from Kentucky and Tennessee and other southern states swarmed into the wooded bottom lands north of the Ohio. They came by way of the Ohio River and the National Road. Favorable terms for the purchase of land under more liberal federal laws made the land available to them. The competition of wheat and corn produced on these newly opened cheap lands accelerated the movement from New England and older areas. In the 1820's the demand for wool in the New England textile mills and the resulting "sheep craze" brought the abandonment of New England fields. Farmers displaced by wool growers moved to the West.

When settlers struck the edge of the treeless prairies in Illinois, they hesitated. They were accustomed to timbered lands, which furnished building materials for cabins and fences and fuel for heating their homes. The tough sod of the prairies discouraged them too. Adaptations had to be made. A special type of plow pulled by several yokes of oxen was developed for turning the sod. The soil proved highly productive and heavy corn crops soon repaid the expense of breaking the sod and hauling in rails for fencing.

Crops and livestock were diversified on the individual farm and all over the states north of the Ohio. Corn-hog farming developed early. In 1818 Cincinnati built its first packing plant for pork and the center of meat-packing soon moved across the mountains from Philadelphia. However, droves of cattle and hogs fed on western grains continued to move to Eastern markets. Sheep-growing spread from the East to Ohio. Wheat remained a typical frontier crop. Many kinds of grain and animal products—flour, whisky, live poultry, bacon, butter, cheese, oats, and corn—were floated down the Ohio and Mississippi rivers to American and foreign markets.

Agriculture in the South.—Cotton production proved to be the main economic basis for the rapid westward expansion south of the Ohio, particularly in the deep South. Technological advances in the mechanical conversion of cotton fiber into cloth created a great demand for raw cotton. When the bottleneck of removing the seeds from the lint was cleared by Whitney's invention of the cotton gin in 1792, cotton farming became highly profitable. The cotton gin made it possible to separate seeds of the upland cotton from their innumerable tightly clinging, short fibers. Sea Island cotton production, confined to its favorable climate in the coastal regions of eastern Georgia, was supplanted by varieties that would thrive over most of the South.

The simple routine of cotton farming made it an almost ideal crop for the employment of supervised slave labor. The cotton planter's hunger for Indian-occupied lands helps to explain the forced removal of the Southern tribes during the 1820's and 1830's. Cotton thrived for a time in the old fields in the Southeast, but as these fields became exhausted farmers and planters sought virgin soils to the west where larger yields and profits could be realized.

Ordinarily small frontier farmers moved out to the frontier first. These small planters cleared the timber for new fields, first in western Georgia and then farther to the west into Alabama, Mississippi, Louisiana, Tennessee, Arkansas, and Texas. Various formations of fertile soil in the warm, moist climate combined to produce large yields in various extensive areas of these states. Well-to-do planters, with large numbers of slaves, surveyed the prospects in the West and then bought out small farmers. These yeomen farmers, displaced by the economic power of the planters, took up less fertile upland soils and engaged in mixed farming. The planters continued to clear more land with slave labor and their profits enabled them to buy out other neighboring small farmers.

18

THE FUR BUSINESS

The fur business is significant both for its economic importance and its role in opening up unknown country. The first large-scale enterprise in America on any new frontier was the collection of furs—whether by trapping or trading with the Indians. (Some of the fur trappers who proved to be important as trail blazers are discussed in the succeeding section on explorations in the Far West.)

Beginnings of the Fur Trade in North America.—The fur trade originated with the crews of French fishing expeditions in Newfoundland. On their fishing vessels they carried in their sea chests knives, beads, mirrors, pots, pans, and other manufactured articles. Soon organized trading developed, and then vessels were sent out for this sole purpose, to trade along the St. Lawrence River. The furs were in demand in Europe for hats and clothing. In 1603 French Canada was founded for the purpose of gaining permanent control of the fur trade with the Indian tribes. It was the economic foundation of the company which Champlain headed.

The business was extremely profitable as trinkets and small articles were traded for furs of high value. The Indians did all the work of catching, dressing the pelts, and delivering them to the traders. Indian tribes often fought each other to gain contacts with the fur traders; the trade assured peaceful relations of the Indians with the French.

The French fur trade spread from the St. Lawrence through the Great Lakes to the Mississippi Basin. The French adapted themselves more to both trapping and Indian trading than did other nations. They did not dislike living with the Indians and intermarried with them. Since the fur traders scattered all over the forests, the name *coureurs de bois* was applied to them. The most valuable pelts were the fine furs such as beaver, otter, mink, and fox, but coarse skins such as buffalo, bear, and deer were also marketed in large quantities.

Significance of the Fur Traders on the American Frontier.— The fur men did far more trading than trapping. They blazed the trails in the wilderness into Kentucky, across the Mississippi, into the Rockies, and to the Pacific Ocean. They adapted themselves to native customs and living habits and acquired knowledge of the forest. They introduced guns, knives, whisky, and the white mens diseases and vices to the Indians and thereby inadvertently weakened them for eventual conquest. The traders discovered attractive farm lands, their trading posts often became cities, and their traces were later widened into roads by pioneers.

*Fur Trade in the English Colonies.—*Although early Virginians engaged in the fur trade, the business was much more important to early Carolinians, since they needed an export staple, and it helped to build up alliances with the Indian tribes in the Southeast against the Spanish. The fur trade on the frontier always served as a means of cementing Indian alliances.

In 1690 over 3,000 traders came together to load supplies in the Carolinas to take into the Indian country to the west. With pack trains of horses they went out to the villages of the Cherokees and the Creeks in the fall and winter and returned in the spring to Charlestown loaded with bundles of skins. Deer skins figured prominently in this southern trade. New Englanders very early turned to the fur trade and competed with the Dutch in New York.

*English Supremacy in the Fur Trade.—*When the French, under the Treaty of Paris of 1763, lost their continental territories, the English succeeded them in control of the North American fur trade, even though the personnel of the trade remained French. London came to be the central fur market in the western world. The Hudson's Bay Company, the most important of the British companies, built a reputation for fair dealing with the natives. The North West Company, operating in the West just to the south of Hudson's Bay Company, was absorbed by that firm in 1821. For a géneration after the American Revolution the

Great Lakes region was the most productive of all, and after the colonies achieved their independence rivalry developed there between the Americans and the British. The British held their posts in the Old Northwest and continued the trade with Indians south of the Great Lakes until the signing of the Jay Treaty.

The United States Government and the Fur Trade.—Regulation of the fur trade became a federal function under the Confederation. Laws were passed to license traders and regulate them, but unlicensed traders could not all be excluded from Indian-held territories. Government regulation did not succeed in preventing traders from selling liquor to the Indians and cheating them. In 1795 the federal government went into the business itself and established trading "factories." The chief motive of the government was to prevent friction by treating the Indians fairly. But private traders were still licensed and competed with the government factories. The government lost money and could not compete with private traders. By 1822 the private fur companies had succeeded in abolishing by law the government competition.

Astor's Activities.—The most outstanding leader in the history of the fur trade in the United States was John Jacob Astor. He came to the United States from Germany in 1783 at the age of twenty. He at first planned to sell musical instruments and brought with him his total stock in trade, seven flutes. In New York City he was soon attracted to the fur business and began collecting furs through his own organization in upstate New York. He became engaged in the China fur trade and by 1800 was operating his own ships. In 1803 he began plans to organize a company to operate in the newly acquired Louisiana Territory, and soon his operations became worldwide in scope. In 1808 he organized the American Fur Company, which came to control the Great Lakes trade; this company grew to be the largest business firm in America before 1850, and its founder became one of the richest men in the nation. In 1810 Astor organized the Pacific Fur Company to take advantage of the fur trade opportunities in the Pacific Northwest.

The Fur Business

The Pacific Fur Company.—Astor established his operations in the Pacific Northwest at a fort built at Astoria, Oregon. Astor's establishment of the post here was dogged by misfortune. Various misadventures were experienced by the party that sailed aboard the *Tonquin* around Cape Horn. The overland party left New York in 1810 and after severe hardships and the loss of many members from Indian attacks reached Astoria in February, 1812. During the War of 1812 Astoria was sold to the British North West Company to prevent its capture by the British navy. Astor then dissolved the Pacific Fur Company and gave up his plans on the Pacific Coast.

Hudson's Bay Company.—Chartered by England in 1670 to operate in the Hudson's Bay region, this firm became a leading contender in the fur trade of the Far Northwest. In 1821 Hudson's Bay Company absorbed the North West Company; earlier the latter had amalgamated all fur-trading operations of British and Canadian companies in Oregon. Dr. John McLoughlin served as the chief agent. In 1825 Hudson's Bay Company established Fort Vancouver on the Columbia River and placed McLoughlin in command. McLoughlin made a reputation as a just and fair trader in his dealings with everyone and ruled with a strong hand in Oregon. He established the first farms in the Oregon country and extended help to the first American settlers when they migrated there. McLoughlin dominated the country until 1843, when the provisional government established by the American settlers became the law in Oregon.

Early Fur Companies at St. Louis.—In 1807 Manuel Lisa took the first of the American fur trading expeditions up the Missouri River. The names of the fur companies and their organization changed so rapidly that it is difficult to follow their history. The Missouri Fur Company, however, was an important early firm set up at St. Louis in 1812. It was organized by the Chouteaus and Manuel Lisa. In spite of many hardships and losses the company was able to show a profit.

The leading successor to the Missouri Fur Company was the Rocky Mountain Fur Company. It was headed by one of the most prominent leaders in this business, William H. Ashley. Its first expedition, which left St. Louis in 1822 and included some of the most famous trappers of the West, spent two years gathering beaver pelts. Among its personnel were Jim Bridger, Hugh Glass, Jedediah S. Smith, and William Sublette.

The American Fur Company.—After his difficulties in Oregon, Astor concentrated his activities in the Great Lakes region and established a monopoly there that almost controlled the whole of the upper Mississippi Valley. The company's trading practices left much to be desired, and Zachary Taylor said of them: "They are the greatest scoundrels the world ever knew."

Agents of the American Fur Company entered the Missouri Valley in 1822 and in a few years came to dominate the fur trade there. In 1834 Astor retired from the company when its business was at a peak, but the firm remained dominant in Missouri for another ten years under the management of the Chouteau family in St. Louis. The establishment of the western headquarters of the American Fur Company at St. Louis helped to make this city the center of the American fur market. Many other companies operating in the Far West also centered their activities at St. Louis.

Conduct of the Fur Business.—Furs were acquired by trading with Indians and by trapping. The Indians gathered the larger part of the furs and traded them at the posts. Two types of white trappers brought in furs. Hired trappers were employed for a year for about $400; they turned over their entire catch to their employers. The "free trapper" worked independently and sold his furs for whatever the market price would bring. Voyageurs, usually of French origin, handled the boats, since the operations required much river transportation.

The most colorful of the personnel were the white trappers, referred to as "mountain men." As an anti-social lot they preferred living alone in the wilds but emerged to spend their earnings riotously. Their life resembled that of the Indians they sometimes lived among. Like the Indians they wore decorative beads and feathers. They usually traveled on horseback. At camp some of them had Indian wives to clean their catches of furs and keep them company.

Furs were sold mainly in Europe and trading goods obtained there. It took about four years to complete the round trip of sending out trading goods, bringing back furs, and marketing them; therefore, much credit had to be used in the business. Profits might be as much as 50 per cent, but the losses suffered in some years made it a difficult and hazardous business.

Trading Posts.—Posts were planned to afford defense against Indian attack. They were enclosed by picket walls with block-houses constructed on the two diagonal corners. It is said that no blockhouse was ever attacked successfully by Indians. Inside the stockade were barracks, shops, and houses. In the south, adobe construction was common.

A substitute for a permanent trading post was the "rendez-vous," a designated meeting place for conducting the trade. Trappers and traders would gather there for several months until all goods were traded or furs had been brought in. The unit of value in the Rockies was the beaver skin.

19

EXPLORATIONS AND TRAILS IN THE FAR WEST

Explorers and fur traders belong to the same phase of the frontier. The same persons or parties interested in exploring usually had an eye out for the fur-bearing animals of the land; likewise, the first hunters and fur men were necessarily explorers in the first zone or phase of the white man's advance. (Further information on the subject matter of this section may be found in the two sections on the Pacific and intermountain regional frontiers and in the preceding section on the fur business.)

PROMINENT TRAIL BLAZERS

The Lewis and Clark Expedition, 1803–1806.—This, the outstanding exploration of the West, indicated President Jefferson's great interest in the Louisiana Territory. Even before the purchase of Louisiana, Jefferson secured a secret appropriation for a military expedition to explore the Missouri Valley for scientific reasons and possibly with a view to seizure of territory. Following the purchase of Louisiana, the plans were carried out immediately through the Lewis and Clark Expedition. To head the expedition Jefferson chose Meriwether Lewis and William Clark, the brother of the conqueror of the Illinois country in the American Revolution.

The expedition was instructed to trace the Missouri River to its source, cross the divide, and follow the Columbia to the Pacific Ocean. The expedition was instructed to find a route across the continent, record the races of Indians, and make observations of animal and plant life. Every member of the party was required to keep a record of the trip and keep his journal with him at all times. Although Jefferson was supposed to have had a strong interest in scientific observations, no scientists accompanied the expedition, only seasoned frontiersmen. They were heavily armed and stocked with trading goods.

The expedition gathered at Pittsburgh in 1803, followed the Ohio, and spent the winter at St. Louis. In May, 1804, they started up the Missouri River by boat, with hunting parties on shore. The Indians were numerous and friendly but practiced petty thievery. The party was fortunate in acquiring a translator of many Indian languages, Sacajawea, the wife of a French guide, who, as a prisoner of war, had been passed among several tribes into the East. After six months they went into winter quarters near present-day Bismarck, North Dakota, and remained there for five months. Lewis encountered fur traders here from the Hudson's Bay Company. In November, 1805, they sighted the Pacific Ocean. In Oregon they entered territory in dispute between England, Spain, Russia, and the United States. They returned to St. Louis in September, 1806.

It was many years before any of the journals of the expedition were published and distributed widely; therefore, the immediate consequences of the journey were not as great as they might have been. They proved the feasibility of an overland crossing to Oregon, gathered scientific information, and stimulated the fur trade.

Pike's Expedition, 1805–1806.—Zebulon Montgomery Pike, a lieutenant in the United States Army, was dispatched by General James Wilkinson in 1805 to determine the sources of the Mississippi River. By agreement with Great Britain the northern boundary of the United States and Canada had been described as originating at the Lake of the Woods and extending due west to the Mississippi River; the expedition, therefore, was to help explore the upper parts of the river. Pike mistakenly decided that Leech Lake was the Mississippi's source and reported back to St. Louis in April, 1806. Pike wrote a highly descriptive account of his observations. He found trading posts of the North West Company flying the British flag and required them to fly the American flag.

Pike's Second Expedition, 1806–1807.—In this exploration Pike was directed to locate the sources of the Arkansas and Red rivers, drive out unlicensed traders, and win the friendship of Indians. He marched straight out from St. Louis to the great bend in the Arkansas River and followed it to the Royal Gorge. He built a fort on the present site of Pueblo and explored the Colorado country but never found the origin of the Red River.

In the spring they went through the mountains into the San Luis Valley and southward down the Rio Grande. Here a Spanish force of one hundred men met his force of twenty-three and escorted them to Santa Fe, where they were questioned endlessly; he pretended to believe he was still on American soil. His band, under arrest, was taken south to Chihuahua for more questioning and then released at Natchitoches in Louisiana on the American side of the border. The Spanish treated Pike and his men well but confiscated his maps and papers. By his excellent memory Pike retained enough to write a report that was both thorough and well received.

Long's Expeditions.—From 1817 to 1819 Major Stephen H. Long was responsible for building two forts prominent in regulating Indians on the frontier, Fort Snelling on the upper Mississippi and Fort Smith on the Arkansas River. In 1820 Long led an expedition up the Platte and South Platte (into present Colorado) and thence to the Royal Gorge. Again the purpose was to find the source of the Red River, but they returned without success. Upon his return he reported regarding the area of the Great Plains he had seen that it was "almost wholly unfit for cultivation." Thus, arose the myth of the Great American Desert in a region later to become the vast wheat-producing areas of Kansas, Nebraska, and Oklahoma.

Jedediah Smith.—Smith opened more new paths and made longer journeys of exploration in the West than anyone since Lewis and Clark. He learned to find his way about in the West as one of the many well-known mountain men who accompanied William H. Ashley in the fur-trapping expedition of 1823. A pious man, who carried the Bible along with his hunting knife, Smith had much curiosity about the West. He made a small fortune in the fur trade under Ashley and later became a partner in the Rocky Mountain Fur Company.

In 1826 Smith began his first independent and most famous exploration. From the Salt Lake region he traveled southward to the Virgin River, followed it to the Colorado River and then crossed the Mojave Desert in southern California to arrive at San Gabriel Mission near Los Angeles; he was the first American to enter California from the East. He traveled on to San Diego, where he was denied his request to explore California. Nevertheless, he led his party into the San Joaquin Valley of California, crossed the Sierra to Walker Lake, and thence made his way across the deserts of Nevada to the Great Salt Lake in 1827.

Within a month he led another party, nineteen men, to return to the men he had left in the San Joaquin Valley on the first trip. The Mexican authorities in California arrested him, but he was released through the good offices of American ship captains. As a result of two Indian attacks, he lost most of his men, but continued on his way north to Fort Vancouver on the Columbia River and thence back to Salt Lake. The main business of his journeys was gathering furs. Smith had done a great deal to open two routes to California and reveal the fertility of her valleys.

The Patties.—In 1824 Sylvester Pattie and his son, James Ohio Pattie, and three others arrived in Santa Fe to begin ten years of adventure and discovery in the Southwest during their trapping and trading career there. In 1825 and 1826 they trapped on the Gila River. In 1828 Sylvester died in prison at San Diego. James Ohio secured his own release because he happened to have a quantity of smallpox vaccine with which he is supposed to have vaccinated 22,000 persons in California. He returned to Kentucky in 1830. The Patties explored much of the intermountain region; they established a regular trail along the Gila River between Santa Fe and southern California that came to be used by many others.

James Ohio Pattie was followed by Ewing Young in 1829; Young traveled from Taos, New Mexico, into southern California and returned in 1830. That same year he became a partner with William Wolfskill; together they opened the "Old Spanish Trail" which extended the Santa Fe trade west to Los Angeles.

The Bonneville Party.—In 1832 Captain Benjamin Bonneville, on leave from the United States Army, was sent out from New York. With a large party and strong financial backing he collected furs in the Rockies. He took Jim Bridger, one of the great scouts, and founded the trading post of Fort Bridger west of South Pass in the Rockies. Washington Irving wrote his famous book *The Rocky Mountains* from Bonneville's notes. This work spread information about the Far West and made it a popular subject of literature. During his second year one of his trapping parties under Joseph R. Walker negotiated the first crossing into California from the east (1833).

Wyeth and Others.—Nathaniel J. Wyeth, from New England, took another party (1832) into the West to trap for furs. In 1834 he made his second trip carrying merchandise for the Indian trade. He founded Fort Hall on the Snake. He tried fishing for salmon, growing grain and tobacco, but failed at everything and returned to the ice business in Boston in 1836. He did much to help open the road to Oregon and give the United States a claim to it. His failures were partly due to competition of the Hudson's Bay Company.

Fremont's Movements in the West.—John Charles Fremont married Jessie Benton and thus became the son-in-law of the famous Senator and Western spokesman from Missouri, Thomas Hart Benton. With his father-in-law's sponsorship and his own daring, this adventuresome, impulsive young army officer made himself famous in five exploring trips through the West. His first three trips in the Rocky Mountain region were made in the service of the army from 1842 to 1847. Although he came to be called "the Pathfinder" of the West, he was guided by men like Kit Carson, who already knew the main paths there. Two later trips in the fifties in search of railroad routes were privately financed and were unsuccessful. His writings about his travels and the excellent maps made by his German draftsman called attention to Fremont's work. Allan Nevins designated him correctly in the title of his biography of Fremont as the *Pathmaker of the West.*

FAMOUS TRAILS OF THE WEST

There are several trails prominently referred to in the literature of the Far West. These routes were blazed by early explorers and traders and became well-established routes for Western trade, emigration, and freight movement. There were two main trails: the Oregon and the Santa Fe; the others are either branches or variations of these two.

The Oregon Trail.—The most famous emigration route in American history, the Oregon Trail, led pioneer farmers from the Missouri frontier across the Plains and Rockies to the Oregon country. The trail began at Independence, Missouri, where wagon caravans made their final preparations for the long march. The trail for the first forty miles followed the same route as the Santa Fe Trail, then led northwestward to the Platte River. It continued along the North Platte to Fort Laramie and thence up the Sweetwater River across the broad South Pass on the Continental Divide into the Colorado River drainage basin of the Green River. The trail then turned southwest to Fort Bridger and from there northwest across the Pacific divide to Fort Hall, Idaho. From here the trail followed the Snake River to Fort Boise and from there across the mountains northwesterly until it struck the Columbia River. It continued along the south bank of the Columbia to the Willamette River; the Willamette Valley was the destination of most of those who took the trail.

The western part of the trail was probably first taken by Astor's overland party to Astoria. In 1824 Jedediah Smith rediscovered the western part of the trail and it thereafter came to be used annually by fur trading parties. The first emigrant train of settlers was led over it by John Bidwell in 1841; he turned off it at Fort Hall to take what became known as the California Trail. After the Gold Rush began most of the emigrants who used the trail turned off at Fort Hall for California.

The California Trail.—This branch of the Oregon Trail beginning at Fort Bridger, Soda Springs, or Fort Hall followed the Humboldt River to its sink, thence across the desert and through the Sierra into the Central Valley of California. The route across the desert and through the Sierra was opened by Joseph R. Walker in 1833.

The Mormon Trail.—This trail may be considered a variation of the Oregon Trail. Opened by the Mormons in their exodus from Nauvoo, it began at Council Bluffs and followed the north bank of the Platte River. The Mormons chose this opposite bank to avoid friction with those taking the Oregon Trail on the south bank. At Fort Bridger the Mormon Trail turned in the direction of the Great Salt Lake.

The Santa Fe Trail.—The opening of the Santa Fe trade coincided with the independence of Mexico from Spain. The Spanish maintained a rigid monopoly and forebade trade by Americans at Santa Fe, but enough trade had occurred to reveal its profitability. In 1821 William Becknell, an American fur trader, was invited by a band of Mexican soldiers to visit Santa Fe. He realized a profit of several hundred per cent from the trip. After a second

[175]

trip he reported back to Missouri in 1822. Parts of the trail had been traversed earlier but Becknell defined the route and called attention to it. Beginning in 1823, wagon trains assembled at different points in Missouri, particularly Independence, to trade Yankee manufactured goods at Santa Fe. The traders carried out iron, cutlery, tools, notions, and brightly colored textiles. They received in exchange silver, silverware, mules, furs, skins, and chinaware. Silver received by the traders helped considerably to provide a medium of exchange on the Missouri frontier.

The route of the trail approximated a straight line from Independence to Santa Fe. In the earlier years the longer but safer route followed the Arkansas River all the way from Big Bend to Bent's Fort just inside present Colorado state. The main, more direct route used later left the Arkansas earlier and cut across the Cimarron Desert. There were branches, and alternate routes at places were used depending on whether the terrain was wet or dry. The trail is significant in opening another route to the West, and the Santa Fe trade developed an interest in the Southwest.

The "Old Spanish Trail."—This trail was an extension of the Santa Fe Trail to Los Angeles. It was blazed by the Young-Wolfskill fur trading party in 1830. The route led northwestward from either Santa Fe or Taos, thence due west, but north of the Grand Canyon of the Colorado, down the Colorado to the southern tip of present Nevada and across the Mojave Desert to Los Angeles. It was used by traders bringing horses and mules east from California and later by California immigrants during the Gold Rush.

The Gila River Route.—The most southerly route used by the fur traders and later by California immigrants followed the Rio Grande River south from Santa Fe southwesterly to the Gila River basin. It followed the Gila all the way to the Colorado at Fort Yuma on the California border and thence to either San Diego or Los Angeles.

The Mining Booms

20

THE MINING BOOMS

The rich discoveries and lootings of gold and silver by the Spanish whetted the appetite of the English for these precious metals. At Jamestown the settlers wasted much time searching for gold, but no precious metals of great importance affected any of the American frontier east of the Rockies. There are two mineral booms, however, that deserve mention. A small gold mining boom in Georgia in 1828 caused white men to overrun the Indian reserves there; many who had taken part in the gold mining in Georgia went to California later during the Gold Rush. Extensive lead deposits along the Mississippi River were mined also. (For relation of the mining booms to political developments, see sections on the Pacific and intermountain regional frontiers.)

Lead Mining Along the Mississippi.—The lead deposits along the Mississippi extended from southeast Missouri into Wisconsin. These mines produced much of the lead used by frontier riflemen. Beginning about 1800, lead deposits gave rise to a mining frontier in Missouri, Iowa, and Illinois. Stephen F. Austin's father, Moses Austin, and Henry Dodge were engaged in this business, which centered at Galena, Illinois. Systematic exploitation began in 1822, when a Kentucky promoter brought in 150 slaves to northern Illinois. A typical mining boom with its violence developed after the success of the Kentucky miner.

The Discovery of Gold in California, 1848.—In the winter of 1847 John A. Sutter undertook to manufacture lumber for the American community at San Francisco. He chose a site for a sawmill on the south branch of the American River and employed J. W. Marshall to build the mill. On January 24, 1848, Marshall found loose flakes of gold in the bottom of a sluice being dug as a tailrace for the mill's water power. In spite of efforts to keep it secret, the newspapers printed items about the discovery and individuals also spread the news. At first the gold rush began among the population in California when they realized that gold was abundant and easy to find. Prospectors without experience went to work with simple equipment—shovel, pick, and pan—and washed sand and gravel for the shiny particles. Innumerable individuals realized quick fortunes in rich deposits in the streams of the Mother Lode country on the western slopes of the Sierra.

The Gold Rush, 1849.—As the news spread up and down the Pacific Coast, men streamed in from the settlements in Oregon, southern California, Mexico, and the countries of Spanish America. Passengers and crews aboard ships vacated, sailors and soldiers deserted, and, individuals regardless of their calling, abandoned their regular work for the gold fields. When President Polk announced the discovery in December, 1848, shiploads of passengers from the East coast and Europe departed for California. Within a year California gained over 90,000 population in one of the greatest migrations in man's history.

Routes to California.—The great mass of gold seekers came West by the same methods as used by the Oregon settlers and the Mormons—in wagons or on foot with their livestock. They followed the routes already opened by the overland traders. The Mormon settlements at Salt Lake provided an opportunity for immigrants to sell worn out livestock and buy fresh horses, oxen, and provisions.

The water routes were used by those who could afford to pay the passage. One went around South America and Cape Horn, the other took passengers to Panama where they crossed the Isthmus and took passage on another vessel for San Francisco.

Early Mining Law.—When large numbers of miners had entered a district, it was organized and laws adopted to determine the size of claims and how they might be established and held. Claims and their transfers were recorded. Here again the pioneer American put to use his experience in self-government. The experience of Welsh and Spanish miners had some influence, but chiefly practical adjustments reached on the location by American miners determined the development of the mining code. The

[178]

provisions of these codes were enacted into law in California and were recognized by the national government.

Establishment of Law and Order.—The population of the camps was unusually heterogeneous in race, nationality, background, and character. Lawless outcasts were attracted after a time. The whole population was trespassing on government or Indian land where there was no organized law enforcement.

Law and order were sometimes provided through mass meetings of those who wished to punish criminals, usually after crimes became unbearable. The law-abiding majority soon organized in secret meetings to create vigilance committees with written constitutions. When the vigilantes had gathered enough members to challenge the outlaws, they selected, hunted down, and hurriedly tried the accused. The decision of guilt was made by the crowd, usually by voice. Information was passed from one vigilante group to another; criminals who had been banished would be watched upon their arrival at another community.

The vigilance committees were looked upon as a temporary expedient until duly constituted law enforcing agencies could be established. When the mining booms spread over the whole Rocky Mountain region, territorial governments had to be organized. The settlers took the initiative in asking Congress to provide territorial government. There was an unusual proportion of able, intelligent, and ambitious men to assume leadership in the mining areas.

Nevada Mining Booms.—In 1859 the famous Comstock Lode was opened at Virginia City, Nevada. Virginia City flourished in the next four years as more than $15,000,000 was taken out of Mount Davidson. In 1873 Consolidated Virginia company bored a great shaft into Mount Davidson to get to the Comstock Lode at a deeper level. The lode there was found to be 54 feet wide and filled with extremely rich gold and silver ore. Those who organized the company made a fortune of $200,000,000. These mining activities in the Washoe district in the early seventies became the basis of feverish speculation in San Francisco: the

[179]

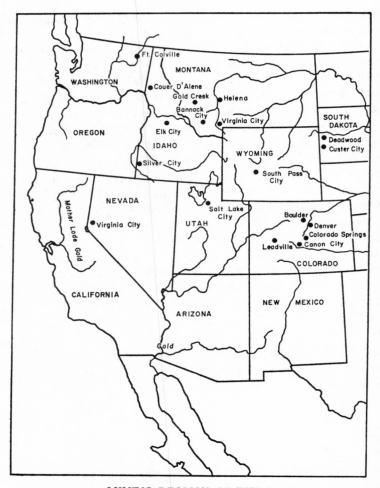

MINING REGIONS OF THE WEST

city more firmly established itself as the financial capital of the West.

Mining in Colorado.—In July, 1858, a party struck gold near Denver, and after further searching others made a number of small strikes during the summer. Newspapers filled their columns with stories of the findings and another gold rush was on, over the Pike's Peak country, as the region was called. The city of Denver originated from mining camps of prospectors. By 1859 a great mining rush was underway. Large numbers of prospectors departed from the outfitting points such as Independence, Missouri, with "Pike's Peak or Bust" as their motto. By the end of June, 100,000 "fifty-niners" were in the region. They filled mining camps at Pueblo, Canon City, Boulder, and other locations. They found little or nothing and in a few months 50,000 had returned to their homes in the East.

Significance of the Miners' Frontier.—As the easily recoverable surface gold was exhausted in California, prospectors spread eastward from California over the whole West in search of new deposits. As new discoveries of gold and silver were made, miners moved from one boom to another, but much of the population often remained in the vicinity of the discoveries. Between 1858 and 1875 the regions of Colorado, Nevada, Arizona, Oregon, Washington, Idaho, Montana, and the Black Hills were dotted with various sized mining communities. (The organization of government in these areas is discussed in Section 8.)

The mining frontier is significant in that it brought a flood of population into the West and peopled the mountain regions more rapidly than any other would have. The immense quantities of gold and silver helped to finance the Civil War. The large quantity of specie poured into the channels of trade stimulated American and world prosperity during the 1850's. The mining booms brought population into these areas without regard to the Civil War.

21

THE CATTLEMEN'S FRONTIER

The open-range cattle industry on the Great Plains developed soon after the Indians.had been removed. It was the most spectacular phase of the frontier on the Great Plains.

Early Origins of the Cattle Industry.—The cattle kingdom on the Plains originated in Texas, where the industry was introduced by the Spanish and propagated by the Mexicans. It developed on present soil of the United States in south Texas between the Nueces and Rio Grande rivers. Even though Americans brought cattle with them to Texas, the bulk of the cattle in south Texas at the time of Texas Independence were of Spanish origin.

From the time of the Texas Revolution until after the Civil War cattle grew wild in Texas and multiplied rapidly. After 1837 cowboys started gathering herds and driving them to New Orleans and other points in the East. In 1846 one man drove 1,000 head to Ohio. In 1850 drives to California were begun to provide beef for the Gold Rush population that had quickly consumed surplus Mexican cattle there.

The Civil War and the Cattle Industry.—An estimated four or five million cattle were grazing in Texas at the opening of the Civil War. The control of the Mississippi River by the Union forces cut off the flow of cattle to the Confederate armies and the multiplication of the herds continued. These cattle bred rapidly even though neglected; their outstanding quality was their ability to survive.

The rapid growth of the cities in the North created a demand for meat. The cattle drives were begun to meet this demand. Cattle in Texas could be bought for three or four dollars per head and driven north and sold for ten times their purchase price; the first drives were made in March, 1866, in herds of about 1,000. Within fifteen years after the Civil War, Texans drove 5,000,000 cattle north and still cattle in Texas were more numerous than before.

The Cattle Drives.—The first cattle drovers encountered trouble in Arkansas and Missouri from cattle thieves who stampeded the herds and from farmers who sought to keep out the Texas fever carried by the Texas longhorns.

An enterprising cattleman, J. G. McCoy, conceived the idea of connecting the cattle drives with the railroads. He induced a railroad official to sign a contract which gave them favorable rates

to Chicago and then McCoy selected a site where the cattle would
be sold and loaded on railroad cars. Stockyard facilities were
built. The word was passed to drovers on the trail to drive their

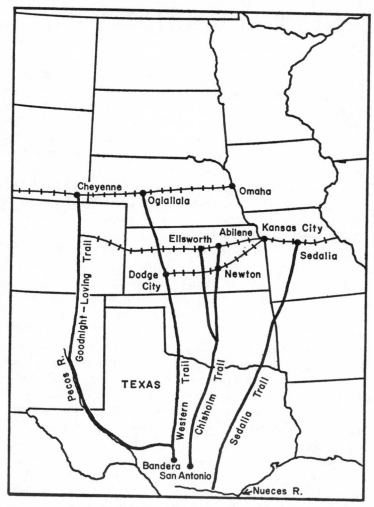

CATTLE TRAILS AND COWTOWNS

herds into the new cow town for marketing. Abilene soon became a rip-roaring town where cowboys celebrated the end of the long drives and spent their pay. As the railroads extended their lines to the west and settlements sprang up, new "cow towns" were created—Newton, Ellsworth, Dodge City, and others. The railroads linked the cattle herds and the Eastern markets. The large profits realized caused the cattle kingdom to spread all over the West.

The Western Range Cattle Industry.—As Texans learned of the lush profits to be made, cattle grazing spread over west Texas, into the Texas Plains, into the Indian Territory, and into Kansas. The confinement of the wild Plains tribes to reservations cleared the West of this most serious obstacle to ranching. The unsurveyed public domain provided vast free grazing grounds, a great boon to the cattlemen since no heavy capital investment in land or the production of feedstuffs was required. It was discovered earlier along the immigrant trails that cattle would thrive on the dry winter grass of the northern Plains; the herds spread into Colorado, Wyoming, Montana, and the Dakotas in the 1870's.

Better cattle were developed by breeding with Hereford bulls and Eastern cattle. The destruction of the buffalo in the 1870's opened vast areas naturally suited for grazing. By 1880 cattle had spread all over the Great Plains, and the grasslands came to be called the "Cattle Kingdom." The canning of meat and development of refrigeration in railroad cars and ships increased the market. In 1871 the practice of selling cattle to be fattened in the Northern corn belt began. The profits of the range cattle industry attracted large investments by land and cattle companies, many of them of English or Scottish origin. Most important of all, the extension of the railroads into the whole Great Plains area in the 1870's and 1880's made the spread of cattle grazing possible by enabling the producers to tap the market for cattle in Eastern cities and in Europe.

The Cattle Boom and Bust.—Rising prices for cattle in the last half of the 1870's caused boom conditions to develop. More and more enterprisers figured that great fortunes could be amassed. The prices of breeding cattle went above prices of steers as the boom gathered momentum and men from all over the world came to invest. But like other economic booms, it came to an end—in 1885. The ranges became overstocked. Any event that would start a wave of sales would drive the market down. Prices weakened when drouth began in 1883, continued down in 1884, and the crash came in 1885 when $35 cattle sold for $10. Prolonged drouth kept prices sliding until 1887. Other causes of the decline of the open-range industry played their part. The construction of fences by homesteaders—"nesters"—began to take over the bounty of free grasslands, to cut off water holes, and to impede the drives. Heavy losses were sustained because of the unusually cold winters and overstocking of the range in the late eighties. During the eighties, as sheepherders invaded the Rockies and then moved east into the Plains, open warfare sometimes broke out, resulting in killings and large-scale destruction of sheep by driving them over cliffs.

Range Customs and Livestock Associations.—The ranchers who first took over the free grasslands (without legal right) found it necessary to protect their claims to the grazing lands and the streams that provided water for their livestock. Boundaries were not marked by fences; instead a "range right" usually extended from a stream to the divide separating it from the drainage basin of the next stream. Cowboys maintained patrols to try to keep cattle within the limits of the owner's range. Branding the livestock provided identification of straying animals. Unmarked calves would be identified at the "round-ups" and branded by their proper owners. These rights of a rancher were enforced by voluntary extralegal livestock associations. Like the gold miners and the squatters, the cattlemen developed their extralegal enforcement agencies and codes on their own initiative whenever they advanced beyond legally constituted agencies of government.

The Beginning of Modern Ranching.—Cattlemen learned from their experience in the 1880's that they would need to acquire their own land and fence their livestock in. They replaced scrub stock with a better grade of beef cattle. The investment in better cattle required an assured supply of winter feed; ranchers began to cultivate hay fields. The water problem was solved by drilling wells and pumping them with windmills. The network of railroads made the long drives unnecessary and the farmers' fences made them impossible. Thus, ranching became a settled, more stable business like farming.

22

THE FARMERS' FRONTIER IN THE FAR WEST

A new frontier in agriculture was opened when farmers occupied the semi-arid Great Plains and the intermountain region where similar conditions of insufficient rainfall prevailed. New crops and techniques had to be found; these changes came to be known as dry-farming.

Dry-farming.—A type of agriculture designed for conditions of insufficient rainfall where irrigation is not practicable is called dry-farming. Its methods and crops were introduced or developed on the Great Plains or where similar conditions existed. Dry-farming is possible because of special kinds of cultivation practices and by the use of crops adapted to relatively little moisture. It is practiced where rainfall is more than 10 inches but less than 30 inches. It requires that moisture be conserved by plowing the ground deep at first and afterward frequently, especially after rainfall. The so-called dust mulch, formed by plowing, prevents the evaporation of moisture through cracks in the crust of the soil.

The Beginnings of Dry-Farming.—It is said that a Mormon colony of Scandinavians first practiced dry-farming when they plowed up sagebrush lands and found that wheat would grow.

Dry-farming as a movement first centered in Nebraska. The pioneers settling there, coming from the humid regions of the East or from Europe, found that their old methods failed in dry years. Their plant varieties were not adapted to the climate. These farmers had to change their practices in the unfamiliar climate. They learned to loosen the soil deeply so it would hold

[186]

and store water from one year to the next. Capillary action of the soil brings stored moisture up from below to the roots of plants. Harrows and other plows were used to pulverize the soil and prevent evaporation in either growing crops or in fallow land. A common practice in dry-farming is to leave land fallow or idle for a year to accumulate enough moisture from precipitation for the next year's crop. Large machines had to be developed so that an entire farm could be covered quickly and mulched soon after rainfall or crops could be harvested quickly.

Introduction of Wheat for Dry-farming.—Wheat came to be the leading crop in the dry-farming areas, especially in the northern parts of the Plains. The soft, white wheat varieties of the East and of Europe were too easily killed by the sudden weather changes and hard freezes of the Plains and suffered from a lack of moisture. They were not hardy enough for the severe weather.

The first knowledge of wheat varieties that would withstand the sudden sharp freezes and cold dry winds of the Great Plains came from experience with varieties introduced by German-Russian Mennonite immigrants to Kansas in 1873. The wheat varieties they brought succeeded but the kernels proved too hard for the millers to grind into satisfactory flour. But these varieties did show that there were wheats that could withstand the severe climate of the Plains.

Mark Carleton of the United States Department of Agriculture experimented with hundreds of varieties of wheat. Carleton realized the possibilities of finding better varieties of wheat in other similar climates of the Old World. In 1898 and 1900 he made trips of exploration to the arid wheat lands of Russia and introduced many successful varieties. These were *durum* or hard varieties of spring and winter wheat. The cultivation of these spread rapidly over the West in the decade of 1900–1910 and improvements have continued since then through programs of breeding and selection. These new wheat varieties provided a crop that settlers could grow over millions of acres of the central and northern Plains.

Wheat Milling.—Technological developments in milling were

essential to the marketing of the hard kernel varieties of spring and winter wheats that thrived on the Plains. The process of grinding between two millstones used with soft-kerneled grains produced a "dirty" flour and made it impossible to separate the bran from other parts of the grain. The grains were too hard and brittle. After experimenting, the Washburn Mills at Minneapolis in 1871 perfected a new process of revolving corrugated steel rollers. These steel roller mills were arranged in a series; as the grain passed through the successive rollers, it was crushed into smaller particles and run through purifiers and sieves at the same time to separate the parts of the broken kernels. The method reduced the cost, hastened the grinding, and produced a highly marketable flour and thereby opened a vast market for the varieties of hard wheat.

Grain Sorghums.—In the late 1850's when the semi-arid lands of west Texas were being settled the drouth-resistant qualities of grain sorghums were observed by farmers there. Drouth-resistant varieties of sorghum were introduced from Africa during the fifties. Interest in dry-land agriculture caused the Department of Agriculture to introduce further varieties from Africa soon after 1900. This crop came to be grown over millions of semi-arid acres in the Plains where corn or wheat could not be grown. These lands were made more productive than if they had been left to grass. The grain sorghums proved ideal for feeding and fattening livestock and poultry.

Other Dry-Land Crops.—The United States Department of Agriculture, the land-grant colleges, and the agricultural experiment stations (created under the Hatch Act of 1887) undertook programs to import and adapt new crop varieties of many kinds and to distribute free seeds and plant materials to farmers. Special attention was given to spreading dry-land varieties in the West to discover crops suitable for the many combinations of climate and soil there. Both new crops and new varieties of the old crops were sought and distributed. This was especially true of small grains, grasses, trees, and fruit crops. Russia and China, with their vast continental areas, had climates similar to those of the American West. It was from these regions that many new plant varieties were introduced.

Large-scale Farming.—The opening of the Plains stimulated the use of machines for large-scale farming. Farm machines had not developed earlier because they could not be accommodated to the small stump-filled fields of the East. But they succeeded in the large, level fields of the Plains. The West gave impetus to the agricultural equipment industry by the use of these machines. Large-scale farming is done with little manpower relative to the acreage cultivated; it is necessary where yields are reduced by an insufficiency of moisture. Large farm units had to be cultivated to support a farm family. Also ranches in the thin bunch grass country of the West had to be large to support enough livestock to enable a family to earn a living.

Effect of Rainfall Cycles.—The pioneers learned from prolonged drouths that successive wet and dry years occur on the Great Plains. During wet years, as during the early eighties, farmers on the Plains enjoyed abundant crops from the fertile soils. There was a strong tendency after two or three wet years to believe that the climate was changing. In such times a tide of immigration would sweep over the Plains states. But after a few years the drouth phase of the cycle returned. When drouth came settlers hoped and prayed for rain but watched their crops wither and burn, sometimes when only half-grown. After a year or two of crop failure followed by bankruptcy, settlers would be forced out.

Attempts To Produce Rainfall.—Various theories advocated for producing or increasing rainfall reflect the desperation of drouth-stricken communities. It was thought that transpiration of moisture by trees would change the climate or produce rainfall, but such reasoning only confused cause and effect. Trees were planted, however, to serve as windbreaks to reduce evaporation and proved of some value. Many communities were victimized by rainmakers. Explosives were set off in experiments in Texas without producing rain. The Timber Culture Act was supported partly on the supposition that planting trees would help change the climate, and in 1934 the New Deal encouraged planting of shelter-belts of trees.

Irrigation.—Large-scale irrigation by American pioneers was first practiced in the West by the Mormons. It is the one important development in the West that called for smaller farm units.

It has been estimated that only about a sixteenth of the dry land of the West could be irrigated from precipitation, no matter by what means the water might be collected. Irrigation is possible because water is collected in reservoirs or pumped up from the underground water table. Both sources of water depend upon precipitation and there is no proven means of increasing rainfall.

Before the Mormons came to the West, irrigation was practiced at some of the Spanish missions in Arizona and California, but these works had fallen into decay with the secularization of the missions by Mexico. Irrigation by private individuals usually did not pay when it was practiced at first; its success seemed to depend upon government assistance.

The Carey Act, 1894.—This was the first federal law to attempt to encourage cooperative irrigation projects. It provided that proceeds from the sale of arid lands in the Western states be paid to these states for irrigation projects. Very little success followed this effort because the land sales did not provide enough revenue, and the law was not drafted for the interstate nature of the projects. The act showed the need for federally sponsored projects.

The Newlands Act, 1902.—The Newlands Act was the first successful federal enactment to promote cooperative irrigation projects. The act provided that irrigation projects would be constructed by the federal government from revenues of land sales in the arid states. Users of the water were to repay the cost of the projects and the funds would then be made available for financing similar new projects. Under this revolving fund principle, 20,000,000 acres was brought under irrigation by 1920. Since then much more land has been added, but such projects serve only oases in the great spaces of the West.

Political Radicalism on the Plains.—The seemingly radical demands of the Grangers (discussed in connection with railroad regulation, Section 14), the Greenbackers, the free-silverites, the Alliance men, and later of the Populists—who supported William Jennings Bryan from the Plains state of Nebraska—arose from the difficulty of adjusting to that region. (The West in movements for monetary reform is discussed in Section 12, pp. 111 ff.) Of course, part of the difficulty was due to overproduction, but the fact remains that the Plains states were the loudest in demanding reform. There were difficulties of economic adjustment as well as of harsh conditions of climate.

The farmers all over the Far West were far from markets, scorched by drouth and hot winds, burned by prairie fires, suffered from hail, were frozen by blizzards, eaten out by grasshoppers, and felt victimized by monopolists, money-lenders, and the railroads. There has been more advocacy of socialism in the Plains states than in any other agricultural region of the United States.

23

THE URBAN FRONTIER

Students of the frontier have recently shown increased interest in both the functions of the towns in the conquest of the wilderness and in the evolution of frontier towns. At first thought, urban life seems to be and is, in the spectrum of civilization, the extreme opposite of the frontier's sparse settlement and the savagery of the wilderness. Even excluding such transitory or specialized concentrations of humanity as missions, military and trading posts, mining camps, the rendezvous of fur traders, and construction camps, urban centers begun in the wilderness and planned for permanency were a part of the frontier scene and in their early years at least exhibited frontier characteristics and were centers of frontier economic and social activities. These towns, often beginning with a crossroads store, served the frontier primarily as trading or commercial centers. Though beginning with some primitive industries, they soon developed more advanced kinds of manufacturing; later they added a wide choice of social amenities associated with urban living. These towns, often planted in the remote wilderness, were "spearheads" of frontier advance, sometimes under harassment or siege; they constituted the commissary and service centers back of the figurative or actual infiltrators, rangers, and shock troops of the frontier.

Wade's Thesis of the Urban Frontier.—Richard Wade in *The Urban Frontier* asserts the thesis that the towns were the "spearheads of the frontier . . . far in advance of the line of settlement." They were sometimes actual precursers of frontier farmers in the region west of the Appalachians. Wade's research calls attention to town life, which is usually regarded as the final stage in the evolution of any frontier and is the stage most neglected by historians. He helps confirm the supporting role of Mississippi Valley towns in subduing the surrounding wilderness.

The "spearheads" of the frontier studied in detail by Wade are the early and prominent frontier cities of St. Louis, Pittsburgh, Louisville, Lexington, and Cincinnati. These towns and others similar to them sprang up along waterways or in the center of fertile farm areas. St. Louis originated when the New Orleans trading firm of Maxent, Laclede and Company was granted an eight-year monopoly of trade with the Indians of the Missouri region. In 1763 the company chose the site of St. Louis for its proximity to the mouth of the Missouri, freedom from flooding, and for strategic location with reference to the fur trade. Pittsburgh, formally planned in 1764, was identified about ten years earlier, by both George Washington and the French, as an inviting site and strategic location for a military post. Its location in reference to water transportation, where the Allegheny and Monongahela met to form the Ohio, gave it a great advantage in commerce.

Louisville, at the rapids on the Ohio, sprang up to facilitate transshipment around this only serious hazard on the whole stretch of that river. Louisville enjoyed the advantage of proximity to a large farming population on an extensive fertile plain and location at the mouth of a small tributary to the Ohio. In 1778 George Rogers Clark began the first permanent settlement there as a base for military operations in the Northwest Territory. Cincinnati was settled in 1788; its location near rich land in Ohio and Indiana and nearness to the mouth of the Licking River, which gave access to the Blue Grass country, recommended it to settlers. Freedom from floods gave the site an advantage over rival spots in the vicinity. For several years Cincinnati was a garrison town. Only Lexington, of the five towns studied by Wade, was not located on a navigable stream, but it centered in the main routes of immigration and trade and in the rich Blue Grass farming country of central Kentucky. In 1779 Lexington, like Pittsburgh, Louisville, and Cincinnati, was begun as a "wilderness fortress." The importance of all these towns as military centers does entitle them to be designated as "spearheads of the frontier."

Factors in the Founding and Growth of Frontier Towns.— Trade and manufacturing were the main economic foundations of the early cities, but most towns over the nation at first served only as market centers for large farming and grazing communities. Transportation was the determinant of city growth, since it was essential to both commerce and manufacturing. The rivers furnished the best transport before roads and railroads were built, but the construction of canals gave rise to and nourished many cities that became prominent in New York state and in the states north of the Ohio River. The early development of steamboats gave the river towns a great head start before most of the canals were built. Cities grew up wherever goods had to be transshipped, as at harbors, rapids, and waterfalls. Cities varied in their degree of preoccupation with trade or with manufacturing: some became primarily commercial centers, some manufacturing, and others developed both about equally. Manufacturing came after the cities had gained commercial importance. Raw materials at hand naturally helped determine the kinds of industries. Nearby deposits of iron and coal allowed Pittsburgh to manufacture household utensils, hardware, glass, and steam engines; shipbuilding, too, was important. Lexington used Kentucky hemp to make cordage and bagging; also cotton and woolen textiles, milling, and paper industries were established there. Cincinnati gave her greatest attention to commerce but after the War of 1812 joined the national drive to foster industry. The fur trade, lead mining, and commerce dominated the economy of St. Louis. The main business of Louisville was the transshipment of goods around the rapids of the Ohio; the coming of steam navigation made her a great commercial center, but manufacturing moved into Louisville also about the time of the War of 1812. The army stimulated the business life of the cities and so did the trade of immigrants passing through. The coming of the river steamboat after 1815 provided the greatest stimulus of all to the growth of the towns and enormously favored towns on the rivers.

Just as immigrants moved into new areas to locate good farms, so did they hope to locate in towns with a future. As the fertile soils attracted settlers so did the towns, and the towns were often built before the outlying lands were settled. The city-making mania engaged the energies of speculative businessmen in every region of the country as settlement proceeded. The towns expected to attract such people as mechanics and businessmen who preferred urban life. It is well known that a great many towns died in infancy, remained villages, or became ghost towns. Speculation in town-founding and the sale of town lots raged during frontier days.

River mouths and central farming areas were favorite locations for cities. In the Far West the railroads determined the location and growth of the towns; the influence of politicians in locating county seats and capitals gave many towns a decided advantage over their rivals. As a way of promoting the sale of town lots advertisements boasted of a glorious future. Many towns failed to live up to the dreams of their founders: their location near more successful rivals, flooding, or remoteness from navigable streams were frequent causes of failure. Not only geographic and economic factors but the efforts of aggressive and farsighted leaders caused many to outgrow others, regardless of natural advantages. With the coming of the railroads, transportation was provided to serve other promising settlements.

Most of the great cities, from the Appalachians to the Pacific, had their origin during the early frontier days. The very fact of primacy gave cities a momentum that kept them ahead of towns founded later. Healthful or congenial climate fostered the growth of towns in the Southwest. After the Civil War, the stimulating life of the cities and attractive wages in urban industries attracted migrants from the rural areas. In the South towns played a less significant role on the frontier, since the plantation system checked urban growth.

Planning the Frontier Towns.—Planning of the western cities shows much similarity among them. Philadelphia served as the model for the almost universal checkerboard pattern of streets. Such rectangular lines set the city apart from the surrounding country where nature's irregular, curving lines prevailed. The frontier towns failed to provide sufficient space for public buildings, markets, wharves, and parks. A feature common to the river towns was that of drawing the main streets parallel to the waterfront. The residential centers were pushed away from the rivers to the back of the towns. In planning their towns as well as in meeting their various problems, the Western settlements looked to Eastern cities for standards and models. In various respects the influence of Philadelphia was especially prominent.

Problems of Frontier Cities.—One of the earliest problems of the cities was their lack of authority to solve local problems. Cities are created legally by the state governments when charters are granted. Western states were dominated by rural interests and state constitutions were drawn up before towns had become organized. Early city charters allowed only limited privileges and had to be amended repeatedly or the cities had to go to the legislatures frequently for authority to deal with their problems. The problems of all cities were those of regulating public markets, paving and maintaining streets, providing a water supply, fire and police protection, and raising revenue to meet expenses. The more successful merchants provided leadership in the towns.

Cities in time came to exercise considerable authority in performing their various functions and in regulating the wide range of activities within their limits. In the regulation of public markets ordinances sought to prevent the sale of unsound foodstuffs; they sought to insure correct weights and measures, to fix prices, and to prevent monopolistic practices. Much attention was given to street paving and the improvement of roads. Manure and dead animals consequent to the presence of large numbers of cows and pigs and the use of streets as depositaries of garbage and trash made the towns dangerous and filthy until these problems were solved.

Policing was necessitated by the presence of slaves and criminal elements. Lack of street lighting made crime common. Western communities were haunted by the likelihood of fast-spreading fires, and indeed every city did suffer destructive conflagrations. Every man was expected to respond to fire alarms; fire engines were in use in all cities by 1815. Cities very early dug wells to supplant private wells from which water was sold at first. The water problem was one of avoiding contamination rather than that of assuring an adequate supply. Problems of sewage disposal were met by regulation of private facilities and quarantines were enforced to prevent the spread of disease.

Social Stratification in the Cities.—As centers of a great variety of occupations and callings ranging from the crudest forms of labor to professional and business skills, cities developed social stratification as various groups either attracted or excluded each other. The egalitarianism of the frontier soon disappeared in the Western cities as it did elsewhere. Economic differences operated more than any other factor in establishing different levels, but professional skills gave some a preferred position. Lawyers were nearly always in good supply and were active in frontier towns. Differences of color and race everywhere gave certain groups inferior status. The social structure paralleled fairly closely that of older cities. Well-to-do merchants topped the social structure and just below them stood the professionals—lawyers, journalists, doctors, ministers, and teachers. The middle ranks included skilled workers, storekeepers, and clerks. At the bottom were whatever racial group was confined to the menial jobs. Frontier towns often attracted a large bottom-layer population of riffraff, transients, scarlet women, and criminals. There existed both mobility and a strong drive for status in frontier cities. As the cities grew older and more complex, stratification and rigidity of social classes increased.

Cultural Beginnings in the Towns.—The towns introduced various cultural opportunities to the frontiers everywhere. They brought people together for cultural association and attracted leaders for such activities. Newspapers were soon established in the larger settlements. Editors commented on local events and filled their newspapers with clippings from Eastern papers. After a time various religious denominations formed congregations, provided fellowship, and brought different classes together. Elementary schools varied a great deal according to place and time on the frontier, but were more likely to meet the needs of children in the towns. Not only were public elementary schools provided in the towns, but academies and colleges were organized very early. Not only schools but less formal associations from agricultural societies to "philosophical societies" promoted discussion and the exchange of knowledge. Frontier towns provided libraries and local theaters. The importance and the efficiency of the cultural function increased as the cities grew older. (The subject of the cities as cultural centers is developed further in Section 16, "Culture on the Frontier.")

The Role of the Towns in the Growth of the West.—At first the cities were more clearly tied to the surrounding areas than later. In their beginnings towns were fortified trading posts or other centers for defense, if not actual military posts. After the Indian menace had been eliminated, the common early function was that of the crossroads store and the trading center. The towns supplied merchandise for local settlers, travelers, and immigrants. As the surrounding area developed its particular economy, the towns became still more important for gathering and shipping items of local production. They provided shipping centers and markets for agricultural, mineral, and forest raw materials and supply centers for producer's equipment, such as tools and machinery, and for consumer goods, such as food, clothing, and luxury goods. Afterward, manufacturing developed as local demand supplied a sufficient market or available raw materials provided a basis for processing industries such as sawmills, gristmills, or slaughterhouses. After a time financial services were provided by banks. County seats served significantly as centers of local government and politics. As the towns became better established, their social and cultural functions increased, and newspapers, entertainment, schools, and libraries were established. The economic functions and the cultural services provided by business and professional pioneers of the urban centers hastened the conversion of the wilderness from savagery to civilization.

Appendix

Virginia	June 25, 1788
New York	July 26, 1788
Massachusetts	February 6, 1788
New Hampshire	June 21, 1788
Maryland	April 28, 1788
Connecticut	January 9, 1788
Rhode Island	May 29, 1790
Delaware	December 7, 1787
North Carolina	November 21, 1789
New Jersey	December 18, 1787
South Carolina	May 23, 1788
Pennsylvania	December 12, 1787
Georgia	January 2, 1788
Vermont	March 4, 1791
Kentucky	June 1, 1792
Tennessee	June 1, 1796
Ohio	March 1, 1803
Louisiana	April 30, 1812
Indiana	December 11, 1816
Mississippi	December 10, 1817
Illinois	December 3, 1818
Alabama	December 14, 1819
Maine	March 15, 1820
Missouri	August 10, 1821
Arkansas	June 15, 1836
Michigan	January 26, 1837
Florida	March 3, 1845
Texas	December 29, 1845
Iowa	December 28, 1846
Wisconsin	May 29, 1848

California	September 9, 1850
Minnesota	May 11, 1858
Oregon	February 14, 1859
Kansas	January 29, 1861
West Virginia	June 19, 1863
Nevada	October 31, 1864
Nebraska	March 1, 1867
Colorado	August 1, 1876
North Dakota	November 2, 1889
South Dakota	November 2, 1889
Montana	November 8, 1889
Washington	November 11, 1889
Idaho	July 3, 1890
Wyoming	July 10, 1890
Utah	January 4, 1896
Oklahoma	November 16, 1907
New Mexico	January 6, 1912
Arizona	February 14, 1912
Alaska	January 3, 1959
Hawaii	August 21, 1959

Selected Paperbacks on the American Frontier

*Especially recommended. For listings of paperbacks currently in print, see Bowker's *Paperbound Books in Print,* issued quarterly.

*ATHEARN, ROBERT G. *Westward the Briton.* Bison. 1.60.

BAKELESS, JOHN. *Eyes of Discovery: America as Seen by the First Explorers.* Dover. 2.00.

*BALDWIN, JOSEPH G. *The Flush Times of Alabama and Mississippi.* American Century. 1.25.

*BILLINGTON, RAY A. *Far Western Frontier: 1830–1860.* Torchbooks. 1.85.

——. *Westward Movement in the United States.* Anvil. 1.25.

——. *The American Frontier.* Macmillan. .50 (Publication No. 8, Service Center for Teachers of History, American Historical Association).

BOURNE, EDWARD G. *Spain in America.* Barnes and Noble. 1.95.

*BRANCH, E. DOUGLAS. *Hunting of the Buffalo.* Bison. 1.40.

BRANDES, RAY. *Frontier Military Posts of Arizona.* Dale Stuart King. 1.00.

*BRONSON, EDGAR B. *Reminiscences of a Ranchman.* Bison. 1.50.

*BUCK, SOLON. *The Granger Movement.* Bison. 1.60.

BURTON, RICHARD. *Look of the West, 1860.* Bison. 1.60.

CONWAY, JOHN. *Apache Wars.* Monarch. .35.

——. *The Texas Rangers.* Monarch. .35.

CRANE, VERNER W. *Southern Frontier, 1670–1732.* Ann Arbor. 1.75.

*CREVECOEUR, J. H. ST. JOHN. *Letters from an American Farmer.* Dolphin. .95 (Everyman. 1.35).

*DANA, RICHARD HENRY. *Two Years Before the Mast.* Bantam. .50 (Dolphin. .95).

DAVIS, BRITTON. *Truth About Geronimo.* Yale. 1.95.

DE VOTO, BERNARD. *Course of Empire.* Sentry. 2.65.

——. *Journals of Lewis and Clark.* Sentry. 2.65.

——. *Year of Decision: 1846.* Sentry. 2.35.

DIAZ, BERNAL. *Chronicles.* Dolphin. 1.45.

DOBIE, J. FRANK. *Longhorns.* Universal. 1.45.

———. *The Voice of the Coyote.* Bison. 1.40.

*FILSON, JOHN. *Discovery, Settlement and Present State of Kentucke.* Citadel. 1.25.

*GARLAND, HAMLIN. *Boy Life on the Prairie.* Bison. 1.40.

*GOLDMAN, ERIC. *Rendezvous with Destiny.* Vintage. 1.50.

GRAHAM, W. A. *Story of the Little Big Horn: Custer's Last Fight.* Collier. .95.

*GREGG, JOSIAH. *Commerce of the Prairies.* 2 vols. Keystone. 2.25 each.

GRINNELL, GEORGE B. *Blackfoot Lodge Tales.* Bison. 1.50.

———. *Pawnee Hero Stories and Folk Tales.* Bison. 1.65.

HANDLIN, OSCAR. *Immigration as a Factor in American History.* Spectrum. 1.95.

HANSEN, MARCUS LEE. *Atlantic Migration, 1607–1860.* Torchbooks. 2.25.

HESSELTINE, WILLIAM B. *Third Party Movements in the United States.* Anvil. 1.45.

*HICKS, JOHN D. *Populist Revolt.* Bison. 1.75.

HOFSTADTER, RICHARD. *Age of Reform: From Bryan to Franklin D. Roosevelt.* Vintage. 1.50.

INNIS, HAROLD A. *Fur Trade in Canada.* Yale. 1.95.

IRVING, WASHINGTON. *Astoria, or Anecdotes of an Enterprise Beyond the Rocky Mountains.* Dolphin. 1.45 (Keystone, 2 vols. 1.95 each).

*JAMES, MARQUIS. *Andrew Jackson: Border Captain.* Universal. 1.65.

*———. *Andrew Jackson, Portrait of a President.* Universal. 1.95.

*JAMES, THOMAS. *Three Years Among the Indians and Mexicans.* Keystone. 1.95.

KIRKPATRICK, F. A. *Spanish Conquistadores.* Meridian. 1.95.

*LAVENDER, DAVID. *Bent's Fort.* Dolphin. 1.45.

LEWIS, MERIWETHER. *Lewis and Clark Expedition.* 3 vols., Keystone. 1.95 each.

LINDERMAN, FRANK B. *Plenty-Coups, Chief of the Crows: The Life Story of a Great Indian.* Bison. 1.50.

*LONGSTREET, A. B. *Georgia Scenes.* American Century. 1.25.

McKEOWN, MARTHA FERGUSON. *Them Was the Days: An American Saga of the '70's.* Bison. 1.25.

*McNICKLE, D'ARCY. *Indian Tribes of the United States.* Oxford. 1.75.

MAGOFFIN, SUSAN SHELBY. *Down the Santa Fe Trail and into Mexico: The Diary of Susan Shelby Magoffin.* Yale. 1.95.

*MARCY, RANDOLPH B. *Thirty Years of Army Life on the Border.* Keystone. 1.95.

MARRYAT, FRANCIS. *Mountains and Molehills.* Keystone. 1.85.

NEIHARDT, JOHN G. *Black Elk Speaks: Being the Life Story of a Holy Man of the Oglala Sioux.* Bison. 1.50.

OLMSTEAD, FREDERICK LAW. *Slave States.* Capricorn. 1.25.

*OSGOOD, ERNEST S. *Day of the Cattleman.* Phoenix. 1.50.

OWEN, DEAN. *Sam Houston Story.* Monarch. .35.

PARKHILL, FORBES. *Last of the Indian Wars.* Collier. .95.

*PARKMAN, FRANCIS. *Conspiracy of Pontiac.* Collier. 1.50.

———. *Discovery of the Great West: La Salle.* Rinehart. 1.65.

———. *Montcalm and Wolfe.* Collier. 1.50.

*———. *Oregon Trail.* Signet. .50.

*PATTIE, JAMES O. *Personal Narrative.* Keystone. 1.95.

PECKHAM, HOWARD. *Pontiac and the Indian Uprising.* Phoenix. 1.95.

PEITHMAN, IRVIN. *Unconquered Seminoles.* Great Outdoors. 1.25.

POTTER, DAVID M. *Trail to California.* Yale. 1.75.

REED, V. B., and J. D. WILLIAMS. *Case of Aaron Burr.* Houghton Mifflin. 1.75

*ROBBINS, ROY M. *Our Landed Heritage: The Public Domain, 1776–1936.* Bison. 1.95.

ROOSEVELT, THEODORE. *Rough Riders.* Signet. .50.

———. *Winning of the West.* Capricorn. 1.25.

RUSSELL, CARL P. *Guns on the Early Frontiers: A History of Firearms from Colonial Times Through the Years of the Western Fur Trade.* California. 2.45.

SANDOZ, MARI. *Crazy Horse.* Bison. 1.65.

*———. *Old Jules.* Bison. 1.60.

SCHLESINGER, ARTHUR M., JR., *Age of Jackson.* New American Library. .50.

*SHANNON, FRED. *American Farmers' Movements.* Anvil. 1.25.

SHIRLEY, GLEN. *Law West of Fort Smith: A History of Frontier Justice in the Indian Territory.* Collier. .95.

*SINGLETARY, OTIS A. *The Mexican War.* Chicago. 1.75.

*SMITH, HENRY NASH. *Virgin Land.* Vintage. 1.25.

STEGNER, WALLACE. *Beyond the Hundredth Meridian.* Sentry. 2.45.

STEPHENSON, W. H. *Basic History of the Old South.* Anvil. 1.25.

STEWART, ELINORE PRUITT. *Letters of a Woman Homesteader.* Bison. 1.25

STEWART, GEORGE R. *Donner Pass.* Lane. 1.95.

*———. *Ordeal by Hunger.* Ace. .50.

*STILL, BAYARD. *West: Collection of Primary Sources on the Westward Expansion.* Capricorn. 1.45.

STOVER, JOHN F. *American Railroads.* Chicago. 1.95.

TIBBLES, THOMAS H. *Buckskin and Blanket Days.* Bantam. .60.

TINKLE, LON. *Alamo.* New American Library. .35.

*TOCQUEVILLE, ALEXIS DE. *Democracy in America.* 2 vols. Schocken. 1.95 each.

*TROLLOPE, FRANCES. *Domestic Manners of the Americans.* Vintage. 1.65.

*TURNER, FREDERICK J. *Rise of the New West, 1819–1829.* Collier. .95.

*———. *Frontier and Section: Selected Essays of Frederick Jackson Turner.* (Introduction and notes by R. A. Billington.) Spectrum. 1.95.

*TWAIN, MARK. *Roughing It.* Rinehart. .95.

*VAN EVERY, DALE. *Forth to the Wilderness: The First American Wilderness.* Mentor. .75.

———. *Company of Heroes: The First American Frontier, 1775–1783.* Mentor. .75.

*VESTAL, STANLEY. *Dodge City: Queen of Cowtowns.* Bantam. .50.

*WEBB, WALTER P. *The Great Plains.* Universal. 1.65.

WEINBERG, ALBERT K. *Manifest Destiny: A Study of Nationalist Expansion in American History.* Encounter. 2.65.

*WITTKE, CARL. *We Who Built America.* Western Reserve. 3.00.

*WRIGHT, LOUIS B. *Culture on the Moving Frontier.* Torchbooks. 1.60.

———. *The Atlantic Frontier.* Great Seal Books. 1.85.

WYMAN, WALKER D. *The Wild Horse of the West.* Bison. 1.60.

A Bibliography of Frontier History

1. THE FRONTIER HYPOTHESIS OR TURNER THESIS

*BILLINGTON, RAY ALLEN. *The American Frontier* (New York: Macmillan, 1958). A booklet published for the American Historical Association, Service Center for Teachers of History. An evaluation and statement of writings about Turner's frontier thesis.

———. "How the Frontier Shaped American Character," *American Heritage*, Vol. IX, No. 3 (April, 1958).

FOX, DIXON R., ed. *Sources of Culture in the Middle West: Backgrounds Versus Frontier* (New York: Appleton-Century, 1934). Denies frontier origin of political democracy.

HUTCHINSON, WILLIAM T., ed. *Marcus W. Jernegan Essays in American Historiography* (Chicago: University of Chicago Press, 1937). See essay by Avery Craven, "Frederick Jackson Turner."

JACOBS, WILBUR R. "Frederick Jackson Turner—Master Teacher," *Pacific Historical Review*, Vol. XXIII (Feb., 1954).

KRAUS, MICHAEL. *A History of American History* (New York: Farrar and Rinehart, 1937). A later edition has been published under the title *The Writings of American History* (Norman: University of Oklahoma Press, 1953).

MOOD, FULMER. "The Historiographic Setting of Turner's Frontier Essay," *Agricultural History*, Vol. XVII (July, 1943).

PAXSON, FREDERIC L. "Generation of Frontier Hypothesis," *Pacific Historical Review*, Vol. II (March, 1933).

SHANNON, FRED A. "A Post Mortem on the Labor-Safety-Valve Theory," *Agricultural History*, Vol. XIX (Jan., 1945).

*SMITH, HENRY NASH. *Virgin Land: The American West as Symbol and Myth* (Cambridge: Harvard University Press, 1950). About the West and literature relating to it; criticizes the Turner thesis.

*TAYLOR, GEORGE ROGERS, ed. *The Turner Thesis Concerning the Role of the Frontier in American History* (rev. ed. Boston: Heath, 1956). Readings selected by the Department of American Studies, Amherst

*Books marked with an asterisk are available as paperback editions, either reprints or originals. The student is referred to the special list of paperback books on the frontier for special information about the paperback editions.

College. Well selected essays from leading critics and defenders of the Turner thesis.

*Tocqueville, Alexis de. *Democracy in America* (2 vols. New York: Knopf, 1945; other editions also).

*Turner, Frederick Jackson. *The Frontier in American History* (New York: Holt, 1950). Includes the famous paper of 1893 and twelve essays and addresses.

——. *The Significance of Sections in American History* (New York: Holt, 1932).

Wade, Richard D. *The Urban Frontier: The Rise of Western Cities, 1790–1830* (Cambridge: Harvard University Press, 1959). See Chapter 1. Best single treatment of the role of cities on the frontier.

Also consult bibliography for Section 2.

2. THE FRONTIER IN WIDE PERSPECTIVE

*Bakeless, John. *The Eyes of Discovery: The Pageant of North America as Seen by the First Explorers* (Philadelphia: Lippincott, 1950). Describes North America as seen by first explorers.

Barraclough, G. "Metropolis and Macrocosm," *Past and Present,* Vol. III (May, 1954).

Carter, Harvey L. *The Far West in American History* (New York: Macmillan, 1960). A booklet published for the American Historical Association, Service Center for Teachers of History. What historians have written on the history of the West.

Coleman, Peter J. "The New Zealand Frontier and the Turner Thesis," *Pacific Historical Review,* Vol. XXVII (August, 1958).

Nettels, Curtis. "Frederick Jackson Turner and the New Deal," *Magazine of History,* Vol. XVII (March, 1934).

Paxson, Frederic L. *When the West Is Gone* (New York: Holt, 1930).

Semple, Ellen Churchill. *American History and Its Geographic Conditions* (rev. Boston: Houghton Mifflin, 1933).

Sharp, Paul F. "Three Frontiers: Some Comparative Studies of Canadian, American, and Australian Settlement," *Pacific Historical Review,* Vol. XXIV (Nov., 1955).

*Taylor, George Rogers, ed. *The Turner Thesis Concerning the Role of the Frontier in American History* (rev. ed. Boston: Heath, 1956).

Toole, K. Ross, *et al.,* eds. *Probing the American West: Papers from the Santa Fe Conference* (Santa Fe: Museum of New Mexico Press, 1962).

TREADGOLD, DONALD W. "Russian Expansion in the Light of Turner's Study of the American Frontier," *Agricultural History*, Vol. XXVI (Oct., 1952).

TURNER, FREDERICK JACKSON. *The Frontier in American History* (New York: Holt, 1950).

WALLACE, HENRY A. *New Frontiers* (New York: Reynal and Hitchcock, 1934).

WEBB, WALTER PRESCOTT. *Divided We Stand: The Crisis of a Frontierless Democracy* (New York: Farrar and Rinehart, 1937).

———. *The Great Frontier* (Boston: Houghton Mifflin, 1952). Courageously applies the frontier thesis to world history.

WILLIAMS, WILLIAM A. "The Frontier Thesis and American Foreign Policy," *Pacific Historical Review*, Vol. XXIV (Nov., 1955).

WYMAN, WALKER D., and CLIFTON B. KROEBER, eds. *The Frontier in Perspective* (Madison: University of Wisconsin Press, 1957).

3. THE SEABOARD-COLONIAL FRONTIER, 1492–1700

EARLY FRENCH AND SPANISH FRONTIERS

BISHOP, MORRIS. *Champlain: The Life of Fortitude* (New York: Knopf, 1948). The idealistic Frenchman's activities in America.

BOLTON, HERBERT E. *The Spanish Borderlands: A Chronicle of Old Florida and the Southwest* (New Haven: Yale University Press, 1921).

BREBNER, JOHN B. *The Explorers of North America, 1492–1806* (New York: Macmillan, 1933). A survey closing with Lewis and Clark's return; brief.

CHATELAIN, VERNE E. *The Defenses of Spanish Florida, 1565–1763* (Washington, D. C.: Carnegie Institution of Washington, Pub. 511, 1941). Describes Spain's efforts to hold her North American empire.

*DE VOTO, BERNARD. *The Course of Empire* (Boston: Houghton Mifflin, 1952). Chapter 1–5. The westward movement up to 1806, an outstanding work and the major work of De Voto.

KIRKPATRICK, F. A. *The Spanish Conquistadores* (2d ed. London: A. & C. Black, 1946). Coherent survey of all Spanish conquests in North and South America; detailed.

Bibliography

MARQUIS, THOMAS G. *The Jesuit Missions: A Chronicle of the Cross in the Wilderness* (Toronto: Brook & Co., 1916).

PARKMAN, FRANCIS. *Pioneers of France in the New World* (Boston: Little, Brown, 1887). Still the best account.

SAUER, CARL. *The Road to Cibola* (Berkeley: University of California Press, 1932). Exploration and discovery in the Southwest.

THE ENGLISH COLONIES IN THE SOUTH

ABERNETHY, THOMAS P. *Three Virginia Frontiers* (Baton Rouge: University of Louisiana, 1941).

BRIDENBAUGH, CARL. *Myths and Realities: Societies of the Colonial South* (Baton Rouge: Louisiana State University Press, 1952). Discusses back settlements as well as Eastern society in the South.

*CRANE, VERNER W. *The Southern Frontier, 1670–1732* (Durham: Duke University Press, 1928). The Charles Town Indian traders and their contribution to American expansion; conflicts with Spain.

GOBER-TEMPLE, SARAH B., and KENNETH COLEMAN. *Georgia Journeys: An Account of the Lives of Georgia's Original Settlers* (Athens: University of Georgia Press, 1961). Social history of early Georgia.

JOHNSON, MARY. *Pioneers of the Old South* (Chronicles of America Series. New Haven: Yale University Press, 1918).

MERIWETHER, ROBERT L. *The Expansion of South Carolina, 1729–1765* (Kingsport, Tenn.: Southern Publishers, 1940). A careful study.

WASHBURN, WIDCOMB E. *The Governor and the Rebel: A History of Bacon's Rebellion in Virginia* (Chapel Hill: University of North Carolina Press, 1957). Critical of Bacon's motives.

WERTENBAKER, THOMAS J. *Virginia Under the Stuarts, 1607–1688* (Princeton: Princeton University Press, 1914).

*WRIGHT, LOUIS R. *The Atlantic Frontier: Colonial American Civilization, 1607–1763* (New York: Knopf, 1947).

THE FRONTIER IN NEW ENGLAND AND MIDDLE COLONIES

GOODWIN, MAUDE W. *Dutch and English on the Hudson: A Chronicle of Colonial New York* (New Haven: Yale University Press, 1919). A general history of the middle colonies.

HALLER, WILLIAM. *The Puritan Frontier: Town-Planting in New England Colonial Development, 1630–1660* (New York: Columbia University Press, 1951).

HALSEY, FRANCIS W. *The Old New York Frontier, Its Wars with Indians and Tories* (New York: Scribners, 1901).

[208]

HARE, LLOYD C. M. *Thomas Mayhew, Patriarch to the Indians* (New York: Appleton, 1932). New England missionary activity among Indians.

INNIS, H. A. *The Fur Trade in Canada* (New Haven: Yale University Press, 1930). Deals with the fur trade as a cause of expansion.

LEACH, DOUGLAS E. *Flintlock and Tomahawk: New England in King Philip's War* (New York: Macmillan, 1959).

MATHEWS, LOIS K. *The Expansion of New England: The Spread of New England Settlement and Institutions to the Mississippi River, 1620–1865* (Boston: Houghton Mifflin, 1909).

WERTENBAKER, THOMAS J. *The Founding of American Civilization; The Middle Colonies* (New York: Scribner, 1938). About social and everyday life of the people in the middle colonies.

*———. *The Puritan Oligarchy: The Founding of American Civilization* (New York: Scribner's, 1947). A useful general history.

4. THE OLD WEST, 1700–1776

SETTLEMENT OF THE OLD WEST

ABERNETHY, THOMAS P. *Three Virginia Frontiers* (Baton Rouge: University of Louisiana, 1941).

ALVORD, CLARENCE W., and LEE BIDGOOD, *The First Explorations of the Trans-Allegheny Region by the Virginians, 1650–1674* (Cleveland: A. H. Clark, 1912).

BREWSTER, WILLIAM. *The Pennsylvania and New York Frontier—History from 1720 to the Close of the Revolution* (Philadelphia: G. S. MacManus Co., 1954).

BUCK, SOLON J., and ELIZABETH H. *The Planting of Civilization in Western Pennsylvania* (Pittsburgh: University of Pittsburgh Press, 1939).

DILLIN, JOHN G. W. *The Kentucky Rifle: A Study of the Origin and Development of a Purely American Type of Firearm* (Washington, D. C.: National Rifle Association, 1924).

DUNBAR, JOHN R., ed. *The Paxton Boys* (The Hague: M. Nijhoff, 1957).

GLASGOW, MAUDE. *The Scotch-Irish in Northern Ireland and in the American Colonies* (New York: Putnam's, 1936). A popular book.

GRAHAM, IAN C. C. *Colonists from Scotland: Emigration to North America, 1707–1783* (Ithaca: Cornell University Press, 1956). An excellent study.

HIGGINS, RUTH L. *Expansion in New York, with Special Reference to the Eighteenth Century* (Columbus: Ohio State University, 1931). Valuable analysis.

MARK, IRVING. *Agrarian Conflicts in Colonial New York, 1711–1775* (New York: Columbia University, 1940).

MERIWETHER, ROBERT L. *The Expansion of South Carolina, 1729–1765* (Kingsport, Tenn.: Southern Publishers, 1940).

ROSENBERGER, JESSE L. *The Pennsylvania Germans* (Chicago: University of Chicago Press, 1923).

TURNER, FREDERICK JACKSON. *The Frontier in American History* (New York: Holt, 1956). A recent reprint.

WALLACE, PAUL A. W. *Conrad Weiser, 1696–1760, Friend of Colonist and Mohawk* (Philadelphia: University of Pennsylvania Press, 1945). About a Pennsylvania German who mediated between red and white man.

THE FRENCH AND INDIAN WAR

HART, F. H. *The Valley of Virginia in the American Revolution* (Chapel Hill: University of North Carolina Press, 1942). Thorough.

HUNT, GEORGE T. *The Wars of the Iroquois: A Study in Intertribal Trade Relations* (Madison: University of Wisconsin, 1940). Excellent account.

INNIS, H. A. *The Fur Trade in Canada* (New Haven: Yale University Press, 1930). The fur trade as a cause of expansion.

JAHNS, PATRICIA. *The Violent Years: Simon Kenton and the Ohio Kentucky Frontier* (New York: Hastings House, 1962).

KOONTZ, LOUIS K. *Robert Dinwiddie, His Career in American Colonial Government and Westward Expansion* (Glendale, Calif.: A. H. Clark, 1941). Deals with the beginning of the French and Indian War.

MARQUIS, THOMAS G. *The Jesuit Missions: A Chronicle of the Cross in the Wilderness* (Toronto: Brook & Co., 1916).

PARKMAN, FRANCIS. *The Conspiracy of Pontiac and the Indian War After the Conquest of Canada* (2 vols. Boston: Little, Brown, 1933).

PECKHAM, HOWARD H. *Captured by Indians: True Tales of Pioneer Survivors* (New Brunswick, N. H.: Rutgers University Press, 1954). Fourteen true narratives of whites captured by Indians.

THWAITES, REUBEN GOLD. *France in America, 1497–1763* (The American Nation Series. New York: Harper, 1905).

TUCKER, GLENN. *Tecumseh: Vision of Glory* (Indianapolis: Bobbs-Merrill, 1956). Leading biography of possibly the greatest of all Indian leaders.

WAINWRIGHT, NICHOLAS B. *George Croghan: Wilderness Diplomat* (Chapel Hill: University of North Carolina Press, 1959).

WRONG, GEORGE M. *Conquest of New France: A Chronicle of the Colonial Wars* (New Haven: Yale University Press, 1918).

5. THE FRONTIER OF THE EASTERN MISSISSIPPI REGION, 1763–1840

BRITISH WESTERN POLICY AFTER 1763 AND THE AMERICAN REVOLUTION

ALDEN, JOHN R. *The American Revolution, 1775–1783* (New American Nation Series. New York: Harper, 1954). A general history of the Revolution with attention to events in the West.

DRAPER, LYMAN C. *King's Mountain and Its Heroes: History of the Battle of King's Mountain* (Cincinnati: P. G. Thompson, 1881).

HART, F. H. *The Valley of Virginia in the American Revolution* (Chapel Hill: University of North Carolina Press, 1942). Thorough.

HENDERSON, ARCHIBALD. *Conquest of the Old Southwest* (New York: Century Co., 1920).

JAMES, JAMES A. *The Life of George Rogers Clark* (Chicago: University of Chicago Press, 1928). A somewhat impersonal narrative; emphasis on the international background; best single history of the American Revolution in the West.

*PECKHAM, HOWARD. *Pontiac and the Indian Uprising* (Princeton: Princeton University Press, 1947).

PHILLIPS, PAUL C. *The West in the Diplomacy of the American Revolution* (Champaign: University of Illinois Press, 1913).

STEVENS, WAYNE E. *The Northwest Fur Trade, 1763–1800* (Urbana: University of Illinois Press, 1928). Fur trade and British Northwest occupation.

OPENING OF SETTLEMENTS WEST OF THE APPALACHIANS

ABERNETHY, THOMAS P. *From Frontier to Plantation in Tennessee: A Study in Frontier Democracy* (Chapel Hill: University of North Carolina Press, 1932).

ALVORD, CLARENCE W., and LEE BIDGOOD. *The First Explorations of the*

Bibliography

Trans-Allegheny Region by the Virginians, 1650–1674 (Cleveland: A. H. Clark, 1912). Description and travel, a standard work on exploration.

BAILEY, KENNETH. *The Ohio Company of Virginia and the Westward Movement, 1748–1792: A Chapter in the History of the Colonial Frontier* (Glendale, Calif.: A. H. Clark, 1939).

BAKELESS, JOHN. *Daniel Boone* (New York: Morrow, 1939). Documented, critical, favorable, the best biography of Boone.

CLARK, THOMAS D. *A History of Kentucky* (New York: Prentice-Hall, 1937). A college textbook.

DRIVER, CARL S. *John Sevier, Pioneer of the Old Southwest* (Chapel Hill: University of North Carolina Press, 1932). The best biography of a true representative of the Old West.

JACOBS, JAMES R. *Tarnished Warrior: Major-General James Wilkinson* (New York: Macmillan, 1938).

MASON, KATHRYN H. *James Harrod of Kentucky* (Baton Rouge: Louisiana State University Press, 1951).

TALBERT, CHARLES G. *Benjamin Logan: Kentucky Frontiersman* (Lexington: University of Kentucky Press, 1962).

THWAITES, REUBEN G. *Daniel Boone* (New York: Appleton, 1902).

WHITAKER, ARTHUR P. *The Mississippi Question: A Study in Trade, Politics, and Diplomacy, 1795–1803* (New York: Appleton, 1934).

——. *The Spanish-American Frontier, 1783–1795: The Westward Movement and the Spanish Retreat in the Mississippi Valley* (New York: Houghton Mifflin, 1927). A standard work.

AMERICAN GOVERNMENT NORTH OF THE OHIO AND THE PROBLEMS RELATING TO THE INDIANS, BRITISH, AND SPANISH

ABERNETHY, THOMAS P. *Western Lands and the American Revolution* (New York: Appleton-Century, 1937). Development of the trans-Appalachian West from 1750–1789 with reference especially to land policies in effect.

——. *The Burr Conspiracy* (New York: Oxford University Press, 1954). A detailed account.

——. *The South in the New Nation, 1789–1819—A History of the South*, Vol. IV, edited by WENDELL HOLMES STEPHENSON and E. MERTON COULTER. (Baton Rouge: Louisiana State University Press, 1961.) Emphasis upon acquisition of the western part of the South and West Florida, Wilkinson, and Burr.

Bibliography

BARNHART, JOHN D. *Valley of Democracy: The Frontier Versus the Plantation in the Ohio Valley, 1775–1818* (Bloomington: Indiana University Press, 1953).

BOND, BEVERLEY W., JR. *The Civilization of the Old Northwest: A Study of Political, Social, and Economic Development, 1788–1812* (New York: Macmillan, 1934).

BOYD, THOMAS. *Mad Anthony Wayne* (New York: Scribner's, 1929). Full history of Indian wars in the Old Northwest.

DOWNES, RANDOLPH C. *Council Fires on the Upper Ohio: A Narrative of Indian Affairs in the Upper Ohio Valley Until 1795* (Pittsburgh: University of Pittsburgh Press, 1940). Excellent.

JACOBS, JAMES R. *Tarnished Warrior: Major-General James Wilkinson* (New York: Macmillan, 1938).

JENSEN, MERRILL. *The Articles of Confederation: An Interpretation of the Social-Constitutional History of the American Revolution, 1774–1781* (Madison: University of Wisconsin Press, 1948). Emphasizes influence of land speculators in dealing with Western problems.

LYON, E. W. *Louisiana in French Diplomacy, 1759–1804* (Norman: University of Oklahoma Press, 1934). Includes a good history of the Louisiana Purchase.

McCALEB, W. F. *The Aaron Burr Conspiracy* (New York: Wilson-Erickson, 1936).

OGG, FREDERICK A. *The Old Northwest* (New Haven: Yale University Press, 1920).

WHITAKER, ARTHUR P. *The Mississippi Question: A Study in Trade, Politics, and Diplomacy, 1795–1803* (New York: Appleton, 1934). ———. *The Spanish-American Frontier, 1783–1795: The Westward Movement and the Spanish Retreat in the Mississippi Valley* (New York: Houghton Mifflin, 1927).

WILDES, HARRY E. *Anthony Wayne: Trouble Shooter of the American Revolution* (New York: Harcourt, Brace, 1941).

THE WEST AND THE WAR OF 1812

BASSETT, JOHN SPENCER. *The Life of Andrew Jackson* (2d ed. New York: Macmillan, 1931). The scholarly guide to Jackson's life.

CLEAVES, FREEMAN. *Old Tippecanoe: William Henry Harrison and His Times* (New York: Scribner's, 1939).

DILLIN, JOHN G. W. *The Kentucky Rifle: A Study of the Origin and Development of a Purely American Type of Firearm* (Washington,

Bibliography

D. C.: National Rifle Association of America, 1924).

*JAMES, MARQUIS. *Andrew Jackson, Border Captain* (Indianapolis: Bobbs-Merrill, 1933). Jackson's life up to 1824. The rest of Jackson's life is covered in *Andrew Jackson, Portrait of a President* (Indianapolis: Bobbs-Merrill, 1937). James's books have a fine literary style and present a living image of Jackson.

MAYO, BERNARD. *Henry Clay, Spokesman of the New West* (Boston: Houghton Mifflin, 1937). Goes only to War of 1812 but is the most thorough study to that point.

PRATT, JULIUS W. *Expansionists of 1812* (New York: P. Smith, 1949). Scholarly; considers western expansion a prominent factor in the War of 1812.

ROOSEVELT, THEODORE. *The Winning of the West* (4 vols. New York: Putnam, 1889–1896). Deals with the dramatic aspects of national expansion up to 1807.

TUCKER, GLENN. *Tecumseh: Vision of Glory* (Indianapolis: Bobbs-Merrill, 1956).

VAN DEUSEN, GLYNDON G. *The Life of Henry Clay* (Boston: Little, Brown, 1937). The most complete life of Clay.

RENEWED ADVANCE OF THE FRONTIER AFTER THE WAR OF 1812

ABERNETHY, THOMAS P. *From Frontier to Plantation in Tennessee: A Study in Frontier Democracy* (Chapel Hill: University of North Carolina Press, 1932).

*BALDWIN, JOSEPH G. *The Flush Times of Alabama and Mississippi* (New York: Appleton, 1853).

BULEY, R. C. *The Old Northwest, Pioneer Period, 1815–1840* (2 vols. Bloomington: Indiana University Press, 1951). Large, detailed.

COLTON, CALVIN. *The Life and Times of Henry Clay* (New York: A. S. Barnes, 1946).

COULTER, E. M. *Georgia, a Short History* (Chapel Hill: University of North Carolina Press, 1947). Emphasis on early history of Georgia.

CRAVEN, AVERY O. *Soil Exhaustion as a Factor in the Agricultural History of Virginia and Maryland, 1606–1860* (Urbana: University of Illinois, 1926).

DICK, EVERETT. *The Dixie Frontier: A Social History of the Southern Frontier from the First Transmontane Beginnings to the Civil War* (New York: Knopf, 1948).

DODD, WILLIAM E. *The Cotton Kingdom: A Chronicle of the Old*

South (New Haven: Yale University Press, 1919). Brief, interpretive, valuable.

EATON, CLEMENT. *A History of the Old South* (New York: Macmillan, 1949).

FOREMAN, GRANT. *Pioneer Days in the Early Southwest* (Cleveland: A. H. Clark, 1926).

HESSELTINE, WILLIAM B. *The South in American History* (New York: Prentice-Hall, 1943). Textbook and survey of Southern history.

JOHNSON, MARY. *Pioneers of the Old South* (Chronicles of America Series; New Haven: Yale University Press, 1918).

McREYNOLDS, EDWIN C. *Oklahoma: A History of the Sooner State* (Norman: University of Oklahoma Press, 1954).

OGG, F. A. *The Reign of Andrew Jackson: A Chronicle of the Frontier in Politics* (New Haven: Yale University Press, 1919).

PELZER, LOUIS. *Henry Dodge* (Iowa City: State Historical Society of Iowa, 1911).

PHILLIPS, ULLRICH BONNELL. *Life and Labor in the Old South* (Boston: Little, Brown, 1929). Excellent social and economic history.

————. *American Negro Slavery: A Survey of the Supply, Employment, and Control of Negro Labor as Determined by the Plantation Regime* (New York: Appleton, 1918). Deals with the plantation frontier.

SCHACKFORD, JAMES ATKINS. *David Crockett, the Man and the Legend* (Chapel Hill: University of North Carolina Press, 1956). Best and most accurate account.

SCHLESINGER, ARTHUR M., JR. *The Age of Jackson* (Boston: Little, Brown, 1945). Stimulating account of the nature of Jacksonian Democracy.

SKINNER, CONSTANCE L. *Pioneers of the Old Southwest* (New Haven: Yale University Press, 1921). Brief; early migration west of the Appalachians.

*TURNER, FREDERICK JACKSON. *Rise of the New West, 1819–1829* (New York: Harper, 1906). History of the decade with attention to the rise of sectionalism.

————. *The United States, 1830–1850: The Nation and Its Sections* (New York: Holt, 1935). Studies of the sections and sectionalism and the influence of the frontier.

WADE, RICHARD C. *The Urban Frontier: The Rise of Western Cities,*

1790–1830 (Cambridge: Harvard University Press, 1959). An important only book.

WILTSE, CHARLES M. *John C. Calhoun* (3 vols. Indianapolis: Bobbs-Merrill, 1944–1951).

Also consult Sections 10–16 for books on special topics.

6. FROM THE MISSISSIPPI TO THE 98TH MERIDIAN, 1800–1860

SETTLEMENT OF THE LOUISIANA TERRITORY AND TEXAS

BARKER, EUGENE C. *The Life of Stephen F. Austin, Founder of Texas, 1793–1836: A Chapter in the Westward Movement of the Anglo-American People* (Nashville: Cokesbury Press, 1925).

———. *Mexico and Texas, 1821–1835* (Dallas: P. L. Turner Co., 1928).

BEALS, CARLETON. *Stephen F. Austin, Father of Texas* (New York: McGraw-Hill, 1953).

BEERS, HENRY P. *The Western Military Frontier, 1815–1846* (Philadelphia: University of Pennsylvania, 1935).

BINKLEY, WILLIAM C. *The Expansionist Movement in Texas, 1836–1850* (Berkeley: University of California Press, 1935).

———. *The Texas Revolution* (Baton Rouge: Louisiana State University Press, 1952). Texas history to 1846, scholarly.

CHITWOOD, O. P. *John Tyler, Champion of the Old South* (New York: Appleton-Century, 1939). Political biography.

CREEL, GEORGE. *Sam Houston, Colossus in Buckskin* (New York: Cosmopolitan Book Corporation, 1928).

DAVIS, EDWIN A. *Louisiana: The Pelican State* (Baton Rouge: University of Louisiana Press, 1959).

FLETCHER, JOHN G. *Arkansas* (Chapel Hill: University of North Carolina Press, 1947).

FOREMAN, GRANT. *The Five Civilized Tribes* (Norman: University of Oklahoma Press, 1934). About the removal of the tribes from 1830–1843.

———. *The Last Trek of the Indians* (Chicago: University of Chicago Press, 1946). Deals with Black Hawk War and Sauk and Fox Indians.

HANSEN, MARCUS L. *Old Fort Snelling* (Iowa City: State Historical Society of Iowa, 1917).

Bibliography

HOGAN, WILLIAM R. *The Texas Republic—a Social and Economic History* (Norman: University of Oklahoma Press, 1946).

HOLLON, W. EUGENE. *The Lost Pathfinder: Zebulon Montgomery Pike* (Norman: University of Oklahoma Press, 1949). The best account.

JAMES, MARQUIS. *The Raven: A Biography of Sam Houston* (Indianapolis: Bobbs-Merrill, 1929). Literary, Pulitzer prize winner in 1930.

LOOMIS, NOEL M. *The Texan–Santa Fe Pioneers* (Norman: University of Oklahoma Press, 1958).

MCREYNOLDS, EDWIN C. *Missouri: A History of the Crossroads State* (Norman: University of Oklahoma Press, 1962). Comprehensive study of a state that played an important role in American expansion.

RANEY, WILLIAM F. *Wisconsin: A Story of Progress* (New York: Prentice-Hall, 1940). History of Wisconsin from early to recent times.

RICHARDSON, RUPERT N. *Texas, the Lone Star State* (New York: Prentice-Hall, 1943). Textbook history.

SCHMITZ, JOSEPH W. *Texan Statecraft, 1836–1845* (San Antonio: Naylor Co., 1941).

STEVENS, HARRY R. *The Middle West* (New York: Macmillan, 1958). A booklet published for the American Historical Association, Service Center for Teachers of History. A discussion of the historical literature of the Middle West.

THE COMPROMISE OF 1850 AND THE KANSAS-NEBRASKA ACT

GOING, CHARLES B. *David Wilmot, Free Soiler* (New York: Appleton, 1924).

HODDER, FRANK H. "The Authorship of the Compromise of 1850," *Mississippi Valley Historical Review*, Vol. XXII (March, 1936).

———. "The Railroad Background of the Kansas-Nebraska Act," *Mississippi Valley Historical Review*, Vol. XII (June, 1925).

MALIN, JAMES C. *The Nebraska Question, 1852–1854* (Lawrence: University of Kansas Press, 1953).

MONAGHAN, JAY. *Civil War on the Western Border, 1854–1865* (Boston: Little, Brown, 1955).

POAGE, GEORGE R. *Henry Clay and the Whig Party* (Chapel Hill: University of North Carolina Press, 1936). See account of the Compromise of 1850.

SIMMS, HENRY H. *A Decade of Sectional Controversy, 1851–1861* (Chapel Hill: University of North Carolina Press, 1942).

ZORNOW, WILLIAM F. *Kansas: A History of the Jayhawk State* (Norman: University of Oklahoma Press, 1957).

7. THE PACIFIC FRONTIER (1769–1869) AND THE MEXICAN WAR

CALIFORNIA AND THE FAR WEST

BANCROFT, HUBERT HOWE. *History of California* (7 vols. San Francisco: History Co., 1884–1890). The longest history of California.

*BILLINGTON, RAY ALLEN. *The Far Western Frontier, 1830–1860* (New American Nation Series; New York: Harper, 1956).

CAUGHEY, JOHN. *California* (2d ed. New York: Prentice-Hall, 1953). Textbook.

CHAPMAN, CHARLES E. *The Founding of Spanish California: The Northwestward Expansion of Newspain, 1687–1783* (New York: Macmillan Co., 1916).

———. *A History of California—the Spanish Period* (New York: Macmillan, 1921).

CLELAND, ROBERT G. *From Wilderness to Empire: A History of California, 1542–1900* (New York: Knopf, 1944). Popular.

———. *A History of California—the American Period* (New York: Knopf, 1922).

*DANA, RICHARD HENRY. *Two Years Before the Mast* (New York: Harper, 1840, many later editions).

ELLISON, WILLIAM H. *A Self-Governing Domain: California, 1849–1860* (Berkeley: University of California Press, 1950).

GARRISON, GEORGE P. *Westward Extension, 1841–1850* (New York: Harper, 1906). About territorial expansion.

GHENT, W. J. *The Early Far West, 1540–1850* (New York: Tudor Publishing Co., 1936).

GOODWIN, CARDINAL. *The Trans-Mississippi West* (New York: Appleton, 1922).

GUDDE, ERWIN G. *Bigler's Chronicle of the West: The Conquest of California, Discovery of Gold, and Mormon Settlement as Reflected in Henry William Bigler's Diaries* (Berkeley: University of California Press, 1962).

HOOKER, WILLIAM F. *The Prairie Schooner* (Chicago: Saul Bros., 1918). Frontier and pioneer life in the West.

HUNT, RICKWELL D. *John Bidwell: A Prince of California Pioneers* (Caldwell, Idaho: Caxton Printers, 1942).

Bibliography

McCaleb, Walter F. *The Conquest of the West* (New York: Prentice-Hall, 1947).

Merk, Frederick. *Manifest Destiny and Mission in American History: A Reinterpretation* (New York: Alfred A. Knopf, 1963).

Paxson, Frederick L. *The Last American Frontier* (New York: Macmillan, 1910). Pioneer life in the West.

Richman, Irving B. *California Under Spain and Mexico, 1535–1847* (New York: Houghton Mifflin, 1911).

Robinson, Alfred. *Life in California* (New York: Wiley & Putnam, 1846). A contemporary account.

Rolle, Andrew F. *California, a History* (New York: T. Y. Crowell, 1960). Most recent, helpful.

Stewart, George R. *Ordeal by Hunger* (New York: Holt, 1936). A full account of the Donner tragedy.

Zollinger, James P. *Sutter: The Man and His Empire* (New York: Oxford University Press, 1939). A distinguished biography.

THE MEXICAN WAR

*Billington, Ray Allen. *The Far Western Frontier, 1830–1860* (New American Nation Series; New York: Harper, 1956).

Clarke, Dwight L. *Stephen Watts Kearny: Soldier of the West* (Norman: University of Oklahoma Press, 1961). Workmanlike biography, favorable to Kearny, tells of his achievements in the West.

*De Voto, Bernard. *The Year of Decision, 1846* (Boston: Little, Brown, 1943). Literary account of the important events in the Far West in 1846.

Dyer, Brainerd. *Zachary Taylor* (Baton Rouge: Louisiana State University Press, 1946).

Elliott, Charles Winslow. *Winfield Scott: The Soldier and the Man* (New York: Macmillan, 1937).

Garber, Paul N. *The Gadsden Treaty* (Philadelphia: University of Pennsylvania Press, 1923).

Graebner, Norman A. *Empire on the Pacific: A Study in American Continental Expansion* (New York: Ronald Press, 1955). Attributes the expansion to the Pacific to pressure of Eastern merchants for ports on the Pacific.

Hamilton, Holman. *Zachary Taylor, Soldier of the Republic* (2 vols. Indianapolis: Bobbs-Merrill, 1941–1951).

[219]

Sellers, Charles G. *James K. Polk* (Princeton: Princeton University Press, 1957).

*Singletary, Otis. *The Mexican War* (Chicago: University of Chicago Press, 1960).

Smith, Justin H. *The War with Mexico* (2 vols. New York: Macmillan, 1919). The standard history of the war.

THE OREGON COUNTRY

Caughey, John W. *History of the Pacific Coast* (Los Angeles: privately published by the author, 1933).

Drury, C. M. *Marcus Whitman, M.D., Pioneer and Martyr* (Caldwell, Idaho: Caxton Printers, 1937).

Fuller, George W. *A History of the Pacific Northwest* (New York: Knopf, 1931).

Ghent, W. J. *The Road to Oregon: A Chronicle of the Great Emigrant Trail* (New York: Longmans, Green, 1929). An accurate and readable history of the use made of the famous trail.

Goodwin, Cardinal. *The Trans-Mississippi West* (New York: Appleton, 1922).

Jacobs, Melvin C. *Winning Oregon: A Study of an Expansionist Movement* (Caldwell, Idaho: Caxton Printers, 1938).

Johansen, Dorothy O., and Charles M. Gates. *Empire of the Columbia: A History of the Pacific Northwest* (New York: Harper, 1957).

Merk, Frederick. *Albert Gallatin and the Oregon Problem* (Cambridge: Harvard University Press, 1950).

Monoghan, Jay. *The Overland Trail* (Indianapolis: Bobbs-Merrill, 1947). A full account of the Oregon Trail and the various travelers over the north central route to the West.

Powell, Fred W. *Hall Jackson Kelley, Prophet of Oregon* (Portland: Ivy Press, 1917).

Winther, Oscar O. *The Great Northwest—a History* (2d ed. New York: Knopf, 1950). Covers Oregon and Washington and their early history.

Also consult bibliographies for Sections 8, 9, 13, 16.

8. THE INTERMOUNTAIN FRONTIER (1803–1890) AND THE ADMISSION OF THE LAST WESTERN STATES

FIRST PENETRATIONS OF THE WEST

Bakeless, John. *Lewis and Clark, Partners in Discovery* (New York:

Morrow, 1947). Readable narrative of the great expedition and the lives of the two leaders.

BARTLETT, RICHARD A. *Great Surveys of the American West* (Norman: University of Oklahoma Press, 1962).

BOLTON, HERBERT E. *Coronado, Knight of Pueblos and Plains* (New York: Whittlesey House, 1949).

——. *The Padre on Horseback: A Sketch of Eusebio Francisco Kino, S.J., Apostle to the Pimas* (San Francisco: Sonora Press, 1932).

——. *Rim of Christendom: A Biography of Eusebio Francisco Kino, Pacific Coast Pioneer* (New York: Macmillan, 1936). Spanish beginnings in Arizona.

CLELAND, ROBERT G. *This Reckless Breed of Men: The Trappers and Fur Traders of the Southwest* (New York: Knopf, 1950).

GHENT, W. J. *The Early Far West, 1540–1800* (New York: Tudor Publishing Co., 1936).

HAKOLA, JOHN W., ed. *Frontier Omnibus* (Missoula: Montana State University Press, 1962). First-hand accounts of frontier experiences, centers in Montana.

SAUER, CARL. *The Road to Cibola* (Berkeley: University of California Press, 1932). Southwest discovery and exploration.

THE MORMON COLONIZATION OF UTAH

ANDERSON, NELS. *Desert Saints: The Mormon Frontier in Utah* (Chicago: University of Chicago Press, 1942). Vivid picture of the Mormon community in Utah to 1877 and expansion of settlements.

BANCROFT, HUBERT HOWE. *History of Utah, 1540–1886* (San Francisco: History Co., 1889).

CREER, LELAND H. *Utah and the Nation* (Seattle: University of Washington Press, 1929). Relations between the United States and the Mormons.

FURNISS, NORMAN F. *The Mormon Conflict, 1850–1859* (New Haven: Yale University Press, 1960). A discussion of all the factors involved in this conflict.

HAFEN, LE ROY R., and ANN W. HAFEN, eds. *The Utah Expedition, 1857–1858: A Documentary Account of the United States Military Movement Under Colonel Albert Sidney Johnston; and the Resistance by Brigham Young and the Mormon Nauvoo Legion* (Glendale, Calif.: A. H. Clark, 1958).

HUNTER, MILTON R. *Brigham Young the Colonizer* (Salt Lake City:

Deseret News Press, 1940). Good narrative of expansion of the Mormon settlements.

MORGAN, DALE L. *The Great Salt Lake* (Indianapolis: Bobbs-Merrill, 1947).

MULDER, WILLIAM. *Homeward to Zion: The Mormon Migration from Scandinavia* (Minneapolis: University of Minnesota Press, 1957). Scholarly.

WERNER, M. R. *Brigham Young* (New York: Harcourt, Brace, 1925). A popular biography.

YOUNG, LEVI E. *The Founding of Utah* (New York: Scribner's, 1923). Economic history.

STATE-MAKING WEST OF THE MISSISSIPPI

ATHEARN, ROBERT G. *High Country Empire: The High Plains and Rockies* (New York: McGraw-Hill, 1960). About the seven states around Wyoming, their history, and miners' and farmers' protests.

BECK, WARREN A. *New Mexico: A History of Four Centuries* (Norman: University of Oklahoma Press, 1962). Brief.

BRANCH, E. DOUGLAS. *Westward: The Romance of the American Frontier* (New York: Appleton, 1930). History of the West—frontier and pioneer life.

BRIGGS, HAROLD E. *Frontiers of the Northwest: A History of the Upper Missouri Valley* (New York: Appleton-Century, 1940). Treats the various frontiers in the Dakotas, Montana, Wyoming.

BURLINGAME, MERRILL G. *The Montana Frontier* (Helena: State Publishing Co., 1942). Frontier and pioneer life in Montana.

FERGUSON, ERNA. *New Mexico: A Pageant of Three Peoples* (New York: Knopf, 1951). A state history.

FOREMAN, GRANT. *Advancing the Frontier, 1830–1860* (Norman: University of Oklahoma Press, 1933). Deals with the Indian removals; scholarly.

———. *Fort Gibson—a Brief History* (Norman: University of Oklahoma Press, 1936).

FRITZ, PERCY STANLEY. *Colorado, the Centennial State* (New York: Prentice-Hall, 1941). Standard textbook.

HOMSHER, LOLA M., ed. *South Pass, 1868: James Chisholm's Journal of the Wyoming Gold Rush* (Lincoln: University of Nebraska Press, 1960). The main contribution is in social history; a journal of exceptional quality.

Bibliography

HOWARD, JOSEPH KINSEY. *Montana: High, Wide, and Handsome* (New Haven: Yale University Press, 1943). Exploitation and economic problems of Montana. Useful, accurate.

HUNTER, MILTON R. *Utah, the Story of Her People, 1540–1947: A Centennial History of Utah* (Salt Lake City: Deseret News Press, 1946). A state history.

JOHANSEN, DOROTHY O., and CHARLES M. GATES. *Empire of the Columbia: A History of the Pacific Northwest* (New York: Harper, 1957).

KELEHER, WILLIAM A. *The Fabulous Frontier* (Rev. ed. Albuquerque: University of New Mexico Press, 1962). Basic source book on southeastern New Mexico since 1846.

LAMAR, HOWARD ROBERTS. *Dakota Territory, 1861–1889: A Study of Frontier Politics* (New Haven: Yale University Press, 1956).

LOCKWOOD, FRANCIS CUMMINS. *Pioneer Days in Arizona, from the Spanish Occupation to Statehood* (New York: Macmillan, 1932).

McREYNOLDS, EDWIN C. *Oklahoma: A History of the Sooner State* (Norman: University of Oklahoma Press, 1954).

OLSON, JAMES C. *History of Nebraska* (Lincoln: University of Nebraska Press, 1955). Probably best written of any state history up to its time; for student and general reader.

RICHARDSON, RUPERT N., and CARL COKE RISTER. *The Greater Southwest: The Economic, Social, and Cultural Development of Kansas, Oklahoma, Texas, Utah, Colorado, Nevada, New Mexico, Arizona, and California from the Spanish Conquest to the Twentieth Century* (Glendale, Calif.: A. H. Clark, 1934).

RISTER, CARL C. *Land Hunger: David L. Payne and the Oklahoma Boomers* (Norman: University of Oklahoma Press, 1942).

SCHELL, HERBERT S. *History of South Dakota* (Lincoln: University of Nebraska Press, 1961). Well-balanced survey of a state's history; emphasizes problems inherent in the Northern Plains environment.

———. *South Dakota, Its Beginnings and Growth* (New York: American Book Co., 1942).

*STEGNER, WALLACE. *Beyond the Hundredth Meridian: John Wesley Powell and the Second Opening of the West* (Boston: Houghton Mifflin, 1954). Interesting book on a most important student of the West.

Also consult bibliographies for Sections 7, 9, 10,
and 17–23 for special subjects.

9. THE GREAT PLAINS, 1865–1890

ATHEARN, ROBERT G. *High Country Empire: The High Plains and Rockies* (New York: McGraw-Hill, 1960).

BABCOCK, KENDRIC C. *The Scandinavian Element in the United States* (Urbana: University of Illinois, 1914). Combines the story of Danish, Swedish, and Norwegian immigration.

BLEGEN, THEODORE C. *Norwegian Migration to America* (2 vols. Northfield, Minn.: Norwegian-American Historical Association, 1931–1940).

*BRANCH, E. DOUGLAS. *The Hunting of the Buffalo* (New York: Appleton, 1929).

BRILL, CHARLES J. *Conquest of the Southern Plains: Uncensored Narrative of the Battle of the Washita and Custer's Southern Campaign* (Oklahoma City: Golden Saga Publishers, 1938).

COOK, JOHN R. *The Border and the Buffalo: The Untold Story of the Southwest Plains* (Chicago: R. R. Donnelley, 1938).

DALE, EDWARD E. *The Indians of the Southwest: A Century of Development Under the United States* (Norman: University of Oklahoma Press, 1949). A broad survey of Indian administration in the Southwest.

DICK, EVERETT. *The Sod-House Frontier, 1854–1890: A Social History of the Northern Plains from the Creation of Kansas and Nebraska to the Admission of the Dakotas* (New York: Appleton-Century, 1937). The settlement of Kansas, Nebraska, and the Dakotas.

GODDARD, PLINY E. *Indians of the Southwest* (New York: American Museum Press, 1927).

HYDE, GEORGE E. *A Sioux Chronicle* (Norman: University of Oklahoma Press, 1956).

PAXSON, FREDERICK L. *The Last American Frontier* (New York: Macmillan, 1910).

POWELL, JOHN WESLEY. *Report on the Lands of the Arid Region of the United States* (Cambridge, Mass.: Harvard University Press, 1962). An important pioneer study of the Western environment.

RICHARDSON, RUPERT N. *The Comanche Barrier to South Plains Settlement: A Century and a Half of Savage Resistance to the Advancing White Frontier* (Glendale, Calif.: A. H. Clark, 1933).

RISTER, CARL COKE. *Fort Griffin on the Texas Frontier* (Norman: University of Oklahoma, 1956).

ROE, FRANK G. *The Indian and the Horse* (Norman: University of Oklahoma Press, 1955). Influence of the introduction of horses on Indian culture.

SANDOZ, MARI. *The Buffalo Hunters: The Story of the Hide Men* (New York: Hastings House, 1954).

SHANNON, FRED A. *The Farmers' Last Frontier, Agriculture, 1860–1897* (New York: Farrar & Rinehart, 1945).

SMITH, CHARLES HENRY. *The Coming of the Russian Mennonites* (Berne, Indiana: Mennonite Book Concern, 1927).

*WEBB, WALTER PRESCOTT. *The Great Plains* (Boston: Ginn, 1931). The great survey of the problems of conquering the unique environment of the West beyond the 98th meridian.

———. *The Texas Rangers* (New York: Houghton Mifflin, 1935).

WELLMAN, PAUL I. *Death on the Prairie: The Thirty Years' Struggle for the Western Plains* (New York: Macmillan, 1934).

———. *The Trampling Herd* (New York: Carrick & Evans, 1939). Popular story of range cattle industry.

WISSLER, CLARK. *North American Indians of the Plains* (New York: American Museum of Natural History, 1934).

WYMAN, WALKER D. *The Wild Horse of the West* (Reissue; Lincoln: University of Nebraska Press, 1962).

Also consult bibliographies for Sections 10, 21, and 22.

10. THE PACIFICATION OF THE INDIANS

CAUGHEY, JOHN W. *McGillivray of the Creeks* (Norman: University of Oklahoma Press, 1938). Careful study.

DOWNES, RANDOLPH C. *Council Fires on the Upper Ohio: A Narrative of Indian Affairs in the Upper Ohio Valley Until 1795* (Pittsburgh: University of Pittsburgh Press, 1940). Excellent.

FOREMAN, GRANT. *Indians and Pioneers* (New Haven: Yale University Press, 1930). Deals with Indian removals.

GABRIEL, RALPH H. *The Lure of the Frontier: A Story of Race Conflict* (New Haven: Yale University Press, 1929). Illustrated history of the whole American frontier; text explains pictures.

HAGAN, WILLIAM T. *American Indians* (Reissue, Chicago: University of Chicago Press, 1962).

HODGE, FREDERICK W., ed. *Handbook of American Indians North of Mexico* (2 vols. Washington, D.C.: Government Printing Office,

1907–1910). Meticulous, encyclopedic, immense.

HORSMAN, REGINALD. "American Indian Policy in the Old Northwest, 1783–1812," *William and Mary Quarterly* (Jan., 1961).

KROEBER, ALFRED L. *Cultural and Natural Areas of Native North America* (Berkeley: University of California Press, 1939). Classification and admirable treatment of American Indians.

MacLEOD, WILLIAM CHRISTIE. *The American Indian Frontier* (New York: Knopf, 1928). Synthesis of Indian-white relations in America from Indian viewpoint.

*McNICKLE, D'ARCY. *The Indian Tribes of the United States. Ethnic and Cultural Survival* (London and New York: Oxford University Press, 1962). Excellent brief survey of Indian policy and history.

McNITT, FRANK. *The Indian Traders* (Norman: University of Oklahoma Press, 1962). Delineations of personalities of leading traders.

*NEIHARDT, JOHN G. *Black Elk Speaks, Being the Life Story of a Holy Man of the Oglala Sioux* (Lincoln: University of Nebraska, 1961).

PECKHAM, HOWARD H. *Captured by Indians: True Tales of Pioneer Survivors* (New Brunswick, N.J.: Rutgers University Press, 1954). Fourteen true narratives.

POUND, MERRITT B. *Benjamin Hawkins, Indian Agent* (Athens: University of Georgia Press, 1951).

PRIESTLEY, HERBERT I. *The Coming of the White Man, 1492–1848* (New York: Macmillan, 1929).

TEBBEL, JOHN, and KEITH JENNISON. *The American Indian Wars* (New York: Harper, 1960).

UNDERHILL, RUTH M. *Red Man's America: A History of Indians in the United States* (Chicago: University of Chicago Press, 1953). Excellent one-volume survey; deals with Indian culture.

WISSLER, CLARK. *The American Indian: An Introduction to the Anthropology of the New World* (3d ed. New York: P. Smith, 1950). Considered best introductory book having an anthropological approach.

———. *Indians of the United States: Four Centuries of Their History and Culture* (Garden City, N.Y.: Doubleday, 1946).

———. *North American Indians of the Plains* (New York: American Museum of Natural History, 1934).

INDIAN WARS AND GOVERNMENT INDIAN POLICY TO 1850

BEERS, HENRY P. *The Western Military Frontier, 1815–1846* (Philadelphia: University of Pennsylvania, 1935).

CORKRAN, DAVID H. *The Cherokee Frontier: Conflict and Survival, 1740–62* (Norman: University of Oklahoma Press, 1962).

DEBO, ANGIE. *And Still the Waters Run* (Princeton: Princeton University Press, 1940). About the exploitation of the Five Civilized Tribes after 1800.

FOREMAN, GRANT. *Advancing the Frontier, 1830–1860* (Norman: University of Oklahoma Press, 1933). Indian removals.

———. *The Five Civilized Tribes* (Norman: University of Oklahoma Press, 1934).

———. *Indian Removal: The Emigration of the Five Civilized Tribes of Indians* (Norman: University of Oklahoma Press, 1932).

———. *The Last Trek of the Indians* (Chicago: University of Chicago Press, 1946). Deals with Black Hawk War and Sauk and Fox Indians.

HARMON, GEORGE D. *Sixty Years of Indian Affairs—Political, Economic, and Diplomatic, 1789–1850* (Chapel Hill: University of North Carolina Press, 1941). A review of federal Indian policy and removals.

McREYNOLDS, EDWIN C. *The Seminoles* (Norman: University of Oklahoma Press, 1957).

*MARCY, RANDOLPH B. *Thirty Years of Army Life on the Border* (Reprint of the 1866 edition, Philadelphia: Lippincott, 1963).

MORRISON, WILLIAM B. *Military Posts and Camps in Oklahoma* (Oklahoma City: Harlow Publishing Corp., 1936).

NYE, WILBUR S. *Carbine and Lance: The Story of Old Fort Sill* (Norman: University of Oklahoma Press, 1937). Accurate.

PRUCHA, FRANCIS PAUL. *American Indian Policy in the Formative Years: The Indian Trade and Intercourse Acts, 1790–1834* (Cambridge, Mass.: Harvard University Press, 1962). Thorough study and fair, understanding analysis of federal Indian policy.

SEYMOUR, FLORA W. *Indian Agents of the Old Frontier* (New York: Appleton-Century, 1941). Federal administrators among the Indians after 1869 under the peace policy of Grant.

INDIAN WARFARE AND POLICY AFTER 1850

BEAL, MERRILL D. *Chief Joseph and the Nez Perce War* (Seattle: University of Washington Press, 1962). A full account of the Nez Perce War.

BIGELOW, JOHN, JR. *On the Bloody Trail of Geronimo* (Los Angeles:

Westernlore Press, 1958). Reminiscences of an army officer.

*Brandes, Ray. *Frontier Military Posts of Arizona* (Globe, Ariz.: Dale Stuart King, 1960).

Brown, Dee. *Fort Phil Kearny: An American Saga* (New York: Putnam's, 1962). Lively narrative about the Bozeman Trail and the Fetterman disaster.

*Conway, John. *The Apache Wars: The Exciting True Saga of the Bloody Conflict Between the White Men and the Apache Indians on the Southwest Frontier* (Derby, Conn.: Monarch Books, 1961).

*————. *The Texas Rangers: A Concise History of the Most Colorful Law Enforcement Group in the Frontier West* (Derby, Conn.: Monarch Books, 1963).

Dale, Edward E. *The Indians of the Southwest: A Century of Development Under the United States* (Norman: University of Oklahoma Press, 1949).

Danker, Donald F., ed. *Man of the Plains: Recollections of Luther North, 1856–1882* (Lincoln: University of Nebraska Press, 1961).

Dunn, Jacob P. *Massacres of the Mountains: A History of Indian Wars of the Far West* (New York: Harper, 1886).

Estergreen, M. Morgan. *Kit Carson—a Portrait in Courage* (Norman: University of Oklahoma Press, 1963).

Ewers, J. C. *The Blackfeet: Raiders on the Northwestern Plains* (Norman: University of Oklahoma Press, 1958).

Fee, Chester A. *Chief Joseph: The Biography of a Great Indian* (New York: Wilson-Erickson, 1936).

Goddard, Pliny E. *Indians of the Southwest* (New York: American Museum Press, 1927).

Hodge, Frederick W., ed. *Handbook of American Indians North of Mexico* (2 vols. Washington, D.C.: Government Printing Office, 1908–1910).

Hyde, George E. *A Sioux Chronicle* (Norman: University of Oklahoma Press, 1956).

Jackson, Helen Hunt. *A Century of Dishonor: A Sketch of the U.S. Government's Dealings with Some of the Indian Tribes* (New York: Harper, 1881).

Lockwood, Frank C. *The Apache Indians* (New York: Macmillan, 1938). A history; realistic in approach.

Mazzanovich, Anton. *Trailing Geronimo* (Los Angeles: Gem Publishing Co., 1926).

Bibliography

MONAGHAN, JAY. *Custer: The Life of General George Armstrong Custer* (Boston: Little, Brown, 1959).

OEHLER, C. M. *The Great Sioux Uprising* (New York: Oxford University Press, 1959).

PRIEST, LORING B. *Uncle Sam's Stepchildren: The Reformation of United States Indian Policy, 1865–1887* (New Brunswick, N.J.: Rutgers University Press, 1942). Indian policy before the Dawes Act; the standard work.

SABIN, EDWIN L. *Kit Carson Days, 1809–1868* (2 vols. New York: Press of the Pioneers, 1935). An accurate account of Carson's life.

*SANDOZ, MARI. *Crazy Horse, the Strange Man of the Oglalas: A Biography* (New York: Hastings House, 1942).

SHERIDAN, PHILIP H. *Personal Memoirs* (New York: Appleton, 1902).

STEWART, EDGAR I. *Custer's Luck* (Norman: University of Oklahoma Press, 1955). A minute reconstruction of the background and events of the disaster. Best work on the subject.

UNDERHILL, RUTH M. *Red Man's America: A History of Indians in the United States* (Chicago: University of Chicago Press, 1953). Good survey.

VESTAL, STANLEY. *Sitting Bull, Champion of the Sioux* (Norman: University of Oklahoma Press, 1957). Takes Indian point of view.

WELLMAN, PAUL I. *Death on the Desert: Seventy Years of War for the American West* (Philadelphia: Lippincott, 1947).

———. *Death on the Prairie: The Thirty Years' Struggle for the Western Plains* (New York: Macmillan, 1934).

Also consult bibliographies for Sections 5, 9, and 22.

11. THE DISTRIBUTION OF THE PUBLIC DOMAIN

ABERNETHY, THOMAS P. *Western Lands and the American Revolution* (New York: Appleton-Century, 1937). Development of the trans-Appalachian West from 1750 to 1789 with reference especially to land policies.

CARSTENSEN, VERNON. *The Public Lands: Studies in the History of the Public Domain* (Madison: University of Wisconsin Press, 1963).

CHAMBERS, WILLIAM N. *Old Bullion Benton, Senator from the New West: Thomas Hart Benton, 1782–1858* (Boston: Little, Brown, 1956). Best biography of Benton.

FORD, AMELIA C. *Colonial Precedents of Our National Land System*

Bibliography

(Madison: University of Wisconsin Press, 1910).

GATES, PAUL W. *Fifty Million Acres: Conflicts over Kansas Land Policy, 1854–1890* (Ithaca: Cornell University Press, 1954).

———. "The Homestead Act in an Incongruous Land System," *American Historical Review*, Vol. XLI (July, 1936).

———. "The Role of the Land Speculator in Western Development," *Pennsylvania Magazine of History and Biography*, Vol. LXVI (July, 1942).

DONALDSON, THOMAS C., ed. *The Public Domain, Its History* (Washington, D.C.: Government Printing Office, 1881). A book of documents.

HARRIS, MARSHALL. *Origin of the Land Tenure System in the United States* (Ames: Iowa State College Press, 1953). Shows the colonial influences.

HIBBARD, BENJAMIN H. *A History of the Public Land Policies* (New York: P. Smith, 1939). The basic history of federal land distribution.

ISE, JOHN. *The United States Forest Policy* (New Haven: Yale University Press, 1920).

PATTISON, WILLIAM D. *The Beginnings of the American Rectangular Land Survey System, 1754–1800* (Chicago: University of Chicago, 1957).

*ROBBINS, ROY M. *Our Landed Heritage: The Public Domain, 1776–1936* (New York: P. Smith, 1950). Traces effects of land distribution policies.

SAKOLSKI, AARON M. *The Great American Land Bubble: The Amazing Story of Land-Grabbing, Speculations, and Booms from Colonial Days to the Present Time* (New York: Harper, 1932).

———. *Land Tenure and Land Taxation in America* (New York: R. Shcalkenback Foundation, 1957).

SANBORN, JOHN B. *Congressional Grants of Land in Aid of Railways* (Madison: University of Wisconsin, 1899).

SHANNON, FRED A. *The Farmers' Last Frontier, 1860–1897* (New York: Farrar & Rinehart, 1945).

SMITH, ELBERT B. *Magnificent Missourian: The Life of Thomas Hart Benton* (Philadelphia: Lippincott, 1957).

STEPHENSON, GEORGE M. *The Political History of the Public Lands from 1840–1862, from Preemption to Homestead* (Boston: R. G. Badger, 1917).

Tatter, Henry. "State and Federal Land Policy During the Confederation," *Agricultural History*, Vol. IX (Oct., 1955).

Treat, Payson J. *The National Land System, 1785–1820* (New York: E. G. Treat & Co., 1910).

Wellington, Raynor G. *Political and Sectional Influence of the Public Lands, 1828–1842* (Cambridge, Mass.: Riverside Press, 1914).

Young, Mary E. "Indian Removal and Land Allotment: The Civilized Tribes and Jacksonian Justice," *American Historical Review*, Vol. LXIV (Oct., 1958).

12. FINANCIAL PROBLEMS OF FRONTIER AREAS

Atherton, Lewis. *Pioneer Merchant in Mid-America* (Columbia: University of Missouri Press, 1939).

——. *The Southern Country Store* (Baton Rouge: Louisiana State University, 1950).

Baldwin, Leland. *Whisky Rebels: The Story of a Frontier Uprising* (Pittsburgh: University of Pittsburgh Press, 1939). Spirited narrative and sympathetic with the Westerners.

Brown, Richard Maxwell. *The South Carolina Regulators* (Cambridge, Mass.: Belknap Press, Harvard University, 1963).

Cable, J. R. *The Bank of the State of Missouri* (New York: Columbia University Press, 1923).

Catterall, Ralph C. H. *The Second Bank of the United States* (Chicago: University of Chicago Press, 1902, 1960).

Dewey, Davis R. *Financial History of the United States* (12th ed. New York: Longmans, Green, 1934). A standard work since 1903.

——. *States Banking Before the Civil War* (Washington, D.C.: Government Printing Office, 1910).

Esarey, Logan. *State Banking in Indiana, 1814–1873* (Bloomington: University of Indiana Press, 1912).

Fine, Nathan. *Labor and Farmer Parties* (New York: Rand School of Social Science, 1928).

Gammon, Samuel R. *The Presidential Campaign of 1832* (Baltimore: Johns Hopkins Press, 1922).

Hammond, Bray. *Banks and Politics in America from the Revolution to the Civil War* (Princeton: Princeton University Press, 1957).

Helderman, Leonard C. *National and State Banks* (Boston: Houghton Mifflin, 1931).

Bibliography

HEPBURN, A. BARTON. *A History of the Currency in the United States* (Rev. ed. New York: Macmillan, 1924).

JENKS, LELAND H. *The Migration of British Capital to 1875* (New York: Knopf, 1927).

MCCRANE, REGINALD C. *The Panic of 1837* (Chicago: University of Chicago Press, 1924).

SCOTT, WILLIAM A. *The Repudiation of State Debts* (New York: T. Y. Crowell, 1893).

SELLERS, CHARLES G., JR. "Banking and Politics in Jackson's Tennessee, 1817–1827," *Mississippi Valley Historical Review*, Vol. XLI (June, 1954).

SHANNON, FRED A. *The Farmer's Last Frontier, Agriculture, 1860–1897* (New York: Farrar & Rinehart, 1945).

SPARKS, EARL S. *History and Theory of Agricultural Credit in the United States* (New York: T. Y. Crowell, 1932).

STEINER, BERNARD C. *Life of Roger Brooke Taney* (Baltimore: Williams & Wilkins, 1922).

SWISHER, CARL B. *Roger B. Taney* (New York: Macmillan, 1935).

WILDMAN, M. S. *Money Inflation in the United States* (New York: Putnam's, 1905).

13. THE SOLUTION OF TRANSPORTATION PROBLEMS

EARLY PROGRESS IN TRANSPORTATION

BALDWIN, LELAND D. *The Keelboat Age on Western Waters* (Pittsburgh: University of Pennsylvania Press, 1941).

CHAPMAN, ARTHUR. *The Pony Express: The Record of a Romantic Adventure in Business* (New York: Putnam, 1932).

DUNBAR, SEYMOUR. *A History of Travel in America* (New York: Tudor, 1937). Includes social history, internal migration; illustrated.

FREDERICK, J. V. *Ben Holliday the Stagecoach King* (Glendale: A. H. Clark, 1940).

GEPHART, WILLIAM F. *Transportation and Industrial Development in the Mid-West* (New York: Columbia University Press, 1909).

HAFEN, LEROY. *The Overland Mail, 1849–1869: Promoter of Settlement, Precurser of Railroads* (Cleveland: A. H. Clark, 1926).

HOOKER, WILLIAM F. *The Prairie Schooner* (Chicago: Saul Bros., 1918). Pioneer life in the West.

Bibliography

HULBERT, ARCHER B. *The Cumberland Road* (Cleveland: A. H. Clark, 1904).

———. *The Great American Canals* (Cleveland: A. H. Clark, 1904).

———. *Waterways of Western Expansion: The Ohio River and Its Tributaries* (Cleveland: A. H. Clark, 1903).

HUNGERFORD, EDWARD. *Wells Fargo—Advancing the American Frontier* (New York: Random House, 1949).

HUNTER, LOUIS C. *Steamboats on the Western Rivers: An Economic and Technological History* (Cambridge, Mass.: Harvard University Press, 1949). A thorough and standard survey of the steamboat era.

JACKSON, W. TURRENTINE. *Wagon Roads West: A Study of Federal Road Surveys and Construction in the Trans-Mississippi West, 1846–1869* (Berkeley: University of California Press, 1952).

JORDAN, P. D. *National Road* (Indianapolis: Bobbs-Merrill, 1948). A narrative history of the Cumberland Road.

KEIR, ROBERT MALCOLM. *The March of Commerce* (New Haven: Yale University Press, 1927). Transportation history.

LASS, WILLIAM E. *A History of Steamboating on the Upper Missouri* (Lincoln: University of Nebraska Press, 1962). About steamboats and life on the Missouri River between Sioux City and Fort Benton in the 1800's.

MEYER, BALTHASAR H., ed. *History of Transportation in the United States Before 1860* (Washington, D.C.: Carnegie Institution, 1917).

SETTLE, RAYMOND W., and MARY L. *Empire on Wheels* (Stanford, Calif.: Stanford University Press, 1949). Freighting in the West.

———. *Saddles and Spurs: The Pony Express Saga* (Harrisburg, Pa.: Stackpole Co., 1955). The best history of the Pony Express.

TAYLOR, GEORGE R. *The Transportation Revolution, 1815–1860* (New York: Rinehart, 1951).

WAGGONER, MADELINE S. *The Long Haul West: The Great Canal Era, 1817–1850* (New York: Putnam, 1958). Popular style.

WINTHER, OSCAR O. *Express and Stagecoach Days in California, from the Gold Rush to the Civil War* (Stanford, Calif.: Stanford University Press, 1936).

———. *Via Wesetrn Express and Stagecoach* (Stanford, Calif.: Stanford University Press, 1945).

———. *Transportation on the Trans-Mississippi West Frontier, 1865–1890* (New York: Holt, Rinehart & Winston, 1964).

Bibliography

THE RAILROADS

ATHEARN, ROBERT G. *Rebel of the Rockies: A History of the Denver and Rio Grande Western Railroad* (New Haven: Yale University Press, 1962).

CLARK, IRA G. *Then Came the Railroads: The Century from Steam to Diesel in the Southwest* (Norman: University of Oklahoma Press, 1958).

CORLISS, CARLTON J. *Main Line of Mid-America: The Story of the Illinois Central* (New York: Creative Age Press, 1951).

DAGGETT, STUART. *Chapters on the History of the Southern Pacific* (New York: Ronald Press, 1922).

HEDGES, JAMES B. *Henry Villard and the Railways of the Northwest* (New Haven: Yale University Press, 1930).

HILL, FOREST G. *Roads, Rails, and Waterways: The Army Engineers and Early Transportation* (Norman: University of Oklahoma Press, 1957).

LARSON, HENRIETTA. *Jay Cooke, Private Banker* (Cambridge: Harvard University Press, 1936).

LEWIS, OSCAR. *The Big Four: The Story of Huntington, Stanford, Hopkins, and Crocker, and of the Building of the Central Pacific* (New York: Knopf, 1941). Good reading, authentic.

MARSHALL, JAMES. *Santa Fe, the Railroad That Built an Empire* (New York: Random House, 1945).

MOODY, JOHN. *The Railroad Builders* (New Haven: Yale University Press, 1919).

PYLE, JOSEPH G. *The Life of James J. Hill* (2 vols. New York: Doubleday, Page, 1917).

QUIETT, GLENN C. *They Built the West: An Epic of Rails and Cities* (New York: Appleton-Century, 1934). Influence of railroads and of individuals in the growth of the cities of the West.

RIEGEL, ROBERT E. *The Story of the Western Railroads* (New York: Macmillan, 1926).

SANBORN, JOHN B. *Congressional Grants of Land in Aid of Railways* (Madison: University of Wisconsin, 1899).

STARR, JOHN W., JR. *One Hundred Years of American Railroading* (New York: Dodd, Mead, 1928).

TAYLOR, GEORGE R. *The Transportation Revolution, 1815–1860* (New York: Rinehart, 1951).

THOMPSON, ROBERT L. *Wiring a Continent: The History of the Tele-*

graph Industry in the United States, 1832–1866 (Princeton: Princeton University Press, 1947).

WATERS, L. L. *Steel Rails to Santa Fe* (Lawrence: University of Kansas Press, 1950).

14. GOVERNMENT AND POLITICS ON THE FRONTIER

In most of the literature of the frontier the subject of government and politics is interwoven with other aspects of the frontier experience and is usually described incidentally in connection with the narrative of frontier events. Biographies of political leaders should be consulted for the personal element in local politics. State, territorial, and local histories should be examined for discussions of government and politics.

ABERNETHY, THOMAS P. *Three Virginia Frontiers* (Baton Rouge: University of Louisiana, 1941).

———. *From Frontier to Plantation in Tennessee: A Study in Frontier Democracy* (Chapel Hill: University of North Carolina Press, 1932).

*BALDWIN, JOSEPH G. *The Flush Times of Alabama and Mississippi* (New York: Appleton, 1853). Courthouse experiences of a lawyer and politician in the frontier South.

BROMAGE, ARTHUR W. *American County Government* (New York: Harper, 1933).

*BUCK, SOLON J. *The Agrarian Crusade: A Chronicle of the Farmer in Politics* (New Haven: Yale University Press, 1920). Grangers and Populists in politics.

BULEY, R. C. *The Old Northwest, Pioneer Period, 1815–1840* (2 vols.; Bloomington: Indiana University Press, 1951).

CARTER, C. E., comp. and ed. *The Territorial Papers of the United States* (18 vols.; Washington: Government Printing Office, 1934–1952).

CAUGHEY, JOHN. *Their Majesties, the Mob* (Chicago: University of Chicago Press, 1960). A useful collection of documents on vigilantism; not an apologetic treatment.

DICK, EVERETT. *The Dixie Frontier* (New York: Knopf, 1948).

FAIRLIE, JOHN A., and C. M. KNEIER. *County Government and Administration* (New York: Century Co., 1930).

FERGUSON, R. J. *Early Western Pennsylvania Politics* (Pittsburgh: University of Pittsburgh Press, 1938).

FRINK, MAURICE. *Cow Country Cavalcade: Eighty Years of the Wyoming*

Bibliography

Stock Growers Association (Denver: Old West Publishing Co., 1954).

GARD, WAYNE. *Frontier Justice* (Norman: University of Oklahoma Press, 1949). The rise of order and law west of the Mississippi in the three decades after the Civil War.

HAYWOOD, JOHN. *The Civil and Political History of the State of Tennessee* (Nashville: Heiskell and Brown, 1891).

HENDRICKS, GEORGE D. *The Bad Man of the West* (rev. ed.; San Antonio: Naylor Co., 1959).

*HICKS, JOHN D. *The Populist Revolt: A History of the Farmers' Alliance and the People's Party* (Minneapolis: University of Minnesota Press, 1931).

HOCKETT, H. C. *Western Influence on Political Parties to 1825* (Columbus: Ohio State University, 1917).

JENSEN, MERRILL. *The Articles of Confederation: An Interpretation of the Social-Constitutional History of the American Revolution, 1774–1781* (Madison: University of Wisconsin Press, 1948). Deals with political problems during a formative period.

LAMAR, H. R. *Dakota Territory, 1861–1889: A Study in Frontier Politics* (New Haven: Yale University Press, 1956).

McLAUGHLIN, A. C. *The Confederation and the Constitution, 1783–1789* (New York: Harper, 1905).

———. *A Constitutional History of the United States* (New York: Appleton-Century, 1936). Covers development of state constitutions.

NEVINS, ALLAN. *The American States during and after the Revolution, 1775–1789* (New York: Macmillan, 1924).

*OSGOOD, ERNEST S. *The Day of the Cattleman* (Minneapolis: University of Minnesota Press, 1929). Material on livestock associations.

PAUL, RODMAN W. *Mining Frontiers of the Far West, 1848–1880* (Histories of the American Frontier Series [New York: Holt, Rinehart and Winston, 1963]). Chap. 8, "First Attempts at Self-Government."

POMEROY, EARL S. *The Territories and the United States, 1861–1890: Studies in Colonial Administration* (Philadelphia: University of Pennsylvania Press, 1947).

*ROBBINS, ROY M. *Our Landed Heritage: The Public Domain, 1776–1936* (New York: P. Smith, 1950). Claims associations.

SCHLESINGER, ARTHUR M., JR. *The Age of Jackson* (Boston: Little, Brown, 1945). Jacksonian democracy and politics.

SCHMITZ, JOSEPH W. *Texas Statecraft, 1836–1845* (San Antonio: Naylor

Co., 1941). Solely on government during a period that was e
frontier.

SHAMBAUGH, B. F. *History of the Constitutions of Iowa* (Des M
Iowa State Historical Society, 1902). The Iowa constitution ᴄᴇ.ᴠᴄᴜ
as a model to other states.

SHINN, CHARLES H. *Mining Camps: A Study in American Frontier
Government* (New York: Scribner's, 1885).

*SHIRLEY, GLENN. *Law West of the Pecos: A History of Frontier Justice
in the Indian Territory, 1834–1896* (New York: Holt, Rinehart and
Winston, 1957). The career of a frontier judge who dealt with
outlaws.

SPENCE, CLARK C. "The Territorial Officers of Montana, 1864–1889,"
Pacific Historical Review, Vol. XXX (May, 1961).

THORPE, F. N., comp. *Federal and State Constitutions, Colonial Charters and Other Organic Laws* (7 vols.; Washington: Government
Printing Office, 1909). Covers the whole range of American government.

*TOCQUEVILLE, ALEXIS DE. *Democracy in America* (2 vols.; New York:
Knopf, 1945).

TURNER, F. J. "Western State Making in the Revolutionary Era,"
American Historical Review, Vol. I (New York, 1895——).

WADE, RICHARD. *The Urban Frontier* (Cambridge: Harvard University
Press, 1959). Much discussion of problems of early city governments.

WELLS, MERLE W. "Territorial Governments in the Inland Empire,"
Pacific Northwest Quarterly, Vol. XLIV (April, 1953).

WILLIAMS, SAMUEL C. *History of the Lost State of Franklin* (rev. ed.;
New York: The Press of the Pioneers, 1933) .

15. PEOPLE AND RELIGION ON THE FRONTIER

CHARACTER OF WESTWARD MIGRANTS AND THEIR ACTIVITIES
ON THE FRONTIER

*ATHEARN, ROBERT. *Westward the Briton* (New York: Scribner's, 1953).

BABCOCK, KENDRIC C. *The Scandinavian Element in the United States*
(Urbana: University of Illinois, 1914).

*BALDWIN, JOSEPH G. *The Flush Times of Alabama and Mississippi*
(New York: Appleton, 1853).

BLEGEN, THEODORE C. *Norwegian Migration to America* (2 vols. Northfield, Minn.: Norwegian-American Historical Association, 1931–1940).

BRIDENBAUGH, CARL. *Myths and Realities: Societies of the Colonial South* (Baton Rouge: Louisiana State University Press, 1952).

CLARK, THOMAS D. *The Rampaging Frontier: Manners and Humors of Pioneer Days in the South and the Middle West* (Indianapolis: Bobbs-Merrill, 1939). Humorously told social history.

DICK, EVERETT. *The Dixie Frontier: A Social History of the Southern Frontier from the First Transmontane Beginnings to the Civil War* (New York: Knopf, 1948).

——. *The Sod-House Frontier, 1854–1890: A Social History of the Northern Plains from the Creation of Kansas and Nebraska to the Admission of the Dakotas* (New York: Appleton-Century, 1937).

ESAREY, LOGAN. *The Indiana Home* (Bloomington: Indiana University Press, 1953). Essays on pioneer life.

*FILSON, JOHN. *Discovery, Settlement, and Present State of Kentucky* (New York: Citadel Press, 1962).

GABRIEL, RALPH H. *The Lure of the Frontier; A Story of Race Conflict* (New Haven: Yale University Press, 1929). Illustrated history.

HALL, JAMES. *Sketches of History, Life, and Manners of the West* (2 vols. Philadelphia: H. Hall, 1835).

HANSEN, MARCUS L. *The Atlantic Migration, 1607–1860: A History of the Continuing Settlement of the United States* (Cambridge: Harvard University Press, 1940).

HOUGH, EMERSON. *The Passing of the Frontier* (New Haven: Yale University Press, 1918).

HUMPHREY, SETH K. *Following the Prairie Frontier* (Minneapolis: University of Minnesota Press, 1931). Frontier and pioneer life in the West.

MEINE, FRANKLIN J. *Tall Tales of the Southwest* (New York: Knopf, 1930).

MOORE, ARTHUR K. *The Frontier Mind* (Lexington: University of Kentucky Press, 1957).

OWSLEY, FRANK L. *Plain Folk of the Old South* (Baton Rouge: Louisiana State University Press, 1949). Social and economic history.

*PHILLIPS, ULRICH B. *Life and Labor in the Old South* (Boston: Little, Brown, 1929). Excellent social and economic history.

PICKARD, MADGE E., and R. C. BULEY. *The Midwest Pioneer, His Ills, Cures and Doctors* (Crawfordsville, Indiana: R. E. Banta, 1945).

Non-technical; covers early history of medicine.

POWER, RICHARD L. *Planting Corn Belt Culture: The Impress of the Upland Southerner and Yankee in the Old Northwest* (Indianapolis: Indiana Historical Society, 1953). Studies a kind of culture conflict between Southern and New England immigrants north of the Ohio River.

SCHAFER, JOSEPH. *The Social History of American Agriculture* (New York: Macmillan, 1936). Comprehensive survey; economic as well as social history.

*TOCQUEVILLE, ALEXIS DE. *Democracy in America* (2 vols. New York: Knopf, 1945, many other editions).

THORNTHWAITE, CHARLES W., and HELEN I. SLENTZ. *Internal Migration in the United States* (Philadelphia: University of Pennsylvania Press, 1934).

*TROLLOPE, FRANCES. *Domestic Manners of the Americans* (2 vols. London: Whittaker, Treacher, 1832).

WITTKE, CARL. *We Who Built America: The Saga of the Immigrant* (New York: Prentice-Hall, 1939). Excellent survey of American immigration by ethnic groups.

*WRIGHT, LOUIS. *Culture on the Moving Frontier* (Bloomington: Indiana University Press, 1955).

FRONTIER RELIGION

ASBURY, HERBERT. *A Methodist Saint: The Life of Bishop Asbury* (New York: Knopf, 1927). Satirical description of early Methodism and of backwoods society.

DUREN, WILLIAM LARKIN. *Francis Asbury, Founder of American Methodism and Unofficial Minister of State* (New York: Macmillan, 1928). Laudatory biography.

GOODYKOONTZ, COLIN B. *Home Missions on the American Frontier* (Caldwell, Idaho: Caxton Printers, 1939).

JOHNSON, CHARLES A. *The Frontier Camp Meeting, Religion's Hardest Time* (Dallas: Southern Methodist University Press, 1955). History of camp meetings.

MAYNARD, T. *The Story of American Catholicism* (New York: Macmillan, 1941).

NOTTINGHAM, E. K. *Methodism and the Frontier* (New York: Columbia University Press, 1941).

Bibliography

POSEY, W. B. *The Development of Methodism in the Old Southwest* (Tuscaloosa, Ala.: Weatherford Printing Co., 1933).

SMITH, TIMOTHY L. *Revivalism and Social Reform in Mid-Nineteenth Century America* (New York: Abingdon Press, 1957).

SWEET, WILLIAM WARREN. *The Presbyterians, 1783–1840* (New York: Harper, 1936).

——. *Methodism in American History* (New York: Methodist Book Concern, 1933).

——. *Revivalism in America, Its Origin, Growth, and Decline* (New York: Scribner's, 1944).

——. *Story of Religion in America* (2d rev. ed. New York: Harper, 1950). Survey by the outstanding authority on this subject.

Also consult bibliographies for Sections 16 and 23.

THE MORMONS AND UTOPIAN COLONIES

ANDERSON, NELS. *Desert Saints: The Mormon Frontier in Utah* (Chicago: University of Chicago Press, 1942). Vivid picture of the Mormon community in Utah to 1877 and about expansion of their settlements.

ARRINGTON, LEONARD J. *Great Basin Kingdom: An Economic History of the Latter-Day Saints, 1830–1900* (Cambridge, Mass.: Harvard University Press, 1958).

BANCROFT, HUBERT HOWE. *History of Utah, 1540–1886* (San Francisco: History Co., 1889).

BESTOR, A. E. *Backwoods Utopias: The Sectarian and Owenite Phases of Communitarian Socialism in America, 1663–1829* (Philadelphia: University of Pennsylvania Press, 1950).

BRODIE, F. M. *No Man Knows My History: The Life of Joseph Smith* (New York: Knopf, 1945). Trustworthy account.

BROOKS, JUANITA. *The Mountain Meadows Massacre* (Norman: University of Oklahoma Press, 1963). An updated, comprehensive account; unbiased.

EVANS, JOHN HENRY. *Joseph Smith: An American Prophet* (New York: Macmillan, 1933).

HINDS, W. A. *American Communities and Cooperative Colonies* (Chicago: C. H. Kerr & Co., 1908).

HUNTER, MILTON R. *Brigham Young the Colonizer* (Salt Lake City: Deseret News Press, 1940). Tells of expansion of Mormon settlements.

Bibliography

LINN, W. A. *The Story of the Mormons, from the Date of Their Origin to the Year 1901* (New York: Macmillan, 1923).

McNIFF, WILLIAM J. *Heaven on Earth: A Planned Mormon Society* (Oxford, Ohio: Mississippi Valley Press, 1946). Mormons and their social life.

MULDER, WILLIAM, and A. RUSSELL MORTENSEN, eds. *Among the Mormons: Historic Accounts by Contemporary Observers* (New York: Knopf, 1958).

NORDHOFF, CHARLES. *The Communistic Societies of the United States* (New York: Harper, 1875).

NOYES, JOHN H. *American Socialisms* (Philadelphia: Lippincott, 1870).

O'DEA, THOMAS F. *The Mormons* (Chicago: University of Chicago Press, 1957). Objective and thorough; best general history of Mormons.

SHAMBAUGH, B. M. H. *Amana: The Community of True Inspiration* (Iowa City: State Historical Society, 1908). An account of the most successful of the religious communitarians.

SHAW, ALBERT. *Icaria: A Chapter in the History of Communism* (New York: Putnam's, 1884).

WERNER, M. R. *Brigham Young* (New York: Harcourt, Brace, 1925). A popular biography.

YOUNG, LEVI E. *The Founding of Utah* (New York: Scribner's, 1923). An economic history.

Also consult bibliographies for Sections 8, 16, and 23.

16. CULTURE ON THE FRONTIER

AUDUBON, JOHN JAMES. *Delineations of American Scenery and Character* (New York: G. A. Baker & Co., 1826).

*BALDWIN, JOSEPH G. *The Flush Times of Alabama and Mississippi* (New York: Appleton, 1853).

BARTRAM, WILLIAM. *Travels* (New York: Barnes and Noble, 1900). First published in Philadelphia in 1791.

BRADBURY, JOHN. *Travels in the Interior of America* (Liverpool: Smith & Galway, 1817; Cleveland: A. H. Clark, 1914).

CARTWRIGHT, PETER. *Autobiography* (New York: Carlton & Porter, 1857).

COTTERILL, ROBERT S. *The Old South: The Geographic, Economic, Social, Political, and Cultural Expansion, Institutions, and Nation-*

Bibliography

alism of the Ante-Bellum South (2d ed., rev. Glendale: A. H. Clark, 1939).

DANA, RICHARD HENRY. *Two Years Before the Mast* (New York: Harper, 1840). Describes life in California in the Mexican period.

DRAKE, DANIEL. *Pioneer Life in Kentucky, 1785–1800* (Cincinnati: R. Clarke & Co., 1870).

DUNBAR, SEYMOUR. *A History of Travel in America* (New York: Tudor, 1937).

*FILSON, JOHN. *Discovery, Settlement, and Present State of Kentucky* (1784; Louisville: G. P. Morgan & Co., 1930).

FLANAGAN, J. T. *James Hall, Literary Pioneer of the Ohio Valley* (Minneapolis: University of Minnesota Press, 1941).

FLINT, TIMOTHY. *Recollections of the Last Ten Years* (Boston: Cummings, Hilbard & Co., 1826).

*GARLAND, HAMLIN. *Boy Life on the Prairie* (New York: Macmillan, 1899).

HALL, JAMES. *Notes on the Western States* (Philadelphia: H. Hall, 1836, and many later editions).

HORNE, EMMET FIELD. *Daniel Drake (1785–1852): Pioneer Physician of the Midwest* (Philadelphia: University of Pennsylvania Press, 1961). Thorough, readable treatment of the various activities of Drake.

KENNEDY, MILDRED FILLMORE, and A. F. HARLOW. *Schoolmaster of Yesteryear: A Three-Generation Story, 1820–1919* (New York: Whittlesey House, 1940).

KIRKPATRICK, JOHN E. *Timothy Flint: Pioneer, Missionary, Author, Editor, 1780–1840* (Cleveland: A. H. Clark, 1911).

*LONGSTREET, A. B. *Georgia Scenes* (Augusta, Ga.: privately printed, 1835).

McCRACKEN, HAROLD. *Frederick Remington, Artist of the Old West* (Philadelphia: Lippincott, 1947).

MICHAUX, ANDRE. *Travels* (London: 1825; also in REUBEN G. THWAITES' *Early Western Travels* [Cleveland: A. H. Clark, 1904]).

NUTTALL, THOMAS. *A Journal of Travels into the Arkansas Territory, During the Year 1819* (Philadelphia: T. Palmer, 1821).

PATTIE, JAMES OHIO. *The Personal Narrative of James O. Pattie* (Cincinnati: John H. Wood, 1831).

POWER, RICHARD L. *Planting Corn Belt Culture: The Impress of the Upland Southerner and Yankee in the Old Northwest* (Indianapolis: Indiana Historical Society, 1953).

TAFT, ROBERT. *Artists and Illustrators of the Old West, 1850–1900* (New York: Scribner, 1953).

*TROLLOPE, FRANCES. *Domestic Manners of the Americans* (2 vols. London: Whittaker, Treacher, 1832).

*WRIGHT, LOUIS. *Culture on the Moving Frontier* (Bloomington: Indiana University Press, 1955).

Also consult bibliographies for Sections 15 and 23.

17. EARLY AGRICULTURAL FRONTIERS

BARDOLPH, RICHARD. *Agricultural Literature and the Early Illinois Farmer* (Urbana: University of Illinois Press, 1948).

BIDWELL, PERCY W., and JOHN I. FALCONER. *History of Agriculture in the Northern United States, 1620–1860* (Washington, D.C.: Carnegie Institution of Washington, 1925).

BROOKS, EUGENE C. *The Story of Corn and the Westward Migration* (New York: Rand, McNally, 1916).

BROWN, HARRY B., and JACOB OSBORN WARE. *Cotton* (3d ed. New York: McGraw-Hill, 1958).

COTTERILL, ROBERT S. *The Old South* (2d ed., rev. Glendale: A. H. Clark, 1939).

CRAVEN, AVERY O. *Soil Exhaustion as a Factor in the Agricultural History of Virginia and Maryland, 1606–1860* (Urbana: University of Illinois, 1926).

DODD, WILLIAM E. *The Cotton Kingdom: A Chronicle of the Old South* (New Haven: Yale University Press, 1919).

EATON, CLEMENT. *The Growth of Southern Civilization, 1790–1860* (New York: Harper, 1961). Covers rise of the Cotton Kingdom, slavery, and plantation systems.

——. *A History of the Old South* (New York: Macmillan, 1949).

GATES, PAUL W. *The Farmer's Age: Agriculture, 1815–1860* (New York: Holt, Rinehart, & Winston, 1960). A survey of agricultural history in the North and South during a pioneering age.

GRAY, LEWIS CECIL. *History of Agriculture in the Southern United States to 1860* (2 vols. Washington, D.C.: Carnegie Institution of Washington, 1933).

*HANSEN, MARCUS L. *The Atlantic Migration, 1607–1860: A History of the Continuing Settlement of the United States* (Cambridge: Harvard University Press, 1940).

Bibliography

HENLEIN, PAUL C. *The Cattle Kingdom in the Ohio Valley, 1783–1860* (Lexington: University of Kentucky Press, 1958).

McNALL, NEIL A. *An Agricultural History of the Genesee Valley, 1790–1860* (Philadelphia: University of Pennsylvania Press, 1952).

MOORE, JOHN H. *Agriculture in the Ante-Bellum Mississippi* (New York: Bookman Associates, 1958).

PHILLIPS, ULRICH B. *American Negro Slavery: A Survey of the Supply, Employment, and Control of Negro Labor as Determined by the Plantation Regime* (New York: Appleton, 1918). Deals with the plantation frontier.

*———. *Life and Labor in the Old South* (Boston: Little, Brown, 1929). Excellent economic history.

SCHAFER, JOSEPH. *History of Agriculture in Wisconsin* (Madison: University of Wisconsin, 1922).

———. *The Social History of American Agriculture* (New York: Macmillan, 1936).

THOMPSON, JAMES W. *A History of Livestock Raising in the United States, 1607–1860* (Washington, D.C.: U.S. Department of Agriculture, 1942).

*WITTKE, CARL. *We Who Built America: The Saga of the Immigrant* (New York: Prentice-Hall, 1939). About the immigrant nationalities who settled the land.

Also consult bibliographies for Sections 5 and 22.

18. THE FUR BUSINESS

ALTER, J. CECIL. *James Bridger, Trapper, Frontiersman, Scout, and Guide* (Columbus, Ohio: Long's College Book Co., 1951). Accurate.

BIEBER, RALPH, ed. *James Josiah Webb: Adventures in the Santa Fe Trade, 1844–1847* (Glendale: A. H. Clark, 1931).

BRIGGS, HAROLD E. *Frontiers of the Northwest: A History of the Upper Missouri Valley* (New York: Appleton-Century, 1940). Treats the various frontiers in the Dakotas, Montana, and Wyoming.

CHITTENDEN, H. M. *The American Fur Trade of the Far West: A History of the Pioneer Trading Posts and Early Fur Companies of the Missouri Valley and Rocky Mountains and of the Overland Commerce With Santa Fe* (Academic reprints. 2 vols. Stanford, Calif.: Stanford University Press, 1954). Has long been the authority and most comprehensive work on the fur trade.

Bibliography

CLELAND, ROBERT GLASS. *This Reckless Breed of Men: The Trappers and Fur Traders of the Southwest* (New York: Knopf, 1950).

COMAN, KATHERINE. *Economic Beginnings of the Far West: How We Won the Land Beyond the Mississippi* (2 vols. New York: Macmillan, 1925). See Vol. I.

*DE VOTO, BERNARD. *Across the Wide Missouri* (Boston: Houghton Mifflin, 1947). Description and significance of the fur trade from 1833–1838.

ESTERGREEN, M. MORGAN. *Kit Carson: A Portrait in Courage* (Norman: University of Oklahoma Press, 1963).

FAVOUR, ALPHEUS H. *Old Bill Williams, Mountain Man* (Chapel Hill: University of North Carolina Press, 1936). Accurate.

FOREMAN, GRANT. *Pioneer Days in the Early Southwest* (Cleveland: A. H. Clark, 1926).

GALBRAITH, JOHN S. *The Hudson's Bay Company as an Imperial Factor, 1821–1869* (Berkeley: University of California Press, 1957). Thorough, scholarly.

GOODWIN, CARDINAL. *The Trans-Mississippi West* (New York: Appleton, 1922).

*GREGG, JOSIAH. *Commerce of the Prairies; or the Journal of a Santa Fe Trader* (Norman: University of Oklahoma Press, 1954). Originally published in 1844; first-hand account of the commerce over this famous trail.

HAFEN, LEROY, and W. J. GHENT. *Broken Hand: The Life Story of Thomas Fitzpatrick, Chief of the Mountain Men* (Denver: Old West Publishing Co., 1931).

HARRIS, BURTON. *John Colter—His Years in the Rockies* (New York: Scribner, 1952).

INNIS, H. A. *The Fur Trade in Canada* (New Haven: Yale University Press, 1930). The fur trade as cause of expansion.

*IRVING, WASHINGTON. *Astoria; or Anecdotes of an Enterprise Beyond the Rocky Mountains* (2 vols. Philadelphia: Carey, Lea, & Blanchard, 1836). Sometimes inaccurate.

JOHANSEN, DOROTHY O., and CHARLES M. GATES. *Empire of the Columbia: A History of the Pacific Northwest* (New York: Harper, 1957).

JOHNSON, IDA A. *The Michigan Fur Trade* (Lansing: Michigan Historical Commission, 1919).

LAUT, AGNES. *The Fur Trade of America* (New York: Macmillan, 1921).

Bibliography

*LAVENDER, DAVID S. *Bent's Fort* (Garden City, New York: Doubleday, 1954).

LENT, D. GENEVA. *West of the Mountains: James Sinclair and the Hudson's Bay Company* (Seattle: University of Washington Press, 1963). Considerable detail on Hudson's Bay posts in North America.

MORGAN, DALE L. *Jedidiah Smith and the Opening of the West* (Indianapolis: Bobbs-Merrill, 1953). One of the best histories of the Rocky Mountain fur trade.

NASATIR, A. P., ed. *Before Lewis and Clark: Documents Illustrating the History of Missouri, 1785–1804* (2 vols. St. Louis: St. Louis Historical Documents Foundation, 1952).

*PATTIE, JAMES O. *Personal Narrative* (Cincinnati: E. H. Flint, 1833). Also later editions.

PEAKE, ORA B. *A History of the United States Indian Factory System, 1795–1822* (Denver: Sage Books, 1954). First attempt of the U.S. Government to enter into competition with private business.

PHILLIPS, PAUL C. *The Fur Trade* (2 vols. Norman: University of Oklahoma Press, 1961). Now the most comprehensive story of the North American fur trade.

PORTER, KENNETH W. *John Jacob Astor, Business Man* (2 vols. Cambridge, Mass.: Harvard University Press, 1931).

RICHARDSON, RUPERT N., and CARL COKE RISTER. *The Greater Southwest* (Glendale: A. H. Clark, 1934).

*RUSSELL, CARL P. *Guns on the Early Frontiers* (Berkeley: University of California Press, 1957). Discusses weapons of the mountain men.

SABIN, EDWIN L. *Kit Carson Days, 1809–1868* (2 vols. New York: Press of the Pioneers, 1935).

STEVENS, WAYNE E. *The Northwest Fur Trade, 1763–1800* (Urbana: University of Illinois Press, 1928).

SUNDER, JOHN E. *Bill Sublette, Mountain Man* (Norman: University of Oklahoma Press, 1959). One of the best biographies of the mountain men.

THWAITES, REUBEN GOLD, ed. *Early Western Travels, 1748–1846* (2 vols. Cleveland: A. H. Clark Co., 1904–1907). Check for accounts dealing with the fur trade.

VANDIVEER, CLARENCE A. *The Fur Trade and Early Western Exploration* (Cleveland: A. H. Clark, 1929). About the fur trade in Canada and in the Northwest; useful history.

VESTAL, STANLEY. *Mountain Men* (Boston: Houghton Mifflin, 1937). A succession of dramatic episodes that surveys the story of the fur men in the Rockies.

WINTHER, OSCAR O. *The Great Northwest—a History* (2d ed. New York: Knopf, 1950). Discusses fur trade in early Oregon and Washington.

Also consult bibliographies for Sections 7, 8, and 19.

19. EXPLORATION AND TRAILS IN THE FAR WEST

BAKELESS, JOHN. *Lewis and Clark, Partners in Discovery* (New York: Morrow, 1947). Readable narrative of the great expedition and the lives of the two leaders.

BIDDLE, NICHOLAS. *History of the Expedition Under the Command of Captains Lewis and Clark* (2 vols. Philadelphia: Bradford & Innskeep, 1814).

DALE, H. C., ed. *The Ashley-Smith Explorations and the Discovery of a Central Route to the Pacific, 1822–1829, with the Original Journals* (Cleveland: A. H. Clark, 1918).

DUFFUS, R. L. *The Santa Fe Trail* (New York: Longmans, Green, 1930). Popular.

GHENT, W. J. *The Road to Oregon: A Chronicle of the Great Emigrant Trail* (New York: Longmans, Green, 1929).

GOETZMANN, WILLIAM H. *Army Exploration in the American West, 1803–1863* (New Haven: Yale University Press, 1959). Excellent book.

GOODWIN, CARDINAL. *The Trans-Mississippi West* (New York: Appleton, 1922).

HOLLON, W. EUGENE. *Beyond the Cross Timbers: The Travels of Randolph B. Marcy, 1812–1887* (Norman: University of Oklahoma Press, 1955).

HULBERT, ARCHER B. *Forty-Niners: The Chronicle of the California Trail* (Boston: Little, Brown, 1931). Excerpts from diaries of forty-niners.

JACKSON, DONALD, ed. *Letters of the Lewis and Clark Expedition, 1783–1854* (Urbana: University of Illinois Press, 1962). Probably the most significant contribution relating to the Lewis and Clark Expedition in nearly sixty years.

*JAMES, THOMAS. *Three Years Among the Indians and Mexicans* (First published in 1846; later editions. Publication data for 1846 edition not available).

McCaleb, Walter F. *The Conquest of the West* (New York: Prentice-Hall, 1947).

Monoghan, Jay. *The Overland Trail* (Indianapolis: Bobbs-Merrill, 1947). A full account of the Oregon Trail and its uses.

Nevins, Allen. *Fremont, Pathmarker of the West* (New York: Longmans, Green, 1955).

*Parkman, Francis. *The Oregon Trail: Sketches of Prairie and Rocky Mountain Life* (New York: Modern Library, 1949). Available in many editions. Like an adventure story.

Rollins, Philip A., ed. *The Discovery of the Oregon Trail: Robert Stuart's Narrative of His Overland Trip Eastward from Astoria in 1812–13* (New York: Scribner's, 1935).

Stewart, George R. *The California Trail* (New York: McGraw-Hill, 1962).

Sullivan, Maurice S. *Jedidiah Smith, Trader and Trail Blazer* (New York: Press of the Pioneers, 1936).

——, ed. *The Travels of Jedidiah Smith* (Santa Ana, Calif.: Fine Arts Press, 1934).

Thwaites, Reuben Gold, ed. *Early Western Travels, 1748–1846* (32 vols. Cleveland: A. H. Clark, 1904–1907). Check for accounts of various explorations.

Also consult bibliographies for Sections 7 and 18.

20. MINING BOOMS

Bennett, Estelline. *Old Deadwood Days* (New York: Scribner's, 1935).

Briggs, Harold E. *Frontiers of the Northwest: A History of the Upper Missouri Valley* (New York: Appleton-Century, 1940). Deals with the mining frontiers in the Dakotas, Montana, and Wyoming.

Burlingame, Merrill G. *The Montana Frontier* (Helena, Mont.: State Publishing Co., 1942).

Canfield, Chauncey L., ed. *The Diary of a Forty-Niner* (New York: M. Shapard Co., 1906). About California gold discoveries.

Caughey, John W. *Gold Is the Cornerstone* (Berkeley: University of California Press, 1948). Deals with the significance of the gold rush.

——, ed. *Rushing for Gold* (Berkeley: University of California Press, 1949).

*Coblentz, Stanton A. *Villains and Vigilantes: The Story of James*

Bibliography

King, of William, and Pioneer Justice in California (New York: Wilson-Erickson, 1936).

CONNOR, DANIEL E. Joseph Reddeford Walker and the Arizona Adventure (Norman: University of Oklahoma Press, 1957).

COULTER, E. MERTON. Auraria: The Story of a Georgia Gold-Mining Town (Athens: University of Georgia Press, 1956).

DE QUILLE, DAN. The Big Bonanza (New York: Knopf, 1947). All about Comstock Lode mining in Nevada.

ELLISON, WILLIAM H. A Self-Governing Domain—California, 1849–1860 (Berkeley: University of California Press, 1950).

EMRICH, DUNCAN, ed. Comstock Bonanza (New York: Vanguard Press, 1950). About the frontier in Nevada, selections from Mark Twain, Bret Harte and others.

GARD, WAYNE. Frontier Justice (Norman: University of Oklahoma Press, 1949). Trustworthy.

GLASSCOCK, C. B. Gold in Them Hills: The Story of the West's Last Wild Mining Days (Indianapolis: Bobbs-Merrill, 1932). Popular; deals with Comstock Lode.

GREEVER, WILLIAM S. The Bonanza West: The Story of the Western Mining Rushes, 1848–1900 (Norman: University of Oklahoma Press, 1963).

HULBERT, ARCHER B. Forty-Niners: The Chronicle of the California Trail (Boston: Little, Brown, 1931).

JACKSON, JOSEPH H. Anybody's Gold: The Story of California's Mining Towns (New York: Appleton-Century, 1941). Life in mining towns.

LOCKWOOD, FRANCIS C. Pioneer Days in Arizona, from the Spanish Occupation to Statehood (New York: Macmillan, 1932).

LYMAN, G. D. The Saga of the Comstock Lode: Boom Days in Virginia City (New York: Scribner, 1947). Excitingly written and accurate.

MICHELSON, MIRIAM. The Wonderlode of Silver and Gold (Boston: Stratford Co., 1934). Nevada mining.

MURDOCK, ANGUS. Boom Copper: The Story of the First United States Mining Boom (New York: Macmillan, 1943).

NUNIS, DOYCE B., JR., ed. The Golden Frontier: The Recollections of Herman Francis Reinhart, 1851–1869 (Austin: University of Texas Press, 1962). Covers a wide range of experience of one who took part in many of the mining booms in the West.

PAUL, RODMAN W. California Gold: The Beginning of Mining in the Far West (Cambridge, Mass.: Harvard University Press, 1947).

———. *Mining Frontiers of the Far West, 1848–1880.* (*Histories of the American Frontier* Series; Holt, Rinehart, & Winston, 1963).

PELZER, LOUIS. *Henry Dodge* (Iowa City: State Historical Society of Iowa, 1911).

QUIETT, GLENN C. *Pay Dirt: A Panorama of American Gold-Rushes* (New York: Appleton-Century, 1936). Popular.

RICKARD, THOMAS A. *A History of American Mining* (New York: McGraw-Hill, 1932). Chapters on mining booms and techniques in mining.

SHINN, CHARLES H. *Land Laws of Mining Districts* (Baltimore: Johns Hopkins University, 1885).

———. *Mining Camps: A Study in American Frontier Government* (New York: Scribner's, 1885).

SMITH, GRANT H. *The History of the Comstock Lode, 1850–1920* (Reno, Nevada: State Bureau of Mines, 1943).

SPENCE, CLARK C. *British Investments and the American Mining Frontier, 1860–1901* (Ithaca: Cornell University Press, 1958).

STEWART, ROBERT E., JR., and MARY FRANCES STEWART. *Adolph Sutro— a Biography* (Berkeley: Howell-North, 1962). An accurate biography.

TAYLOR, BAYARD. *Eldorado; or Adventures in the Path of Empire, Comprising a Voyage to California Via Monterey, Pictures of the Gold Region, and Experiences of Mexican Travel* (2 vols. 2d ed. New York: Putnam, 1850).

WHITE, STEWART E. *The Forty Niners: A Chronicle of the California Trail and El Dorado* (New Haven: Yale University Press, 1918).

WILBUR, MARGUERITE E., ed. *A Pioneer at Sutter's Fort, 1846–1850: The Adventures of Heinrich Lienhard* (Los Angeles: Calafia Society, 1941).

WILLISON, G. F. *Here They Dug the Gold* (New York: Brentano's, 1931).

Also consult bibliographies for Sections 7, 8, and 16.

21. CATTLEMEN'S FRONTIER

ADAMS, ANDY. *The Log of a Cowboy* (Boston: Houghton Mifflin, 1903). Accurate description of cowboy life on the trail by one who lived the cowboy's life.

ATHERTON, LEWIS. *The Cattle Kings* (Bloomington: Indiana University

Press, 1961). Careful analysis of the early ranchers of the Cattle Kingdom.

*BRANCH, E. DOUGLAS. *The Cowboy and His Interpreters* (New York: Appleton, 1926).

*BRONSON, EDGAR BEECHER. *Reminiscences of a Ranchman* (Reprint, Lincoln: University of Nebraska Press, 1962).

BROWN, DEE, and MARTIN SCHMITT. *Trail Driving Days* (New York: Scribner, 1952). A picture book mainly.

CLAWSON, MARION. *The Western Range Livestock Industry* (New York: McGraw-Hill, 1950).

COLLINSON, FRANK. *Life in the Saddle* (Norman: University of Oklahoma Press, 1963). Autobiography of a literate cowboy.

DALE, EDWARD E. *The Cow Country* (Norman: University of Oklahoma Press, 1942). Written by a scholar and one-time cowboy.

——. *The Range Cattle Industry* (Norman: University of Oklahoma Press, 1930). A standard work on the significance and the economics of the range cattle industry up to the 1920's.

*DOBIE, J. FRANK. *The Longhorns* (Boston: Little, Brown, 1941).

——. *A Vaquero of the Brush Country* (Dallas: Southwest Press, 1929). Enjoyable reading.

FLETCHER, ROBERT H. *Free Grass to Fences: The Montana Cattle Range Story* (New York: University Publishers for the Historical Society of Montana, 1960).

FRANTZ, JOE B., and JULIAN CHOATE, JR. *The American Cowboy: The Myth and Reality* (Norman: University of Oklahoma Press, 1955). A study of cowboy literature and the cowboy.

FRINK, MAURICE. *Cow Country Cavalcade: Eighty Years of the Wyoming Stock Grower's Association* (Denver: Old West Publishing Co., 1954).

——, et al. *When Grass Was King: Contributions to the Western Range Cattle Industry Study* (Boulder: University of Colorado Press, 1956).

GARD, WAYNE. *The Chisholm Trail* (Norman: University of Oklahoma Press, 1954). Best book on the experiences of cattle drivers and the long drives.

HALEY, J. EVETTS. *Charles Goodnight: Cowman and Plainsman* (Chicago: Lakeside Press, 1929).

——. *The XIT Ranch of Texas, and the Early Days of the Llano*

Bibliography

Estacado (New edition, Norman: University of Oklahoma Press, 1953).

HAZELTON, JOHN M. *History and Handbook of Hereford Cattle and Hereford Bull Index* (Kansas City: Hereford Journal Co., 1925).

HENLEIN, PAUL C. *The Cattle Kingdom in the Ohio Valley, 1783–1860* (Lexington: University of Kentucky Press, 1958).

HOLDEN, WILLIAM C. *The Spur Ranch: A Study of the Inclosed Ranch Phase of the Cattle Industry in Texas* (Boston: Christopher Publishing House, 1934).

HUNTER, J. MARVIN, ed. *Trail Drivers of Texas* (San Antonio: Jackson Printing Co., 1920). Reminiscences of cowmen.

LANG, LINCOLN. *Ranching with Roosevelt, by a Companion Rancher, Lincoln A. Lang* (Philadelphia: Lippincott, 1926).

*OSGOOD, ERNEST S. *The Day of the Cattlemen* (Minneapolis: University of Minnesota Press, 1929). A leading book on the range cattle industry.

PEAKE, O. B. *The Colorado Range Cattle Industry* (Glendale: A. H. Clark, 1939).

PELZER, LOUIS. *The Cattlemen's Frontier: A Record of the Trans-Mississippi Cattle Industry, 1850–1890* (Glendale: A. H. Clark, 1936). Another standard work.

ROLLINS, PHILIP ASHTON. *The Cowboy: An Unconventional History of Civilization on the Old-Time Cattle Range* (Rev. New York: Scribner, 1936).

SANDOZ, MARI. *The Cattlemen from the Rio Grande Across the Far Marias* (New York: Hastings House, 1958).

SHANNON, FRED A. *The Farmer's Last Frontier, Agriculture, 1860–1877* (New York: Farrar & Rinehart, 1945).

THOMPSON, JAMES W. *A History of Livestock Raising in the United States, 1607–1860* (Washington, D.C.: U.S. Department of Agriculture, 1942).

*WEBB, WALTER P. *The Great Plains* (Boston: Ginn, 1931).

WELLMAN, PAUL I. *The Trampling Herd* (New York: Carrick & Evans, 1939). Popular account of range cattle industry.

WENTWORTH, EDWARD N. *America's Sheep Trails—History, Personalities* (Ames: Iowa State College Press, 1948).

———. *Shepherd's Empire* (Norman: University of Oklahoma Press, 1945).

WERSTEIN, IRVING. *The Blizzard of '88* (New York: T. Y. Crowell, 1960).

Bibliography

WYMAN, WALKER D. *Nothing but Prairie and Sky: Life on the Dakota Range in the Early Days* (Norman: University of Oklahoma Press, 1954).

Also consult bibliography for Section 9.

22. FARMERS' FRONTIER IN THE FAR WEST

BABCOCK, KENDRIC C. *The Scandinavian Element in the United States* (Urbana: University of Illinois, 1914).

BRIGGS, HAROLD E. *Frontiers of the Northwest: A History of the Upper Missouri Valley* (New York: Appleton-Century, 1940).

*BUCK, SOLON J. *The Agrarian Crusade: A Chronicle of the Farmer in Politics* (New Haven: Yale University Press, 1920). Influence of Grangers and Populists.

*———. *The Granger Movement: A Study of Agricultural Organization and Its Political, Economic, and Social Manifestations, 1870–1880* (Cambridge, Mass.: Harvard University Press, 1913). The standard work.

BURLINGAME, MERRILL G. *The Montana Frontier* (Helena: State Publishing Co., 1942).

DICK, EVERETT. *The Sod-House Frontier, 1854–1890* (New York: Appleton-Century, 1937).

ELLIS, ELMER. *Henry Moore Teller, Defender of the West* (Caldwell, Idaho: Caxton Printers, 1941).

*GOLDMAN, ERIC F. *Rendezvous with Destiny: A History of Modern American Reform* (New York: Knopf, 1952). Stimulating reading about reform movements beginning in the late 1860's.

HARGREAVES, MARY WILMA. *Dry Farming in the Northern Great Plains, 1900–1925* (Cambridge, Mass.: Harvard University Press, 1957).

HAYNES, FREDERICK EMORY. *James Baird Weaver* (Iowa City: State Historical Society of Iowa, 1919). The biography of a leading Greenbacker.

*HICKS, JOHN D. *The Populist Revolt: A History of the Farmers' Alliance and the People's Party* (Minneapolis: University of Minnesota Press, 1931). Scholarly history of a farmers' movement.

ISE, JOHN. *Sod and Stubble: The Story of a Kansas Homestead* (New York: Wilson-Erickson, 1936). Realistic first-hand account.

KLOSE, NELSON. *America's Crop Heritage* (Ames: Iowa State College Press, 1950). Introduction of drouth-resistant crops for the West.

[253]

Bibliography

KNOLES, GEORGE HARMON. *Presidential Campaign and Election of 1892* (Stanford: Stanford University Press, 1942).

MALIN, JAMES C. *Winter Wheat in the Golden Belt of Kansas* (Lawrence: University of Kansas Press, 1944).

OLSON, JAMES C. *J. Sterling Morton* (Lincoln: University of Nebraska Press, 1942). Biography of an agricultural leader from the Plains.

RICHARDSON, RUPERT N., and CARL COKE RISTER. *The Greater Southwest: The Economic, Social, and Cultural Development of Kansas, Oklahoma, Texas, Utah, Colorado, Nevada, New Mexico, Arizona, and California From the Spanish Conquest to the Twentieth Century* (Glendale: A. H. Clark, 1934).

RIDGE, MARTIN. *Ignatius Donnelly: The Portrait of a Politician* (Chicago: University of Chicago Press, 1962). Biography of a prominent Populist leader.

RISTER, CARL COKE. *Southern Plainsmen* (Norman: University of Oklahoma Press, 1938). Deals with the farmers' frontier south of Nebraska.

——. *The Southwestern Frontier, 1865–1881* (Cleveland: A. H. Clark, 1928).

——. *Land Hunger: David L. Payne and the Oklahoma Boomers* (Norman: University of Oklahoma Press, 1942).

ROGIN, LEO. *The Introduction of Farm Machinery in Its Relation to the Productivity of Labor in the Agriculture of the United States During the Nineteenth Century* (Berkeley: University of California Press, 1931).

*SANDOZ, MARI. *Old Jules* (Boston: Little, Brown, 1935). Account of the author and her father pioneering in Nebraska.

SCHAFER, JOSEPH. *The Social History of American Agriculture* (New York: Macmillan, 1936).

SCHELL, HERBERT S. *Dakota Territory During the Eighteen Sixties* (Vermillion: University of South Dakota, 1954).

——. "Official Immigration Activities of Dakota Territory," *North Dakota Historical Quarterly*, Vol. VII (Oct., 1932).

SHANNON, FRED A. *The Farmers' Last Frontier, Agriculture, 1860–1897* (New York: Farrar & Rinehart, 1945).

SMITH, CHARLES H. *The Coming of the Russian Mennonites* (Berne, Indiana: Mennonite Book Concern, 1927).

*STEGNER, WALLACE. *Beyond the Hundredth Meridian: John Wesley*

Powell and the Second Opening of the West (Boston: Houghton Mifflin, 1954).

TAYLOR, HENRY C. *The Farmers' Movement, 1620–1920* (New York: American Book Co., 1953). Survey of farmers' protests since colonial times.

THORNTHWAITE, CHARLES W., and HELEN I. SLENTZ. *Internal Migration in the United States* (Philadelphia: University of Pennsylvania Press, 1934).

*WEBB, WALTER PRESCOTT. *The Great Plains* (Boston: Ginn, 1931).

WIK, REYNOLD M. *Steam Power on the American Farm* (Philadelphia: University of Pennsylvania Press, 1953).

WINTHER, OSCAR O. *The Great Northwest—a History* (2d ed. New York: Knopf, 1950).

*WITTKE, CARL. *We Who Built America: The Saga of the Immigrant* (New York: Prentice-Hall, 1939).

Also consult bibliographies for Sections 8, 9, and 21; state histories contain much information regarding their agricultural development.

23. THE URBAN FRONTIER

Very little has been written on frontier towns as such, but the histories of American cities usually include chapters on their frontier beginnings. Accounts by travelers and others on the frontier give much scattered information about early towns. Local libraries and historical societies can usually supply several histories and much information on the history of their own town. The student should consult his local library card catalog for city histories he may be interested in. A list of local city histories would be too extensive and any particular work would not be of interest to a large number of readers.

BROCKETT, L. P. *Our Western Empire* (Columbus, Ohio: W. Garretson & Co., 1882).

EATON, CLEMENT. *The Growth of Southern Civilization, 1790–1860* (New York: Harper, 1961).

HUNTER, LOUIS C. *Steamboats on the Western Rivers* (Cambridge, Mass.: Harvard University Press, 1949).

POWELL, LYMAN P., ed. *Historic Towns of the Western States* (New York: Putnam's, 1901).

QUIETT, GLENN C. *They Built the West: An Epic of Rails and Cities* (New York: Appleton-Century, 1934).

STILL, BAYARD. "Patterns of Mid-Nineteenth-Century Urbanization in the Middle West," *Mississippi Valley Historical Review*, Vol. XXVIII (Sept., 1941).

*TROLLOPE, FRANCES. *Domestic Manners of the Americans* (2 vols. London: Whittaker, Treacher, 1832).

WADE, RICHARD. *The Urban Frontier: The Rise of Western Cities, 1790–1830* (Cambridge, Mass.: Harvard University Press, 1959). An important only book. (See "Bibliographical Note," pp. 343–345, for sources used by Wade in his research and for suggestions.)

Also consult bibliography for Section 16.

Some Historical Journals Dealing
with the Frontier

Many historical journals, most of which are quarterlies, include articles on the subject of the frontier. The following list will suggest some of the leading journals where articles may be found; in addition, nearly all states and many counties and towns publish historical journals. Many universities publish "Studies" where results of research are reported. See the Harvard Guide for a more extended list.

Agricultural History Society. *Agricultural History.* 1927.
American Economic Association. *American Economic Review.* 1911.
American Heritage Publishing Co. *American Heritage.* 1949.
American Historical Association. *American Historical Review.* 1895.
American Political Science Association. *American Political Science Review.* 1916.
University of Arizona Press. *Arizona and the West.* 1958.
Arkansas Historical Association. *Arkansas Historical Quarterly.* 1942.
California Historical Society. *Quarterly.* 1922.
Canadian Historical Review. 1920.
State Historical Society of Colorado. *Colorado Magazine.* 1923.
Filson Club. *History Quarterly.* 1926.
Florida Historical Society. *Quarterly.* 1908.
Georgia Historical Society. *Georgia Historical Quarterly.* 1917.
Great Plains Journal.
Illinois State Historical Society. *Journal.* 1908.
Indiana University and Indiana Historical Society. *Indiana Magazine of History.* 1905.
Iowa State Department of History and Archives. *Annals of Iowa.* 1863.
State Historical Society of Iowa. *Iowa Journal of History.* 1903.
Kansas State Historical Society. *Kansas Historical Quarterly.* 1931.
Kentucky Historical Society. *Register.* 1903.
Louisiana Historical Society. *Louisiana Historical Quarterly.* 1917.
Maryland Historical Society. *Maryland Historical Magazine.* 1906.
Michigan Historical Commission. *Michigan History.* 1917.

Minnesota Historical Society. *Minnesota History.* 1915.

Mississippi Historical Society. *Journal of Mississippi History,* 1939.

Mississippi Valley Historical Association. *Mississippi Valley Historical Review.* 1914.

State Historical Society of Missouri. *Missouri Historical Review.* 1906.

Nebraska State Historical Society. *Nebraska History.* 1918.

New England Quarterly. 1928.

Historical Society of New Mexico and the University of New Mexico. *New Mexico Historical Review.* 1926.

North Carolina State Department of Archives and History. *North Carolina Historical Review.* 1924.

New York State Historical Association. *New York History.* 1919.

North Dakota History.

University of North Dakota Press. *North Dakota Quarterly.* 1958.

Ohio Historical Society. *Ohio Historical Quarterly.* 1887.

Oklahoma Historical Society. *Chronicles of Oklahoma.* 1921.

Oregon Historical Society. *Oregon Historical Quarterly.* 1900.

Pacific Coast Branch, American Historical Association. *Pacific Historical Review.* 1932.

Pennsylvania Historical Association. *Pennsylvania History.* 1934.

Historical Society of Western Pennsylvania. *Western Pennsylvania Historical Magazine.* 1918.

South Carolina Historical Society. *South Carolina Historical Magazine.* 1900.

Southern Historical Association. *Journal of Southern History.* 1935.

Tennessee Historical Society. *Tennessee Historical Quarterly.* 1942.

Texas State Historical Association. *Southwestern Historical Quarterly.* 1897.

Utah State Historical Society. *Utah Historical Quarterly.* 1928.

Virginia Historical Society. *Virginia Magazine of History and Biography.* 1893.

Washington State Historical Society. *Pacific Northwest Quarterly.* 1906.

Western History Association. *The American West.* 1964.

Journal of the West. 1963.

Institute of Early American History and Culture. *William and Mary College Quarterly.* 1892.

State Historical Society of Wisconsin. *Wisconsin Magazine of History.* 1917.

State Department of History. *Annals of Wyoming.* 1923.

INDEX

Index

Index

Index

ment, 130; extralegal governments, 129; frontier, 127–134; political characteristics of the West, 127–130; provisional governments, 128; state-making, 131–133; territorial, 131
Graduation Act of 1854, 102
Grangers: opposition to railroads, 125–126; organization of, 126; radicalism, 190
Gray, Robert, discovered Columbia River, 64
Great American Desert, 78, 172
Great Awakening, 139
Great Britain: fur trade, 165–166; interest in Oregon, 64–66; interest in Texas, 54–55; War of 1812, 45–47. *See also* England
Great Migration (after 1812), 47–49, 52; causes, 47, 100, 138
Great Northern Railroad, 125
Great Plains: approach to, 55, 57; dry-farming, 82–84, 186–187; environment and problems, 77–83; fencing, 81–82; Indians, 78–79, 95–97; open-range cattle industry, 181–185; Populism in, 113–114; settlement, 78, 83–84
Great Revival, 139–140, 146
Greenback movement, 112, 191
Greenville, Treaty of, opened Ohio and Indiana to settlement, 43
Gregg, Josiah, Santa Fe trader, 154
Guadalupe Hidalgo, Treaty of, 62, 63

Hall, James, 153
Harmar, Colonel Joseph, in Northwest Territory, 42, 90
Harney, General W. S., in "Utah War," 70
Harrison, William Henry, in battle of Tippecanoe, 46
Hatch Act of 1887, 188
Headrights, 22
Henderson, Judge Richard, land speculation, 39–40
Hill, James J., railroad building, 125
Holladay, Ben, stagecoach operations, 120
Homestead Act: passage and provisions, 102–103, 137; in settlement of Kansas and Nebraska, 56–57
Hopkins, Mark, 123
Horseshoe Bend, battle of, 46
Houston, General Sam: as a frontier

character, 135; won Texas independence, 54
Hudson's Bay Company: in North Dakota, 170; reputation, 165; in Oregon, 64–66, 167
Huntington, Collis P., 123

Idaho: government, 72–73; mining strikes, 72–73, 181; Mormon settlements, 69
Illinois: lead mining at Galena, 177; settlement, 47–48
Illinois Central Railroad, 121
Indian Intercourse Act of 1834, 93
Indian policy: army, 93–94; British, 33; Dawes Act, 97; education, 97; and farmers' frontier, 163; Indian Bureau, 94; Peace Commission, 95, 97; reservation system, 96; United States, 87–98; Wheeler-Howard Act, 97
Indian tribes: 87–89; Apaches, 95–97; Cherokees, 48, 91–92, 165; Cheyennes, 96; Chickasaws, 91; Choctaws, 91–92; Comanches, 79, 95; Creeks, 44, 48, 91–92, 165; "Diggers," 95; Five Civilized Tribes, 75–76, 91–92, 95; Fox, 52, 91; Great Plains, 78–79, 95–97; Kiowa, 96; Navahoes, 95; Sauk, 52, 91; Seminoles, 48, 91; Sioux, 53, 73, 96–97
Indian wars: 87–97; Black Hawk War, 47–48, 91; on Great Plains, 78–80; in Kentucky, 39; King Phillip's War, 28–29; in New York, 39; in Northwest Territory, 42–43; Pequot War, 28; Pontiac's Rebellion, 34; in Tennessee, 43, 46, 90; in Virginia, 24; during War of 1812, 45–47, 90
Indiana, settlement, 47–48
Indians: concepts of property, 87–88; responsibility for conflicts, 89, 94–98; treaties with, 88–89
Interstate Commerce Commission, 126
Iowa: Amana Society, 146; constitution, 133; settlement, 52; statehood delayed, 134
Irish, on frontier, 138
Irrigation, Carey Act, 190; early efforts, 190; Newlands Act, 190
Irving, Washington, writings, 154, 173

Index

Jackson, Andrew: in frontier politics, 127; Indian removals, 48–49, 91–92; and Sam Houston, 54; and the Second Bank of the United States, 107, 110; Specie Circular, 110–111; War of 1812, 46

Jackson, Helen Hunt, *A Century of Dishonor* and *Ramona*, 97

Jacksonian democracy, 7, 127–128, 143

Jamestown, Virginia, 6, 22, 25, 177

Jay Treaty, signed, 166

Jefferson, Thomas: and Aaron Burr, 51–52; and Louisiana, 50–52; sends out explorers, 68, 170

Jesuits: in California, 58–59; in Oregon, 65

Johnston, Colonel Albert Sidney, in "Utah War," 70

Journalism, 150

Judah, Theodore D., promoted Central Pacific Railroad, 123

Kansas: Indians in, 95; settlement, 55–56

Kansas-Nebraska Act, 55–56

Kearny, General Stephen W., in Mexican War, 62–63

Kelley, Hall J., interest in Oregon, 65

Kelley, O. H., organized the Grangers, 126

Kentucky: agriculture, 161; constitution, 132–133; fur trade, 165; government, 44, 131; settlement, 39, 136; statehood, 44; and United States Bank, 109

Kino, Father Eusebio, in Arizona, 58

Kitanning Path, 36, 38

Lancaster Turnpike, 116

Land claims, of the colonies, 33, 40–41

Land law of 1796, provisions, 99

Land law of 1800 (Harrison Act), provisions, 99–100

Land law of 1804, provisions, 100–101

Land law of 1820, provisions, 101

Land speculation (Land jobbing, land companies): in British colonies, 33–36; distribution of land, 137; and Homestead Act, 103; in Indiana, 48; in New England, 160; and state land claims surrender, 41

Larkin, Thomas O., in California, 60

Lead mining: in Illinois, 47; along Mississippi River, 177

Lee, Reverend Jason, in Oregon, 65

Leon, Ponce de, 20

Lewis and Clark Expedition, 51, 68; account of, 169–171

Lexington, Kentucky: educational center, 149; publishing, 152; "spearhead" of the frontier, 192–194

Lisa, Manuel, in fur trade, 68, 167

Livestock associations, 185

Locofocos, 111

Log cabins, 137

Long, Stephen H.: expeditions, 171–172; exploration of Colorado, 68; on Great Plains, 78

Longstreet, A. B., *Georgia Scenes*, 153

Louisiana: agriculture, 163; migration from, 136; settlement, 48, 52, 68

Louisiana Purchase: boundary, 49; treaty, 50, 52

Louisiana Territory: exploration, 169–172; Oklahoma as a part of, 75; settlement, 50–52; in Treaty of Paris (1763), 32

Louisville, "spearhead" of the frontier, 192–194

Lyceum, 149

McCoy, J. G., starts railroad shipment of cattle, 183

McGillivray, Alexander, organized Indian confederation, 90

McGuffey, William Holmes, *Reader*, 148

Mackenzie, Alexander, in Oregon, 64

McLoughlin, Dr. John, in Oregon, 64–65, 167

Marshall, James W., discovery of gold, 63, 177

Maryland: farmers' frontier, 22; and land claims, 40–41, 98; settlement, 23; tobacco, 157–160

Massachusetts, Shays' Rebellion, 107. *See also* Plymouth *and* Massachusetts Bay Colony

Massachusetts Bay Colony, settlement, 26–28

Mayflower Compact, 26, 128

Merchandising and merchants, 137

Methodists: colleges, 149, on the frontier, 137–142; in Oregon, 65

Mexican War, 61–63; six-shooter in, 80

Mexico: and California, 59–63; and Texas, 53–55

Michaux, André, 152–153

Michaux, Francois, 152

Michigan: settlement, 47–48, 136; statehood, 52

Migrants: characteristics, 134–135; sources and direction of migration, 135–136

Mining. *See* specific minerals

Mining codes, 178

Mining frontiers: Arizona, 76, 181; California, 63–64, 155, 177–179; Colorado, 71, 180–181; Georgia, 177; Hispaniola, 20; Idaho, 72, 181; Illinois, 47; Montana, 73, 181; Nevada, 71, 155, 179, 181; significance, 181; South Dakota, 73, 181; Wyoming, 74, 181

Minnesota, Scandinavians, 84; settlement, 53

Mississippi, settlement, 48, 136

Mississippi River, navigation, 43

Missouri: German settlers, 138; settlement, 52, 68, 71, 138; admission, 134

Missouri Fur Company, 167

Monroe, President James, Indian policy, 90–91

Montana: government, 73; Indians in, 97; mining, 73, 181

Mormon Trail, travel, 175

Mormons: in Gold Rush, 178; migration to Utah, 69, 144–145; at Nauvoo, 144–145; origin and early history, 142–145

Morrill Land Grant College Act, 15, 103

Morse, Jedidiah, school geography, by, 148

Mount Davidson, silver mining, 71, 179

Mountain Meadows Massacre, 70

Murray, Lindley, school grammar text, 148

Museum, a frontier institution, 149

Napoleon Bonaparte, sells Louisiana, 50–51

Narvaez, Panfilo de, 20

National (Cumberland) Road, 36, 116–117, 162

Nebraska: Indians in, 95, and Populism, 113, 191; settlement, 56–57; statehood delayed, 134

Nevada: government, 70–71, 134; mining, 179–181; Mormon settlements, 69–70; settlement, 70–71

New England: agriculture, 160, 162; establishment of towns, 28; frontier, 26–30; migrants from, 139

New Mexico: exploration of, 58; settlement and government, 76, 138; Spanish beginnings, 67

New York: agriculture, 160; Amana Society, 146; constitution as a model, 133; settlers, 136

Newlands Act, 190

North Carolina: constitution, 133; governs Tennessee, 39–40, Regulators, 31; settlement, 25, 136

North Dakota: Lewis and Clark explore, 170; settlement and government, 74

North West Company: absorbed by Hudson's Bay Company, 165, 167; in Oregon, 64

Northern Pacific Railroad, 125

Northwest Ordinance (1787): provisions, 41, 131–132, 134; school lands, 148

Northwest Territory: British military posts, 41–43; fur trade, 165; George Rogers Clark in, 193; land law of 1800, 99; Ohio as first state in, 132; settlement, 47

Nuttall, Thomas, 152, 154

Oberlin College, 149–150

Ohio, enabling act, 132; statehood, 44

Ohio Company, 32, 44

Ohio Valley: in American Revolution, 39; contest for, 32; religious colonies, 146; source of settlers, 136

Oklahoma: Indian removal to, 92; Indian reservations, 96; Indian Territory, 48, 75; settlement and government, 75–76, 134

"Old Spanish" Trail, travel, 176

"Old West" frontier, 29–32, 138, 161

Omnibus States, 74, 134

Onate, Juan de, colonized New Mexico, 67

Ordinance of 1785: enacted, 41; land for schools, 15; provisions, 98–99

Ordinance of 1787. *See* Northwest Ordinance

Index

Index

Vaca, Cabeza de, 20

Vermont, statehood, 44

Vigilantes: as extralegal government, 129; in Gold Rush, 179

Villard, Henry, reorganized Northern Pacific Railroad, 125

Virginia: fur trade, 165; migrants from, 136; organizes Kentucky, 39; settlement, 6, 22, 25; tobacco, 159–160

Virginia City, mining, 71, 179

Wabash Decision, 126

Wade, Richard, *The Urban Frontier*, 192

Walker, Joseph R., blazed trail to California, 173, 175

War of 1812: causes, 45; Indian warfare, 45–47

Washburn Mills, 188

Washington: mining, 181; statehood, 58, 66

Washington, George: at Fort Necessity, 32; interest in land speculation, 34; places militia under Joseph Harmar, 42

Watauga settlement, 38–39, 128

Wayne, General Anthony, campaigns against Indians, 42–43, 90

Webb, Walter Prescott: *The Great Frontier*, 12–15; *The Great Plains*, 78

Wells, Fargo Company, 120

Wheat: in dry-farming, 187; milling, 187–188

Whitman, Dr. Marcus, missionary in Oregon, 65

Whitney, Asa, railroad promoter, 122

Whitney, Eli, invented cotton gin, 163

Wilderness Road, 36, 39

Wilkinson, General James: and Aaron Burr, 51–52; in Florida, 49; in Kentucky politics, 132; sent out Pike to explore, 171

Windmills, 82–83

Wisconsin, 47–48; German settlers, 138; settlement, 136

Wolfskill, William, 173, 176

Wright, Louis B., *Culture on the Moving Frontier*, 148 n.

Wyeth, Nathaniel, in Oregon fur trade, 65, 173

Wyoming: settlement and mining, 73; statehood, 74

Yazoo land controversy, 41

Yazoo Strip, disputed, 43

Young, Brigham: arrival in Utah, 69–70; assumed leadership of Mormons, 145

Young, Ewing, 173, 176